WRITTEN ON MY HEART

Creede,
Thank you for
all your encouragement!
I hope you'll enjoy the
fruits of your pastoring!
You mean so much to mr.
many Blessings,
Ann Smith
Gal. 6:14

Smyth & Helwys Publishing, Inc.
6316 Peake Road
Macon, Georgia 31210-3960
1-800-747-3016
©2009 by Smyth & Helwys Publishing
All rights reserved.
Printed in the United States of America.

The paper used in this publication meets the minimum requirements of
American National Standard for Information Sciences—
Permanence of Paper for Printed Library Materials.
ANSI Z39.48–1984. (alk. paper)

Library of Congress Cataloging-in-Publication Data

Smith, Ann, 1942–

Written on my heart / by Ann Smith. p. cm.
Includes bibliographical references and index.
ISBN 978-1-57312-549-9 (pbk. : alk. paper)
1. Bible—Meditations. 2. Devotional calendars.
I. Title. BS491.5.S65 2009 242'.2—dc22 2009049335

Scripture quotations are taken from the Holy Bible,
New Living Translation, copyright 1996, 2004.
Used by permission of Tyndale House Publishers, Inc.,
Wheaton, Illinois 60189. All rights reserved.

Written ON MY Heart

by Ann H. Smith

Dedication

For my husband, Jim, and my sons, J. and Nick,
who give me countless reasons to be thankful every day.

Acknowledgments

It's amazing to me to see this book actually being published! When I felt led to do it, I had no idea what lay ahead. My first affirmation came from my longtime friend and mentor, Joni Woolf. Because she is a book editor, I asked if she would read through the manuscript and let me know if she thought it was worthy of publishing. Her encouragement propelled me to seek a publisher and not to be discouraged by rejection letters! I am grateful for her friendship, support, and comments about the manuscript.

I want to thank Rev. Jimmy Towson and Rev. Creede Hinshaw for reading the manuscript. Because I have learned so much from each of them, I am humbled by their kind words about the manuscript and their willingness to take time out of their busy pastoral schedules to read it.

Henry Beers answered many questions and offered advice about the publishing process.

Keith Gammons, Rachel Stancil, Griff Hogan, and Leslie Andres, all of Smyth & Helwys, were incredibly patient with me as I navigated the process of publishing for the first time. I appreciate them for taking a chance on me! I mean, a CPA writing a devotional book?!

My "cyber-sisters," Susan Middleton, Gail Springstead, and Reverend Cile Mitchell have cheered me on every step of the way.

I especially want to thank my husband, Jim Smith. His support and encouragement with whatever endeavor I undertake (and there have been many) mean more to me than I can say. I also appreciate him "test-driving" the manuscript.

Foreword

For years, I had heard the Bible referred to as the Living Word of God, but I never gave much thought to what that actually meant. Then one day, as a group of friends and I discussed how a particular passage spoke to us differently each time we read it, someone commented, "I guess that's why they call the Bible the Living Word of God. It changes every time you read it." For me, it was one of those "A-ha!" moments because, unlike most books, the Bible truly never grows old or tired. It is always fresh and new, just like the manna the Israelites ate as they wandered in the wilderness. It fills us, giving us exactly what we need when we need it.

Yet, when we are unfamiliar with it, the Bible is intimidating. Memorizing a verse is not the same as plowing through Leviticus! Even so, I am always surprised by the treasures I find in the most unlikely passages of the Bible.

I had read the Bible each year for several years, but I often considered it as something to check off my "to-do" list rather than a spiritual experience. One year, though, I decided to journal each day about the passage I read. I began each reading by asking God to teach me something from the passage that I could apply in my life. As I read, I felt like a small child reading with a loving parent beside me. In certain spots, I paused and allowed God to speak to me, showing me something new.

I was frequently surprised by what I learned. Some days, the passage was so familiar that I felt challenged to read it with fresh eyes. Other times, I was amazed at the lessons I learned in passages I had skimmed in prior readings.

As I experienced the Bible in this new and exciting way, I was troubled when I heard others talk about parts of the Bible they avoided. I wanted to share what God showed me. Thus, the idea for this book was born.

I don't claim any special background as a Bible scholar. I simply share what I feel God has shared with me. You will undoubtedly find your own special treasures as you read. That's what makes the Bible unique. All I ask is that you "Come and see" (John 1:39).

I hope you will find that God speaks to you in new and fresh ways as you read his Living Word!

January 1 ✠ Genesis 1–3

From the beginning of time, we have found it easier to listen to the voices of the world than to the voice of our Creator. Not only is God our creator, but he is also the source of true guidance.

It may seem easier to listen to the world's voices because there are more of them, but when man and woman were first created, they had only two voices to listen to—God's and the serpent's. Even then, they chose to listen to the voice of the serpent!

We often hear the voices of the world over the voice of God because worldly voices shout at us like a car salesman on TV, while God often speaks quietly, not clamoring boisterously for our attention. We need the selective hearing that children employ so successfully. We need to look and listen for God, for he is all around us. He created everything, and we can hear him in a bird's song, a baby's laugh, and in a still, small inner voice that beckons us to tune out the voices of the world and tune in to him.

You have taught children and infants to tell of your strength . . . (Psalm 8:2a)

How intently must you listen to hear God's voice?

Creator God, help me listen for your voice. May I remember your love for me today as I observe the good world you created for me. Grant me a time of quiet to listen for your voice. Amen.

January 2 ✠ Genesis 4–6

In Genesis 4, God distinguished between the gifts of Cain and Abel. While both men brought gifts, Abel offered the best of his flock, while Cain simply presented a gift from his harvest. I sometimes give more like Cain. I give a gift to God, but I don't ask myself if it is a gift of my best. When I give, it may become merely another responsibility to fulfill instead of a way to thank God for his gifts to me.

To what or whom do I give my best?

Before giving a gift to God, I should remember what he has given me—my life, my intellect, the very gift I give to him. I need to approach my giving to God as an act of worship and gratitude, giving not only a part of my blessings, but the best I have to offer.

You must each decide in your heart how much to give. And don't give reluctantly or in response to pressure. "For God loves a person who gives cheerfully." (2 Corinthians 9:7)

What gifts do you offer to God each day?

Gracious God, like a small child clinging to a favorite toy, I cling to what I have, forgetting that it came from you. When I look at everything I have, may I remember that I have nothing that is not a gift from you. Cultivate in me a heart of gratitude so that I desire to give you my best. Amen.

January 3 ✠ Genesis 7–9

After the great flood, people and animals were again fruitful, and they multiplied. So did evil, which grew as prolific as any creature that rode on the ark. In Genesis 8:21, God acknowledges that the flood failed to change our hearts when he says, "everything they think or imagine is bent toward evil from childhood." What a flood could not do, and what we cannot do on our own, Jesus did.

Evil is as persistent as a whiny toddler. Thankfully, God loves us despite our evil ways. God loves us so much that he gave us his best gift, his Son.

I was sinking deep in sin,
Far from the peaceful shore . . .

When nothing else could help,
Love lifted me.
          —James Rowe[1]

How often are you grateful for God's forgiveness of your sins?

Savior God, your love for us is incredible. We cannot help sinning. Evil is in our nature, but you love us so much that you gave your Son to save us. We praise you for this indescribable love! Amen.

January 4 ✠ Genesis 10–12

God told Abram he would make him a great nation, and Abram trusted God enough to leave home and family to travel to an unknown country. However, after Abram arrived in Canaan, famine struck and he headed for Egypt. In Egypt, he lied to Pharaoh about Sarai.

Did he think the famine negated God's promise to him? Why did he put Sarai in such a position, and why did he not trust God in that situation when he trusted him before?

Some days we may feel that our faith is unshakable, especially when we recognize that events are moving according to what we believe is God's plan. Then something derails those plans, like the famine Abram experienced in his new homeland, the very land God told him to inhabit. When plans go awry, our faith is shaken. We begin to question whether we heard God correctly in the first place.

A common expression says, "What God leads you to, he'll lead you through." Adverse circumstances should not shake our faith. When plans change, we should continue to focus solely on Christ, who is with us always.

If I go up to heaven, you are there;
*   if I go down to the grave, you are there.*
If I ride the wings of the morning,
*   if I dwell by the farthest oceans,*

even there your hand will guide me,
and your strength will support me. (Psalm 139:8-10)

How have you tried to alter your path when God took you somewhere you didn't expect?

O Perfect God, thank you for being consistent even when I have doubts. Help me trust you even when plans change. Amen.

January 5 ✠ Genesis 13–15

When God promised Abram great rewards, Abram responded with surprising frankness. He told God that he really wanted a son. Abram had accumulated much wealth and power. In the process of defeating eleven different peoples, he and his men had already attacked four kings who had captured Lot. Yet Abram desired more than these successes.

Before Abram left Haran, God told him that if he left, God would make him into a great nation. Abram experienced many blessings due to his obedience, but a son was not one of them. Even though much time had passed since God's original call to Abram, Genesis 15:6 says Abram "believed the Lord" when God promised that his descendants would be as numerous as the stars in the sky.

And so a whole nation came from this one man who was as good as dead—a nation with so many people that, like the stars in the sky and the sand on the seashore, there is no way to count them. (Hebrews 11:12)

How easily do you believe what God tells you?

Heavenly Father, I want to have the faith of Abraham, such that I believe what you tell me always. Amen.

January 6 ✠ Genesis 16–18

For twenty-five years, God had told Abraham that he would be a great nation, but Abraham had not seen the manifestation of that promise. Can you blame him for laughing when, in Genesis 17, he is again told of this promise, learning that its fulfillment will come when Sarah gives birth to a son?

We live in an instant society. We want answers as soon as we press the button to send an e-mail. We want instant updates to our news. We want to lose ten pounds by the weekend. How can God expect us to wait twenty-five years to see his plans for us fulfilled?

Yet, think of a pebble worn smooth by years of water flowing over it. You can't make a pebble overnight. Likewise, you can't make a diamond without years and years of pressure. If we are to be diamonds for God, we must persevere in our faith. God's timetable is not the same as ours. Part of faith is trusting his timing.

Faith is the confidence that what we hope for will actually happen; it gives us assurance about things we cannot see. (Hebrews 11:1)

In what ways is waiting for God to move difficult for you? How do you cope with it?

Faithful God, grant me patience and faith to trust in your timing. Amen.

January 7 ✠ Genesis 19–21

It's important to listen to God. Lot's wife learned this the hard way, turning into a pillar of salt when she disobeyed by looking back. Hagar had heard God speak to her about Ishmael, but when Abraham sent her away and she ran out of water in the desert, God's words seemed fruitless.

Have you ever forgotten God's promises to you? Do you continue to worry and fear even though God has revealed his plans for you? Have you prayed for guidance and received it? We can all cite instances of answered prayer, and yet, we still forget God's promises because we sometimes fail to listen for his voice.

The Lord always keeps his promises;
he is gracious in all he does. (Psalm 145:13b)

How can you remember God's fulfillment of his promises to you?

Lord, forgive me for being afraid when you have shown me the way. Help me to remember and rest on your promises to me. Amen.

January 8 ✤ Genesis 22–24

Abraham told his servant to travel to Abraham's family and find a wife for Isaac. Due to the distance and unknown circumstances, the servant was concerned that he would not find a woman to come back with him. After all, would you allow a daughter to leave with someone you did not know and travel far away to marry someone you had never met? The servant suggested that he take Isaac along so that Isaac could live with Abraham's family in Haran, but Abraham was emphatic that Isaac must not stray from the land God promised to Abraham and his descendants.

What the servant suggested seemed harmless enough, but as we see later with Jacob, traveling to the land of his relatives might have caused problems when Isaac was ready to return home.

Sometimes opportunities arise that appear reasonable and safe. However, if they take us off God's path for us, what may seem harmless actually causes our disobedience to God. God's ways are not the world's ways. It is important that I listen and follow his direction for my life, even if it violates the advice of well-meaning friends and relatives.

But even as he spoke, a bright cloud came over them, and a voice from the cloud said, "This is my dearly loved Son, who brings me great joy. Listen to him." (Matthew 17:5)

How can you discern which opportunities are godly?

Lord, you have said that you are The Way. Give me the discipline to follow the path you have shown me, even when it seems illogical to those around me. Amen.

January 9 ✠ Genesis 25–27

When famine struck, Isaac moved to Gerar, the land of King Abimelech. When Isaac farmed the land in Gerar, he harvested a hundred times more grain than he had planted. He also acquired many flocks and herds. Abimelech grew jealous of Isaac because Isaac gained great wealth. He made Isaac leave his country.

Isaac moved without protest and continued to prosper. Eventually, Abimelech came to Isaac and wanted to make a treaty. He was afraid of Isaac because God blessed Isaac wherever he lived.

Abimelech reminds us that it is best to do all we can to have peaceful relationships. When a relationship becomes strained, don't hesitate to approach the other person to make peace.

So if you are presenting a sacrifice at the altar in the Temple and you suddenly remember that someone has something against you, leave your sacrifice there at the altar. Go and be reconciled to that person. Then come and offer your sacrifice to God. (Matthew 5:23-24)

Can you think of someone with whom you are in conflict? What steps could you take to make peace?

O Lord, help me to live at peace with everyone. Make me more willing to forgive than to hold a grudge. Amen.

January 10 ✠ Genesis 28-30

Ever the negotiator, Jacob even attempted to negotiate with God. I get the sense that if Jacob lived today, he would be the person pouring over a contract to find a loophole in order to out-maneuver someone else.

I want to laugh when I read Genesis 28:20. Despite the generous blessing God already gave Jacob in verses 13-15, Jacob did not wholeheartedly embrace God as his God. Jacob gave God conditions to meet in order to "earn" Jacob's worship.

Jacob's negotiations are as ridiculous as an ant trying to negotiate with a person. Yet who of us has not attempted to place conditions on our worship of God? We get in a tense situation and "bargain" with God to get us out of it. Does God respond to our bargaining, or does he respond out of his infinite love for us? I hope my faith is strong enough to know God is with me always, not only when I offer him a deal. After all, he already gave us the deal of a lifetime!

For God loved the world so much that he gave his one and only Son, so that everyone who believes in him will not perish but have eternal life. (John 3:16)

Have you negotiated with God? How did God react to you?

Thank you, Lord, for your unconditional love! Amen.

January 11 ✠ Genesis 31-33

Rachel had a Plan B. I can almost hear her saying to herself, "I'll go with my husband, sister, and all these children, servants, and animals to a new land, but I'll be prepared in case Jacob's god doesn't work out."

I have heard many people say that their hesitancy in accepting Christ was due to their concern that if they became Christians, God would make them do something drastic, like becoming a missionary or selling everything they owned. There is fear in stepping into an unknown territory. Having a Plan B makes us feel more secure.

It's fine to go to a new place or do something different, but we often do so with a desire to hold on to something familiar *just in case* things don't work out with the new and unfamiliar. When Jesus calls us, having a Plan B in the back of our minds signifies lack of faith on our part. Do we not trust Christ to take care of us when he calls us to something different?

You go before me and follow me.
You place your hand of blessing on my head. (Psalm 139:5)

How can you let go of your hesitation to follow God fully?

Lord, I believe. Help my unbelief! Amen.

January 12 ✠ Genesis 34–36

Deceitfulness has an unsatisfied appetite. As Genesis 34 shows, hidden agendas and crafty negotiating rarely get good results. Jacob's sons used what God had ordained as a sacred ritual for his people as a means of putting the Hivites in a vulnerable position. On the other hand, the Hivites saw cooperating with Jacob's sons as a means for acquiring the wealth Jacob's family had amassed.

The end result was that nobody won. Simeon and Levi slaughtered the Hivites, but later, as Jacob gave his last words to his sons, Simeon and Levi received curses rather than blessings (Genesis 49:5-7). Ultimately, when the Israelites leave Egypt and settle in the promised land, the descendants of Simeon and Levi will not have a homeland that identifies their tribes. Levi will become the priestly tribe, scattered among the nation of Israel, and Simeon will receive land that is part of the territory of Judah.

Deceit cuts a wider swath than is often intended and hurts many innocent victims. How much better to deal honestly with others!

Deceit fills hearts that are plotting evil; joy fills hearts that are planning peace! (Proverbs 12:20)

How difficult is it for you to be honest with the people you encounter, no matter the situation?

Lord, help me to speak honestly to others. Amen.

January 13 ✠ Genesis 37–39

I wonder how Joseph felt in light of all that happened to him. The author of Genesis gives us no insight into his reactions to being sold by his brothers, working as a servant in the home of Potiphar, or being thrown in prison in Egypt. We are told that God was with him and caused him to prosper in all he did, even in adverse circumstances.

It must have been difficult for Joseph not to despair in his circumstances. I cannot imagine going from being the favorite child of a wealthy father to life as a servant in the house of a foreigner who cares nothing for my background.

How do I look at those I meet every day, particularly those whose work or social standing is not respected in society? I know I am guilty of judging the worth of others in the way the world does, but the story of Joseph reminds me that God made us all in his image. I may be meeting a Joseph in unlikely circumstances.

He will delight in obeying the Lord. He will not judge by appearance nor make a decision based on hearsay. (Isaiah 11:3)

How do you judge the worth of others?

Heavenly Father, help me to see others as you see them. Amen.

January 14 ✠ Genesis 40–42

Yesterday I mused about Joseph and how he handled the continuing adversity he faced. Reading about his interpretation of dreams for Pharaoh's chief cupbearer, chief baker, and Pharaoh himself reveals Joseph's source of strength in adversity. He credited his ability to interpret dreams to God. Through all his trials, his faith in God sustained him.

He could work faithfully as a slave for the Egyptians who owned him because his master was truly God, and he ultimately worked for God's glory.

We don't focus much attention on Joseph's steady faith during the years of his captivity, and yet, when we hear him speak in Genesis 40, we hear the voice of a man whom God has sustained and who trusts in God for his well-being. He did not turn away from God even when he faced trials.

Those trials may be what humbled Joseph and strengthened his faith, making him bold and confident when he had the opportunity to appear before Pharaoh. Joseph knew that God was leading him and providing for him.

I should have the same confidence.

Jesus told him, "I am the way . . . ." (John 14:6a)

Can you imagine being in Joseph's situation? Do you think you would be able to maintain your faith in God as he did?

Lord, help me to trust you even when the way before me seems dark and uncertain. Amen.

January 15 ✠ Genesis 43–45

I am not sure why Joseph waited so long before revealing his identity to his brothers. Did he want to get some measure of revenge, or was he waiting because he was unsure of everyone's reactions?

Whatever the case, it is obvious from the conversations among the brothers that they had carried guilt with them for years due to their treatment of Joseph. I can imagine that while there was fear upon learning that their brother was governor of Egypt, there was probably also relief at knowing what became of him.

I am thankful that God forgives sins. I have certainly done things that caused me to carry guilt around for a long time. Yet if I acknowledge my sin and take it to God, I can experience the relief and freedom that he provides because he loves me!

Have mercy on me, O God,
  because of your unfailing love.
Because of your great compassion,
  blot out the stain of my sins.
Wash me clean from my guilt.
  Purify me from my sin.
For I recognize my rebellion;
  it haunts me day and night. (Psalm 51:1-3)

How have you forgiven others in the past? How has God forgiven you?

Gracious God, thank you for your great compassion. Amen.

January 16 ✠ Genesis 46–48

We have almost read all of Genesis. It has taken a little more than half a month to read, which can lull us into forgetting that the events described in the book took place over a long period.

Jacob had no idea that he would ever see Joseph again. He thought his favorite son was dead and lived for years with that belief. I doubt Joseph ever expected to see his family again. If he recalled the dreams he had shared with his brothers and father as a young man, I wonder what he thought of them during the events of his life in Egypt.

Sustaining faith in light of the unknown and unresolved is not easy. We don't always see God in the events of the day, but often we can look back and recognize God's hand at work in what may seem like unrelated and random events.

I suppose that makes faith what it is. We cannot know the outcome, but we can trust the One we know is in control.

Faith is the confidence that what we hope for will actually happen; it gives us assurance about things we cannot see. (Hebrews 11:1)

What does it mean to you that God sees the end of your journey?

Faithful God, help me to remember that whenever my way seems uncertain to me, you know that my journey always ends in you if I will have faith. Amen.

January 17 ✠ Genesis 49–50

Joseph, who appeared to start his life as the spoiled son of an aging father, shows how far he has come in his faith journey. He holds no resentment toward his brothers for what they did to him years ago. He understands how God's hand has been at work in his experiences to preserve not only his life but the lives of his family members as well.

Joseph could have spent the intervening years building hatred and resentment toward his brothers. I believe if he had chosen that response to his circumstances, God would not have been able to use him to bring life to his family.

Joseph responded to his circumstances by increasing his faith in God instead of wondering whether God loved him. God can take our circumstances and use them for his glory when we are faithful to him.

And we know that God causes everything to work together for the good of those who love God and are called according to his purpose for them. (Romans 8:28)

How difficult is it to hold on to hope when life seems hopeless?

Eternal God, even when things seem bad, help me never to lose hope. Amen.

January 18 ✤ Exodus 1–4

I can relate to Moses. God called him for a great work, but Moses was not confident in what God could do through him. He begged God to find someone else. Sometimes I feel small and inadequate. It's not easy to remain confident when life takes unexpected turns.

God is able to do more in us than we can imagine. Our feeble minds and bodies seem so limited, but God can and does use us to accomplish his purposes if we make ourselves available. God gave each of us gifts and calls on us to use them. Since he knows us better than we know ourselves, I should banish my doubt and confidently go where he leads me.

Then Christ will make his home in your hearts as you trust in him. Your roots will grow down into God's love and keep you strong. (Ephesians 3:17)

What excuses do you regularly offer to God when he asks you to serve in various ways?

Lord, help me remember that you are in control, and my role is to be obedient to you. I want to yield to you today in all I think and do. Amen.

January 19 ✤ Exodus 5–7

God, who is all-powerful, did not reveal his power in one mighty act to free the Israelites from Egypt. Knowing the conclusion of the events makes it difficult to place myself in the story. The Israelites did not know what would come next. Only God knew the whole plan.

Moses and Aaron knew that God's plan was to free the Israelites and dispose the Egyptians toward them, but they did not know the sequence of steps to reach the result. Understanding their limited knowledge, I can see how Moses and Aaron grew discouraged when God's acts did not produce what they thought was the desired result.

When I become discouraged at what seems like unanswered prayer, I should remember that my vision and understanding are limited. At the end of my story, God's plan will make sense, just as his plan made sense in Egypt.

Now we see things imperfectly as in a cloudy mirror, but then we will see everything with perfect clarity. All that I know now is partial and incomplete, but then I will know everything completely, just as God now knows me completely. (1 Corinthians 13:12)

Have you ever prayed an unanswered prayer? What makes you keep praying it?

Author of my life, I want to remember that while I don't understand the twists and turns in my story, you do. May I remember that you work all things together for good. Amen.

January 20 ✠ Exodus 8–10

As frustrating as Pharaoh's behavior was, I know I am also guilty of saying I'll do something and then failing to follow through. I can think of a long list of good intentions I never carried out, from sending cards to the sick and hurting to agreeing to volunteer for projects and then not living up to my commitment.

Most often, I don't live up to the goals I set for myself. I eat dessert when I say I'm on a diet; I stay up too late even when I've promised to go to bed early. If I struggle this much to keep commitments with myself, I wonder how often I must disappoint God.

Oh, what a miserable person I am! Who will free me from this life that is dominated by sin and death? Thank God! The answer is in Jesus Christ our Lord. So you see how it is: In my mind I really want to obey God's law, but because of my sinful nature I am a slave to sin. (Romans 7:24-25)

How can you fulfill godly goals?

Lord, thank you for not giving up on me, even though I am weak and sinful. Amen.

January 21 ✠ Exodus 11–13

Exodus does not tell us much about the Israelites during the plagues, other than to point out plagues that didn't affect them.

When Moses first arrived and told the Israelites that God was at work to release them from their slavery, the people were not terribly excited. The Egyptians worked them harder than ever after Moses approached Pharaoh.

Maybe the reason for so many plagues was not merely because Pharaoh's heart was hard. Maybe these plagues were needed to soften the hearts of the Israelites too.

If I observe God's work in others, it can strengthen my faith as well. The key is for me to be observant, which means I have to focus beyond my own troubles, events, and activities and *be aware* of others' lives.

You know how to interpret the weather signs in the sky, but you don't know how to interpret the signs of the times! (Matthew 16:3b)

What might God teach you through the people around you?

Lord, make me aware of the ways you teach me through others. Amen.

January 22 ✠ Exodus 14–16

The Israelites, despite the Red Sea miracle and the plagues in Egypt, lose faith in God because they are hungry in the wilderness.

Am I faithful even when everything around me looks bleak? Recently I read a verse in 2 Timothy: "Don't be afraid of suffering for the Lord" (4:5).

When life is bleak, I need to trust God more, not less. Whatever my present circumstances, God is steadfast.

God led the Israelites into the wilderness. He did not lead them there to abandon them. Whether God leads me into a difficult time, I create it myself, or circumstances simply cause it to happen, God will not abandon me.

If we endure hardship, we will reign with him. If we deny him, he will deny us. If we are unfaithful, he remains faithful, for he cannot deny who he is. (2 Timothy 2:12-13)

What does it mean to you that God will never abandon you, no matter where you find yourself?

Lord, when my circumstances are bleak, drive me to you. Amen.

January 23 ✠ Exodus 17–19

Jethro's advice to Moses shows that delegation has been around for thousands of years. I've heard this story used as an example in business for the importance of delegating to others so doing too much work doesn't burn one out.

Probably the most significant part of this story is not the delegation, but that Moses should spend his time doing what he is uniquely qualified to do, which is teaching the people and showing them how to conduct their lives.

How often do we, like Moses, work hard at something because we feel we should do it, although it may not be what God gifted us to do? Rather than merely being busy doing the Lord's work, we should listen to God and follow his leading in our lives. We should use the gifts he gives to us. My gift may not be the same as yours, nor yours the same as mine. If we work for God, using the gifts he uniquely gave us, we accomplish his purpose.

God works in different ways, but it is the same God who does the work in all of us. A spiritual gift is given to each of us so we can help each other. (1 Corinthians 12:6-7)

How often do you devote your energy to good activities rather letting God lead you to the places to which you are most suited?

Lord, help me to slow down and listen to you, so that I may do the work you have gifted me to do. Amen.

January 24 ✣ Exodus 20–22

When God gave instructions about how to build the altar, he did not tell the people to build it from silver or gold. They were to build it from earth, from uncut stones. In other words, they were to keep it simple!

He probably feared, and rightly so, that if the altar was beautifully crafted, the people would focus their worship on the altar instead of on God. I can imagine that it would be easy to admire a beautiful altar and forget that its purpose is to offer sacrifices to God.

We face the same dilemmas today. A beautiful sanctuary can enhance our worship of God. It can also cause us to become distracted if we spend more time admiring the beauty than thinking about the One for whom it is made beautiful.

We can also apply the same analogy to our bodies. Are we happy being plain and simple in our appearance and dress, or do we feel it is important to adorn ourselves so that others admire us? That's a tough question!

Maybe the answer lies in our motivation. If our appearance is so important, we may become like an ornate altar. We may distract ourselves from God by such a strong focus on our appearance.

So don't worry about these things, saying, "What will we eat? What will we drink? What will we wear?" These things dominate the thoughts of unbelievers, but your heavenly Father already knows all your needs. Seek the Kingdom of God above all else, and live righteously, and he will give you everything you need. (Matthew 6:31-33)

Are your time, money, and effort focused on making yourself look good or on making God known to others?

Lord, may I live simply and faithfully to bring honor to you instead of to myself. Amen.

January 25 ✤ Exodus 23–25

It is hard for me to understand how fickle the Israelites were while living in the wilderness. God did great miracles for them, and in Exodus 23, he tells the people he is sending an angel before them to protect them and lead them to the promised land.

Am I missing something? Is God doing the same for me, but I am not seeing it? Jesus is the Light of the World, but we don't always realize that we live in darkness when we substitute the "wisdom" of the world for the wisdom of Christ. We tend to look at people like Mother Teresa as outside the norm, since her wisdom was not the wisdom of the world.

God did not promise the angel for only one task. The angel would *lead* and *protect*. Would I be better at following if I thought about the protection I would receive?

Jesus spoke to the people once more and said, "I am the light of the world. If you follow me, you won't have to walk in darkness, because you will have the light that leads to life." (John 8:12)

How might you miss God's leading in your everyday life?

Lord, I don't want to be blind to the angel you send to lead me and protect me. Open my eyes, shine your light into my darkness, and help me see what marvelous gifts you have for me. May I remember that gifts from you are not like the world's gifts, for you are light and the world is darkness. May I boldly live in your light. Amen.

January 26 ✦ Exodus 26–28

Today's passage from Exodus includes some of God's instructions for constructing the tabernacle and clothing for Aaron and his sons. My first thought as I read the level of detail is, "I wish God would be that specific with his instructions for me." Maybe he is, but I'm not listening closely enough. Moses was on the mountain alone with God and probably took notes!

I try to sit alone with God, but my mind ends up wandering all over the place. I begin thinking about what I need to do instead of listening to God for instructions. Maybe that's why I'm not getting the detail Moses received. My brain has already jumped ahead from my quiet time with God into the busyness of the day.

I need the equivalent of Moses' smoke-covered mountain, my own spiritual retreat. Getting away and alone with God both physically and mentally can improve my hearing.

Then Jesus called to the crowd to come and hear. "Listen," he said, "and try to understand." (Matthew 15:10)

What makes it difficult for you to set aside time to be with God?

Lord, I need to be alone with you so I can hear your instructions for me. Today, help me find a time to be with you fully. Amen.

January 27 ✤ Exodus 29–31

In Exodus 30, God tells Moses that every time a census is taken, each person must be ransomed by half a shekel. The ransom is the same amount for everyone, whether rich or poor. God makes no distinction between them. The rich are no better than the poor in God's eyes. They are all the same.

A popular business magazine honors the world's richest people every year, but we should not follow suit. Wealth should not equal honor; what is important is whether a person lives and walks in the light of Christ. In the eyes of the world, a wealthy person who gives everything away is viewed as eccentric or even crazy.

Wealth is not the problem. The problem is how it changes our perception of a person. We judge someone's worth based on his or her wealth. It is so human, and yet so wrong.

The rich and poor have this in common: The Lord made them both. (Proverbs 22:2)

How easily do you see every person—all shapes, sizes, and personality types—as uniquely made by God?

Lord, may I remember that each person is worth the same to you. Forgive me when I look at myself or another person as more or less worthy. Give me your vision so I may see all people as you see them. Amen.

January 28 ✤ Exodus 32–34

Moses came down from the mountain to find the people worshiping a golden calf that Aaron made. God was ready to destroy them all, but Moses was eloquent in his appeal to God to have mercy on the people. When I contrast the appeal of Moses here with his conversation with God in the burning bush, it seems as if two completely different people are speaking.

Whether it's maturity, the mantle of leadership, or time spent with God, Moses, who was once afraid to speak to Pharaoh, is now not afraid to challenge God to change his mind.

On the other hand, Aaron, who was the spokesman before Pharaoh, now shows that he has learned little from God's miracles. His complicity in Israel's idolatry shows that he is more concerned about how people perceive him than how God views him.

Obviously, I'm not trying to win the approval of people, but of God. If pleasing people were my goal, I would not be Christ's servant. (Galatians 1:10)

In what ways can you seek to please God today?

Lord, give me the strength to seek to please you and not people. Remind me of Moses, and how he grew strong in your presence. Your favor, O Lord, is all that matters. Amen.

January 29 ✠ Exodus 35–37

When work was to begin on the tabernacle, the people brought so much stuff to contribute that Bezalel had to stop them. Are we capable of such generosity? We should be capable, but are we willing?

Do you want to do more for God? He gave us everything, even his only Son. We should be generous with our gifts and trust God for our own provisions. It's not always easy, but our love for Christ is our motivation.

You must each decide in your heart how much to give. And don't give reluctantly or in response to pressure. "For God loves a person who gives cheerfully." (2 Corinthians 9:7)

How can you give without holding back?

Lord, may I give generously because of your generous love for me. Amen.

January 30 ✠ Exodus 38–39

In the last chapters of Exodus, the people bring items to construct the tabernacle and all that goes with it. Great care is taken to describe in detail the items, and chapter 39 lists everything made for the tabernacle.

Do I focus as much attention and detail on the work I do for God as the Israelites did on the building of the tabernacle? I recall times when I agreed to serve God in some way and then did not follow through with my best effort.

God knows even the number of hairs on my head. I need to be more attentive to serving him.

All athletes are disciplined in their training. They do it to win a prize that will fade away, but we do it for an eternal prize. So I run with purpose in every step. I am not just shadowboxing. I discipline my body like an athlete, training it to do what it should. Otherwise, I fear that after preaching to others I myself might be disqualified. (1 Corinthians 9:25-27)

How attentive are you to serving God every minute of your day?

Lord, may I be disciplined and attentive in my spiritual life so that I please you. Amen.

January 31 ✠ Exodus 40

As I read Exodus 40 today, I thought about the similarities between the erection of the tabernacle and any major event in our lives that requires great planning, attention to detail, and persistence. The tabernacle's completion marked a new chapter in the lives of the Israelites. They had a structure in which to worship God. Even though they still roamed in the wilderness, something tangible reminded them of God's presence with them. It was a place to identify with their faith.

On the day of my wedding, I awoke with an upset stomach. I had moved almost everything out of my apartment except a mattress and ironing board, so the apartment did not feel like home. When I arrived at the church, my stomach settled. I was in a familiar place, and I had something tangible to comfort me.

We all experience life events in which something happens that marks the beginning of a new chapter. At those moments, do we look to God?

Surround me with your tender mercies so I may live, for your instructions are my delight. (Psalm 119:77)

What comforts you when you undergo a life transition? How can you remember to cling to God?

Lord, remind me always that I belong to you. Amen.

February 1 ✠ Leviticus 1–3

Leviticus 2 describes grain offerings in detail, giving specific instructions about how to prepare them and also what not to do. It's a good reminder that we should not take the holiness of God for granted or treat it lightly.

While we can think of God as our friend, we also must acknowledge his power, his majesty, and his godliness. Because he is God, we revere him and fall down in awe of him. Praise him, for he alone is God!

Give to the Lord the glory he deserves!
  Bring your offering and come into his courts.
Worship the Lord in all his holy splendor.
  Let all the earth tremble before him. (Psalm 96:8-9)

How can you honor the holiness of God?

Holy God, thank you for being God! Thank you for loving me! Amen.

February 2 ✠ Leviticus 4–6

Twice in Leviticus 6, God commands that the fire on the altar should never go out. It is to burn all the time. I don't sacrifice animals on an altar as the Israelites did, but I can see how this admonition relates to me. My heart is the altar, and God commands me never to let his fire go out in my heart.

In Leviticus, this fire is a wood fire. Think about a fire in a fireplace. Such a fire might blaze high and hot at times, and glow only faintly at other times. I'm like that. There are times in my life when I feel unable to contain the flames, and yet there are times when I have to poke my fire with a stick to be sure it still burns.

Wood kept the altar fire burning, and maybe this means God knows we can't maintain a consistent flame for him. Had an oil lamp made the fire, the flame would burn steadily and consistently as long as someone added oil to the reservoir. Not so with a wood fire!

Although I want to be consistent, I am not. Thank God I am at least a wood fire!

I know all the things you do, that you are neither hot nor cold. I wish that you were one or the other! (Revelation 3:15)

How can you keep your fire for God burning?

Lord, keep poking me when my flame dies down. I want to stay lit and burning for you. Amen.

February 3 ✠ Leviticus 7–8

Moses ordained Aaron and his sons to serve God as priests. Their ordination was an elaborate ritual that culminated with them staying in the tabernacle for seven days.

What a great example of the forgiveness of God! Aaron had defied God by making an idol for the people to worship while Moses met with God on the mountain. Now Aaron is in God's presence, in the tabernacle, to serve him as priest. His ordination shows that God is a God of mercy.

Sometimes we tend to think that God in the Old Testament is vengeful. That Aaron served him as priest shows that God is always ready to forgive.

O Lord, you are so good, so ready to forgive, so full of unfailing love for all who ask for your help. (Psalm 86:5)

How has God surprised you with his forgiveness?

Merciful God, thank you for your abundant forgiveness, for I always need your grace. Amen.

February 4 ✠ Leviticus 9–10

In Leviticus 10, God demonstrates how important it is to follow his instructions exactly as he commands. Two of Aaron's sons fail to obey God and burn the wrong kind of fire. God kills them. Aaron's other two sons fail to eat sacrifices that they are allowed to eat. Instead, they burn the parts they could have eaten. However, God does not kill them.

In the first instance, the brothers apparently don't take seriously the holiness of God and the importance of correct worship of him.

The other brothers offer to God their portion of the sacrifice. Their act does not diminish God.

I sometimes fail to acknowledge properly the holiness and sacredness of God. Something that helps me to remember God's holiness is to pray using the PRAY acrostic (Praise, Repent, Ask, Yield), because praising God as the first part of my prayers reminds me that he is more than a friend and benevolent father. He is God, creator and ruler of all things.

O Lord, our Lord, your majestic name fills the earth!
 Your glory is higher than the heavens.
When I look at the night sky and see the work of your fingers—
 the moon and the stars you set in place—
what are people that you should think about them,
 mere mortals that you should care for them?
Yet you made them only a little lower than God
 and crowned them with glory and honor. (Psalm 8:1, 3-5)

Is it easy or difficult for you to accept the holiness of God?

Holy Creator God, I praise you for who you are. All your works are glorious! May I bring glory to you by obeying you. Amen.

February 5 ✠ Leviticus 11–13

It is not easy to read Leviticus 11–13 and apply it to my daily life, other than to learn that God dealt with practical issues such as mildew! Much of the instruction in these chapters is health related, and we learn of certain acts that made people unclean.

God's instructions reinforce his sacredness by reminding us how to prepare ourselves to be in his presence. They also illustrate the importance of being aware of others, because our "uncleanness" can affect others. We have a responsibility to present ourselves clean not only to God but also to those with whom we live.

Live in harmony with each other. Don't be too proud to enjoy the company of ordinary people. And don't think you know it all! (Romans 12:16)

In what ways do you affect others' perception of God?

Lord, may I honor you and my brothers and sisters with my behavior. Amen.

February 6 ✚ Leviticus 14–15

In Leviticus 14, God tells Moses that he may contaminate some houses with mildew when the Israelites reach Canaan (v. 34). Mildew is not something I associate with God!

I had the opportunity to stay in a coastal hotel damaged by Hurricane Katrina. Pictures of the damage were displayed in the lobby. To look out over the calm water and think about the fury that caused such damage reminds me of how little I understand about God. I wonder why God created mosquitoes and wasps and why illnesses can strike for no apparent reason.

Thinking about these things makes me feel small and ignorant. I am humbled because I realize that no matter how much I learn about God, I still know little about his thoughts and actions. I do know that how I behave and act is far removed from the way God thinks and acts. It gives me a better understanding of why Isaiah, upon being in the presence of God, said "Woe unto me."

Have you never heard?
Have you never understood?
The Lord is the everlasting God,
the Creator of all the earth.
He never grows weak or weary.
No one can measure the depths of his understanding.
(Isaiah 40:28)

Do you find that the more you know about God, the more there is to know?

Lord, I am thankful that although there is much I do not understand, I know you love me. Even in times of uncertainty, help me to remember this. Amen.

February 7 ✤ Leviticus 16–18

God gave the Israelites instructions about their sexual behavior. They were to be people who behaved differently than their neighbors in Canaan. As God's chosen people, they were to stand out, not blend in. God knew that for the Israelites to remain faithful to him, they must be disciplined in their behavior.

It's no different today. God expects his followers to be different. Jesus challenges us to behave differently rather than doing what seems acceptable in our society. If we blend into our society, we cannot be the light that leads people to Christ.

But I say, love your enemies! Pray for those who persecute you! In that way, you will be acting as true children of your Father in heaven. For he gives his sunlight to both the evil and the good, and he sends rain on the just and the unjust alike. If you love only those who love you, what reward is there for that? Even corrupt tax collectors do that much. If you are kind only to your friends, how are you different from anyone else? Even pagans do that. But you are to be perfect, even as your Father in heaven is perfect. (Matthew 5:44-48)

In what ways can you honor God by standing apart from the rest of the world?

Lord, give me the strength to stand strong for you in all situations. Amen.

February 8 ✠ Leviticus 19–21

God gives instructions regarding fruit trees in Leviticus 19:23-25. For the first three years that the tree bears fruit, no one should harvest it. In the fourth year, the whole crop is consecrated to the Lord. Only in the fifth year may the people eat the fruit.

This period of waiting helped the people remember who was responsible for the tree's growth and production. The example offers interesting implications for us today. When a person starts a business, the first three years are often referred to as the "starvation period." How much faith would it require for a person to consecrate all the profit of the fourth year to God?

It may seem like a leap of faith, but isn't that what we are called to do—trust God for our provision?

He covers the heavens with clouds,
*   provides rain for the earth,*
*   and makes the grass grow in mountain pastures.*
He gives food to the wild animals
*   and feeds the young ravens when they cry. (Psalm 147:8-9)*

How often do you recognize the source of what you have?

Lord, all I have comes from you. May I behave as though I know that with all my heart. Amen.

February 9 ✠ Leviticus 22–23

Offerings to God were to be without defect—imperfect animals were not acceptable. God is to be honored with our best, not just any old gift we decide to bring. That means God gets my best thinking, my best leadership skills, my best time of day, my best attention, my best effort. I don't raise animals or crops, but the best of my work skills should go to God.

It's not merely about what I earn. It's also about what I do. The Israelites did not only bring the proceeds from their crops or herds; they brought the actual product. Likewise, I am to bring more than money to the Lord. How can I give my abilities to him?

The Lord has gifted Bezalel, Oholiab, and the other skilled craftsmen with wisdom and ability to perform any task involved in building the sanctuary. Let them construct and furnish the tabernacle, just as the Lord has commanded. (Exodus 36:1)

What gifts has God given you? How can you use them in God's service?

Lord, show me how to use my gifts to serve you. Amen.

February 10 ✜ Leviticus 24–25

Leviticus 25 gives the instructions for observing the year of Jubilee. The Israelites were not to worry about storing crops, since crops produced in the year before the Jubilee would be plentiful enough to supply food for three years.

It's sometimes hard for me to overcome logic and allow faith to prevail. When I rely on what I see, what logic tells me to expect, I lose the blessing that living by faith bestows on me. My lack of faith limits what God can do. If I follow in faith the way God leads me, why would I not expect God to provide for me?

And so he did only a few miracles there because of their unbelief. (Matthew 13:58)

How do your expectations fall short of God's capabilities?

Almighty God, help me to follow you faithfully and trust in your infinite power and love. Amen.

February 11 ✠ Leviticus 26–27

God told the Israelites that he would bless them if they followed his commands. He also told them that he would punish them if they were disobedient.

While Leviticus lists numerous commands, they mainly relate to how to worship God and how to live as God's chosen people. The Israelites were to recognize God's holiness and live holy lives as God's children.

It all sounds rather simple—love God, love each other, be holy. But we have as much trouble being obedient to God today as they did then. Thankfully, we worship a patient God!

In your love, you were patient with them for many years. (Nehemiah 9:30a)

How have you experienced God's patience personally?

Loving Father, I thank you for your infinite love and patience with me. May I never take for granted your holiness and your love. Amen.

February 12 ✠ Numbers 1–2

It's not easy to read Numbers 1–2 and find a relevant message from God. Yet God was interested in the details of where the tribes camped and the order in which they struck out when traveling.

Sometimes I think I shouldn't trouble God with specific, maybe even trivial issues. But Numbers 1–2 shows me that God is involved with all my life, not only the big stuff. It is all important to God. He wants me to share the details with him, because even though he already knows all about me, our relationship grows whenever I share my life story with him.

You made all the delicate, inner parts of my body
and knit me together in my mother's womb.
Thank you for making me so wonderfully complex!
Your workmanship is marvelous—how well I know it.
(Psalm 139:13-14)

How often do you share the details with God?

Creator God, thank you for caring about all the details of your creation. May I always go to you with all that is happening in my life. Amen.

February 13 ✠ Numbers 3–4

God gave each Levite clan a specific area of responsibility for the tabernacle. The Kohathites were responsible for preparing and transporting all the sacred objects. The Bible goes into great detail about the process of preparation for moving these items. In contrast, the description of the duties for the other two tribes is brief.

It would be easy to conclude that the Kohathites had the most important job because it involved the sacred objects. However, they also had the riskiest job. To touch or even look at the sacred objects without orders from the priests meant death for the Kohathites.

I can see why God imposed such a rule. Without this potential for punishment, it would be easy for the Kohathites to get an inflated view of themselves and their duties. There is a good lesson for us in this story.

If I am given an area of special responsibility, I need to obey. If I begin to think I did something special to merit the extra responsibility, I doom myself as surely as the Kohathites would if they failed to obey the instructions of the priests.

My abilities for any special task come from God. It is my job to use my gifts appropriately and only at God's direction.

So humble yourselves under the mighty power of God, and at the right time he will lift you up in honor. (1 Peter 5:6)

How difficult is it to be humble as you serve God?

Almighty God, may I never forget that all I am and all I have come from you. Keep me obedient and thankful to you. Amen.

February 14 ✠ Numbers 5–6

Numbers 6:27 says, "Whenever Aaron and his sons bless the people of Israel in my name, I myself will bless them." Giving blessings was an awesome responsibility and privilege given to the priests.

Even today, priests and ministers have a great responsibility before God. They are charged with the care of their congregations and intercede with God on behalf of the church as a whole as well as its individual members.

However, we also have a responsibility as church members to pray for our ministers and encourage them as they fulfill their responsibilities. As members of the church, we are also to pray for the church as a whole and for our brothers and sisters within the church who need prayer.

Confess your sins to each other and pray for each other so that you may be healed. The earnest prayer of a righteous person has great power and produces wonderful results. (James 5:16)

How frequently do you pray for others in your church?

Lord, may I never grow weary of praying to you. May I faithfully lift others to you in prayer. Amen.

February 15 ✠ Numbers 7

Why do you suppose the writer of Numbers repeats the gift of each tribe, when each tribe brings exactly the same gift? Surely it would be more efficient to list the leaders of each tribe and then say, "each leader brought the following gift from his tribe . . . ."

Two things come to mind as I read this repetitious list. The first is that although the tribes differed in size, each contributed identically to the tabernacle. Small or large, each brought the same gift. Are we, although different in terms of gifts, abilities, and economics, expected to give the same gifts to God? Maybe the lesson is that we each bring the best we have to offer. In that way, our gifts are all the same.

The second thought is that by detailing the gift of each tribe, even though identical, the writer treats each tribe's gift as uniquely the gift of that tribe. No one's gift gets lost in the shuffle. Likewise, when we give our best gifts to God, no one's gift is lost or less precious to him. He gives equal honor to what each person brings. Even if I am not as gifted and talented (in the eyes of the world), my gifts are unique and valuable to God.

He created me and gave me these gifts. For me to compare myself to others and judge my gifts as less valuable is to insult the gifts God gave especially to me. The world may treat them differently, but God gives me strength to use them for his glory.

There are different kinds of spiritual gifts, but the same Spirit is the source of them all. There are different kinds of service, but we serve the same Lord. God works in different ways, but it is the same God who does the work in all of us. (1 Corinthians 12:4-6)

When are you tempted to compare your gifts to those of others? How does God help you refocus on using your unique gifts for him?

O Lord, may I be thankful for the gifts you give me, and use them to honor and glorify you. Amen.

February 16 ✠ Numbers 8–9

The Israelites moved or stopped at the movement of the cloud. Numbers 9:22 tells us that sometimes they stopped for one night, but it could be as long as a year.

Am I that obedient? It is difficult for me to wait when God tells me to wait. I want to know the plan, the timetable, the agenda. But God wants me to be obedient, whether I am moving or waiting, whether he has revealed his plan for me or not.

Because he is in control, I can rest. So why do I fret over the unknown?

If it seems slow in coming, wait patiently, for it will surely take place. It will not be delayed. (Habakkuk 2:3b)

When have you had to wait for God? What did you do as you waited?

Lord, help me to be as flexible as the Israelites are in Numbers 9. May I obediently follow your direction for my life, even if you tell me to wait. Amen.

February 17 ✠ Numbers 10–11

In Numbers 11:21-23, Moses questions how God will provide enough meat for all the people for a month, and God responds by saying, "Has my arm lost its power?"

Moses had seen God's miracles and had been with God regularly and frequently, and yet he still, in his mind, put limits on what God could do. I haven't experienced God in the same way Moses did, but I am also guilty of limiting the power of God in my mind.

I need to trust God for *all* things, not only some things. I can trust him in both the big crises of my life and the day-to-day worries. God is in the details as well as in the big picture.

Come and see what our God has done,
  what awesome miracles he performs for people!
He made a dry path through the Red Sea,
  and his people went across on foot.
  There we rejoiced in him. (Psalm 66:5-6)

In what ways do you limit the power of God?

Lord, forgive me for not looking to you for all things. It doesn't make sense for me to try to handle things by myself when you are there, wanting to guide me. I want to have your love and guidance always. Help me to seek you first and in all things. Amen.

February 18 ✤ Numbers 12–13

In Numbers 13, Moses sent spies into Canaan to scout out the land. All came back and discouraged invasion except for Caleb and Joshua. Many times, if we follow God's direction, we have more detractors than supporters.

God's ways don't always make sense to others because people act on what they see, not on faith in what God says he will do.

Gideon led an army of only 300 men against the armies of the Midianites. Anyone would have thought Gideon didn't stand a chance, but he obeyed God, and the Midianites were defeated. When God gives us direction, he also will give us the means to accomplish his purpose.

He has shown his great power to his people
  by giving them the lands of other nations.
All he does is just and good,
  and all his commandments are trustworthy. (Psalm 111:6-7)

How has God surprised you by acting beyond your expectations and above your inadequacies?

All-powerful God, may I always rely on you for direction and support. When I feel inadequate, may I remember that you made me and provide all I need to accomplish the tasks you give me. Amen.

February 19 ✠ Numbers 14–15

God commanded the Israelites to attach tassels to their robes as a reminder to obey God's laws. What physical reminder would help me remember to be obedient?

A few years ago, WWJD (What Would Jesus Do?) bracelets were everywhere. I'm not sure how much they changed the lives of their wearers. Those I knew who wore them didn't seem to behave much differently with the bracelets than they did without them. As the bracelets became familiar, their message was no longer fresh.

How can I maintain freshness in my relationship with God? Can I marvel with fresh eyes the miracles in nature around me?

Sing a new song to the Lord!
Let the whole earth sing to the Lord!
Sing to the Lord; praise his name.
Each day proclaim the good news that he saves.
Publish his glorious deeds among the nations.
Tell everyone about the amazing things he does. (Psalm 96:1-3)

What keeps your relationship with God fresh?

Lord, keep my eyes, ears, and heart aware and seeking you. Keep my faith fresh, vibrant, and growing, so that I am always challenged to seek a closer relationship with you. Amen.

February 20 ✠ Numbers 16–18

Numbers 18:29 repeats an instruction given often to the Israelites as they learned how God wants to be worshiped: "Be sure to give to the Lord the best portions of the gifts given to you." Here, the priests are told to give a tithe of the tithe received from the people.

Though the priests had the right to receive the tithes of the people, they were also expected to give a portion of what they received to God. And not just any portion, but the best portion.

Do I give God the best portion of what he has given me? All I receive is a gift from God, even though to the world it may seem that I earned much of what I receive through my labor. I want to be sure God gets the best portions of the gifts he gives me. This may mean I place a higher priority on my service in the church or clearly communicate that God gets the glory when I am recognized in some way.

Whom have I in heaven but you? I desire you more than anything on earth. (Psalm 73:25)

Do you ever hold your best back from God? How can you be more dedicated about giving your best to God first?

Lord, show me how I can give you the best of what I have received from you. Amen.

February 21 ✠ Numbers 19–20

God gave a specific ritual for cleansing those who were unclean due to association with a dead person. One verse in particular stands out in the description of the cleansing ritual: Numbers 19:12. The purification ritual was so important that failure to do it properly meant the person was still unclean.

I like ritual in my life. I like to have certain ways and certain times to do things. It gives me a sense of order and predictability. It helps me establish new habits if they have a particular place in my daily life.

Lent is a season that encourages a focus on ritual. It is a time to give up what takes our focus away from God, and it is also a time to adopt practices or rituals that draw us closer to God. As Jesus spent forty days in the wilderness to prepare himself for ministry, the forty days of Lent call us to cleanse ourselves from what is impure in our lives so we may present ourselves clean to Christ.

Under the old system, the blood of goats and bulls and the ashes of a young cow could cleanse people's bodies from ceremonial impurity. Just think how much more the blood of Christ will purify our consciences from sinful deeds so that we can worship the living God. For by the power of the eternal Spirit, Christ offered himself to God as a perfect sacrifice for our sins. (Hebrews 9:13-14)

What impurities has God cleansed from you? How did this change your relationship with God?

Perfect God, reveal to me the impurity in me so I can be cleansed. I want to be holy and pure for you. Amen.

February 22 ✜ Numbers 21–22

We tend to criticize the Israelites for their wavering faith in God. God does something amazing for them, and quickly they forget. Numbers 21:4-5 relates their complaints over a long journey. They are impatient and tired of eating manna.

Perseverance is not a characteristic we want to have. We would rather not have to plod along, seeing no visible signs of progress to encourage us. We want to see instant results and score at least small victories along the way. Wandering in the wilderness with no miracles, no excitement, is not appealing at all.

We need to remember that when stone competes with water, stone will always lose because water's persistence wears it down. We need to be content when it feels that all we are doing is plodding, if it is what God seeks from us. He may want us to move slowly, or not at all, so he can wash his cleansing water over our stony hearts. We may not see the change for a long time, but it will come in God's time as long as we are content to persevere.

But if you look carefully into the perfect law that sets you free, and if you do what it says and don't forget what you heard, then God will bless you for doing it. (James 1:25)

When do you struggle to persevere in your faith?

Faithful God, help me to be diligent in following you, even when the way is dull and I feel I am going nowhere. May I only look to you and be obedient. Amen

February 23 ✜ Numbers 23–25

Something about watching a beautiful sunrise reminds me that God is in control and I can be at peace. In Numbers 23 and 24, Balak tries to get Balaam to curse the Israelites, but Balaam says he can only do what God wills. Consequently, he blesses the Israelites three times.

God won't be thwarted. His plans will come to pass regardless of our inability to comply. A gorgeous sunrise occurs because God created another day and gave it to us. What a marvelous gift a day is! It gives us another chance to live for God. I may not have done what I should have done yesterday, but because I see the sun rise, I have the opportunity to live for God and God alone today! Hallelujah!

For the Lord is a great God,
a great King above all gods.
He holds in his hands the depths of the earth
and the mightiest mountains.
The sea belongs to him, for he made it.
His hands formed the dry land, too. (Psalm 95:3-5)

When have you failed to comply with God's plans? How did God show you grace through this situation?

Great God, I am thankful that you are always in control and that you are always merciful. May I strive every day to be more faithful to you. Amen.

February 24 ✠ Numbers 26–27

God commanded Moses to take another census of the Israelites. When it was completed, it was determined that no one from the earlier census remained alive except Caleb and Joshua. Therefore the people would be able to enter the promised land. For forty years they had wandered and waited to receive what God promised them. Could I remain faithful for forty years, waiting for the fulfillment of God's promise?

How does my life look when I think back over the past forty years? Have I been wandering aimlessly in my own wilderness, complaining about where I am? I know I have experienced many periods of disobedience, just as the Israelites did. As I look ahead, I hope I will be more faithful, so that in another forty years I can look back and see obedience and joy.

But my life is worth nothing to me unless I use it for finishing the work assigned me by the Lord Jesus—the work of telling others the Good News about the wonderful grace of God. (Acts 20:24)

What helps you obey God each day?

Faithful Father, I want to be obedient to you all the days of my life. Amen.

February 25 ✠ Numbers 28–29

Numbers 29 details three different festivals to be celebrated in the same month. The first is a one-day festival, the Festival of Trumpets. Ten days later is a Day of Atonement, a day of fasting. Five days later is the eight-day Festival of Shelters. When I initially read this, my first thought was to wonder what it would be like to celebrate God for an entire month.

Then I thought about the seasons of Advent and Lent. Am I attentive to God during these seasons? Do I celebrate God? I should view these seasons as special opportunities to celebrate God and to rejoice in the gift of Christ's birth and the sacrifice he made for us all.

Praise the Lord!
Praise God in his sanctuary;
praise him in his mighty heaven!
Praise him for his mighty works;
praise his unequaled greatness!
Praise him with a blast of the ram's horn;
praise him with the lyre and harp!
Praise him with the tambourine and dancing;
praise him with strings and flutes!
Praise him with a clash of cymbals;
praise him with loud clanging cymbals.
Let everything that breathes sing praises to the Lord!
Praise the Lord! (Psalm 150)

How do you celebrate God?

Lord, when I think of who you are and what you've done for me, how can I help but praise you? Thank you for all you have done for me. Amen.

February 26 ✠ Numbers 30–31

It's hard to read Numbers 30 and 31 and find something from the reading that I can apply in my life. In Numbers 30, God gives instructions that affect relationships between a husband and wife and a father and daughter. In Numbers 31, the Midianites are attacked and destroyed for leading the Israelites away from God.

When I read these chapters, I realize that there is much I do not understand about God. However, I trust that he is good and that he has a reason for the instructions he gives, even if he doesn't always explain them. As his children, we cannot always understand the why, but we can always trust God to be faithful to us.

Just as you cannot understand the path of the wind or the mystery of a tiny baby growing in its mother's womb, so you cannot understand the activity of God, who does all things. (Ecclesiastes 11:5)

Do you find that you need to understand God in order to love God?

Creator God, there is much that I do not know or understand about you. But I do know that you love me and take care of me, and for that I am thankful. Amen.

February 27 ✠ Numbers 32–33

God warned the Israelites to drive out completely the people living in the promised land. To leave any remnant of them or their culture would provide "splinters in your eyes and thorns in your side." Ouch!

Things aren't much different now with regard to our temptation to succumb to the surrounding culture. We may behave in a way that is perfectly acceptable in our society, but is not compatible with a Christian life. It is not always easy to eliminate such behavior from our lives because those around us who still practice that behavior may ridicule us for being different.

Likewise, it is not easy to adopt a behavior that is not valued in our society. A good example is reducing our number of activities. Our society values busyness as a measure of individual worth. God, however, does not value us based on the level of busyness in our lives. Instead, he asks that we spend time with him.

Because we have these promises, dear friends, let us cleanse ourselves from everything that can defile our body or spirit. And let us work toward complete holiness because we fear God. (2 Corinthians 7:1)

When do you struggle between God and the world? What helps you follow God?

Holy and Perfect God, you have called us to be different because we belong to you. It's not easy, Lord, even to know when we are listening to the world's "wisdom" instead of your teaching. Give us discerning minds so that we can hear your voice over that of the world. Amen.

February 28 ✜ Numbers 34–36

The idea of Cities of Refuge is interesting. A City of Refuge gave someone who accidentally killed another person a place to live where he or she was safe from those who would seek revenge.

God realized that forgiveness is not easy. If it was, the accidental killer could have approached the family of the person killed, asked for forgiveness, and received it. Forgiveness is neither easy to ask for nor easy to give.

When Jesus came, he preached forgiveness. While it isn't easy, it should be our aim not only to seek forgiveness when we've hurt another, but to grant forgiveness when someone has hurt us or someone we love.

Love your enemies! Do good to them. Lend to them without expecting to be repaid. Then your reward from heaven will be very great, and you will truly be acting as children of the Most High, for he is kind to those who are unthankful and wicked. You must be compassionate, just as your Father is compassionate. (Luke 6:35-36)

When have you found it difficult to offer compassion to someone who hurt you?

Loving Father, help me to be compassionate to all people, even if they hurt me. Amen.

March 1 ✠ Deuteronomy 1-2

As the people prepared to enter the promised land, Moses addressed them, recalling the events that occurred since they left Egypt. He reminded them that even though God led them by a pillar of cloud and a pillar of fire so that they camped in good places, they failed to trust that he would deliver to them the people living in the promised land.

In *My Utmost for His Highest*, Oswald Chambers says "we impoverish and weaken His ministry in us the moment we forget He is almighty. The impoverishment is in us, not in Him."[2] God's ability to help us is limited only by our faith in him. May we trust him always.

If we are unfaithful, he remains faithful, for he cannot deny who he is. (2 Timothy 2:13)

In what ways have you weakened the ministry of God with your low expectations of him?

Faithful God, may I remember that you are almighty, able to do anything. May I lean on you and trust you with everything in my life. Amen.

March 2 ✠ Deuteronomy 3-4

In Deuteronomy 4, Moses predicted the falling away of the Israelites. He foretold their being scattered among other nations. Yet, in verse 29, Moses says, "But from there you will search again for the Lord your God. And if you search for him with all your heart and soul, you will find him."

This should give us great comfort because no matter how badly we feel we have sinned, God still loves us and is there at the moment we call for him. When you ponder that, it is truly amazing—the absolute depth of God's love for us.

Lord, if you kept a record of our sins,
  who, O Lord, could ever survive?
But you offer forgiveness,
  that we might learn to fear you. (Psalm 130:3-4)

When have you searched for God "with all your heart and soul" and found him?

Loving Father, may I never hesitate to turn to you for forgiveness. Your love for me is beyond my power to understand, and I praise you for it! Amen.

March 3 ✤ Deuteronomy 5–7

Deuteronomy 7:6 says, "Of all the people of the earth, the Lord your God has chosen you to be his own special treasure." We are not to take these words lightly.

Henri Nouwen, in his book, *Life of the Beloved*, says we have a hard time believing we are beloved because people have told us we are not. "In the midst of this extremely painful reality," he writes, "we have to dare to reclaim the truth that we are God's chosen ones, even when our world does not choose us. As long as we allow our parents, siblings, teachers, friends, and lovers to determine whether we are chosen or not, we are caught in the net of a suffocating world that accepts or rejects us according to its own agenda of effectiveness and control."[3]

When God tells the Israelites that they are his special treasure, it is not because of anything they have done. Likewise, God chooses us not because we are smart or eloquent or even obedient to him. He chooses us because he loves us, just as we are.

But now, O Jacob, listen to the Lord who created you.
  O Israel, the one who formed you says,
"Do not be afraid, for I have ransomed you.
  I have called you by name; you are mine." (Isaiah 43:1)

How does it make you feel if you truly believe that you are God's special treasure?

Lord, may I always remember that I am your treasure. Amen.

March 4 ✠ Deuteronomy 8-10

God gave the people manna while they lived in the wilderness. Moses told the people that God fed them this way to humble them. Deuteronomy 8:17 says, "He did all this so you would never say to yourself, 'I have achieved this wealth with my own strength and energy.'"

Because the Israelites owed their "daily bread" to God's love for them, they were to remember that God, not anything they did, provided what they needed.

It's a lesson that applies to us today. It's not always easy to remember when I experience success. At those times, the world holds me up and honors me for what "I" have accomplished. I must always remember that I accomplish nothing on my own. God's manna to me may not be food falling from the sky, but he provides everything I have.

By his divine power, God has given us everything we need for living a godly life. We have received all of this by coming to know him, the one who called us to himself by means of his marvelous glory and excellence. (2 Peter 1:3)

How often do you thank God for your successes in life, both large and small?

Generous God, thank you for creating me, loving me, and giving me everything I need. May I always give you the glory! Amen.

March 5 ✠ Deuteronomy 11–13

I have heard that Christianity is always only one generation away from extinction. Deuteronomy 11:18-20 gives us instructions about how to keep God's word at the forefront of our minds. We are to use physical reminders and share God with family and others we encounter.

For me, the physical reminder may be a Bible verse on an index card or Christian music on my car stereo. But sharing my faith with others is also important. God doesn't say we are to remember God's word for ourselves. When I share my faith, not only do I feed someone else's spiritual hunger, but I also send the roots of my own faith deeper into God's soil.

If I am reluctant to share my faith with others, I need to ask myself why I hesitate. We share what we are excited about, whether it's a movie we've seen or something our children have done. Am I excited about what God is doing for me?

We will not hide these truths from our children;
we will tell the next generation
about the glorious deeds of the Lord,
about his power and his mighty wonders. (Psalm 78:4)

How do you keep God's word at the forefront of your mind?

Glorious God, may I be an enthusiastic witness about what you have done for me. May I rejoice in sharing your great love with others. Amen.

March 6 ✠ Deuteronomy 14–16

I like the instruction God gave the Israelites to cancel debts and free servants every seven years. What a good way to remind both master and servant, creditor and debtor that God is in control, and all we have is really his.

God's instruction protected debtors and servants so that others would not take advantage of them. Lenders and masters found it more difficult to think better of themselves because at the end of seven years, everything was again equal.

But Jesus called them together and said, "You know that the rulers in this world lord it over their people, and officials flaunt their authority over those under them. But among you it will be different. Whoever wants to be a leader among you must be your servant, and whoever wants to be first among you must become your slave. For even the Son of Man came not to be served but to serve others and to give his life as a ransom for many." (Matthew 20:25-28)

What levels you with the rest of humanity? How easy is it to remember this?

Giving Father, may I never think more of myself than I ought to think. May I be gracious to others and serve them as if I were serving you. Amen.

March 7 ✠ Deuteronomy 17–20

"But you must be blameless before the Lord your God" (Deuteronomy 18:13). This is a tall order! Moses told the people not to engage in the practices of the nations around them. It's not easy to live in the world and act differently from those who are of the world.

What I hear and see on television, in music, in the news, and in movies often matches the list of things God wanted the Israelites to avoid. For me to remain faithful and focused on the things of God requires that I surround myself with Christian influences. The people I associate with, what I read and listen to, and how I spend my time should reflect and support my faith. Living a Christian life is hard enough without deliberately placing myself in situations that threaten my faith.

You go before me and follow me.
You place your hand of blessing on my head. (Psalm 139:5)

How do the things you see and hear each day influence you?

Lord, may I surround myself with people and influences that draw me nearer to you. Amen.

March 8 ✠ Deuteronomy 21–23

Jesus tells us not to worry about food or clothing because if God takes care of the birds and the lilies, he will surely take care of us. Deuteronomy 22:6-7 shows us that this idea goes back for centuries before Jesus spoke about it.

Among laws that tell the Israelites how to deal with murder and accidental death, give rules about war, advise on sexual purity, and relate the way to worship are two verses that instruct the people not to take both eggs and the mother bird. This instruction even comes with a blessing: so that we may prosper and enjoy a long life.

Kind treatment of animals, even a bird, is rewarded with prosperity and a long life. One of my great morning joys is listening to the birds. At sunrise, they seem to sing all at once. When I think of how many I hear, it is incredible that the Lord knows each bird and cares for each one! And Jesus says we are of greater value than many birds!

I know every bird on the mountains, and all the animals of the field are mine. (Psalm 50:11)

How does God's creation remind you of how much he loves you?

Creator God, I am so thankful that you made me and treasure me. May I treasure the birds and remember you each time I hear one sing. Amen.

March 9 ✠ Deuteronomy 24–27

Among all the instructions about human relationships, Deuteronomy 25:4 stands out: "You must not muzzle an ox to keep it from eating as it treads out the grain."

Animals are God's creation, just as we are. God cares about animals. Jesus reminded us of God's concern for animals when he said God knows even when a sparrow falls to the ground. When we treat every living creature as a creature of God, we are able to maintain an awareness of God's blessings to us and to all creation.

He gives food to the wild animals and feeds the young ravens when they cry. (Psalm 147:9)

In what ways can you care for God's world?

Creator God, when I experience nature and see the creatures you have made, may I remember your blessings to me. May I be a good steward of this world you created. Amen.

March 10 ✠ Deuteronomy 28

God lists both blessings and curses in Deuteronomy 28. If the Israelites choose to follow him and listen to him, they will receive great material blessings. If they fail to follow him, they will suffer incredible hardships.

It is difficult to read and understand this when I think of faithful and obedient people suffering. Our Savior also suffered and was crucified, and he was perfectly obedient to God.

There is much I don't understand, but I do know that even in the midst of suffering, I can trust God to be with me, to care about me, and to love me always.

The thought of my suffering and homelessness
*   is bitter beyond words.*
I will never forget this awful time,
*   as I grieve over my loss.*
Yet I still dare to hope
*   when I remember this:*
The faithful love of the Lord never ends!
*   His mercies never cease.*
Great is his faithfulness,
*   his mercies begin afresh each morning. (Lamentations 3:19-23)*

How easy is it to have faith in God during the most difficult times?

Lord, whatever happens to me, may I remember that you are ever faithful. Amen.

March 11 ✠ Deuteronomy 29–31

"The Lord our God has secrets known to no one. We are not accountable for them, but we and our children are accountable forever for all that he has revealed to us, so that we may obey all the terms of these instructions" (Deuteronomy 29:29). To think about God having secrets reminds me that I am limited in my ability to know him. No matter how much I learn about God, there are things that I can never know. It helps me to realize that I have a relationship with the almighty and all-knowing One.

However, I have a responsibility in the relationship. The second part of the verse says I am accountable for what I know about God and how he teaches me to live. Just as a child may not know a parent's reasons for particular instructions, I may not understand all that God wants me to do. However, if I know what he wants me to do, I am responsible for doing it.

"My thoughts are nothing like your thoughts," says the Lord.
"And my ways are far beyond anything you could imagine.

For just as the heavens are higher than the earth,
so are my ways higher than your ways
and my thoughts higher than your thoughts." (Isaiah 55:8-9)

What has God revealed to you? How seriously do you take this knowledge?

Almighty God, it is humbling to think that you, the creator of all things, speak to me. May I never lose sight of the wonder of having a relationship with you. Amen.

March 12 ✣ Deuteronomy 32–34

God knew Moses face to face. What a powerful statement! To reflect on the life of Moses is to realize that he was an ordinary man. God saw something in Moses that others might have missed. Moses had killed a man and fled Egypt. He lived with his in-laws and worked for them. He did not want to be God's spokesman before Pharaoh.

Despite his relationship with God, there were times when he did not believe God could do what he promised. Yet he stood up to God when God threatened to destroy the Israelites.

God gave Moses the abilities he needed to confront Pharaoh and lead a nation to the promised land, even when they didn't want to go. Because Moses was obedient, God prepared him to do what God called him to do. If God calls you, be assured that he will equip you for the task.

For the Lord grants wisdom!
From his mouth come knowledge and understanding.
He grants a treasure of common sense to the honest.
He is a shield to those who walk with integrity. (Proverbs 2:6-7)

How do the stories of biblical people encourage you in your own walk with God?

Lord, I am encouraged to know that you see promise in me that I cannot see. May I be obedient when you call me. Amen.

March 13 ✠ Joshua 1–3

God does not always use godly people to accomplish his purposes. Take Rahab, for instance. A prostitute in Jericho, she hid and protected the spies Joshua sent to the promised land. Her actions were motivated by self-preservation, but the result helped assure a successful mission for the Israelites.

Lest we get too elitist in our thinking about God and his love for us, we need to remember that God created us all, even a prostitute in Jericho. Whether or not she acknowledged God as her Father, she still is remembered for the help she gave the Israelite spies.

We need to look for God in all circumstances, in all people, and in all places. God often uses the unlikeliest of people in the unlikeliest places to accomplish his purpose.

I have observed something else under the sun. The fastest runner doesn't always win the race, and the strongest warrior doesn't always win the battle. The wise sometimes go hungry, and the skillful are not necessarily wealthy. And those who are educated don't always lead successful lives. It is all decided by chance, by being in the right place at the right time. (Ecclesiastes 9:11)

How has God used people in surprising ways?

Lord, may I be open to you wherever I go and whatever I do. May I see you in everyone I meet. Amen.

March 14 ✠ Joshua 4–6

Most of us enjoy collecting visible reminders of special events. Who doesn't have a souvenir that keeps alive a memory of a treasured vacation? Parents often proudly display gifts made by their children in their homes or offices.

When God stopped the Jordan River's flow so the Israelites could safely cross on dry ground, Joshua asked each tribe to gather a stone from the riverbed. They erected a memorial to mark the event. When God performed a similar (and more famous to us) miracle as recorded in Exodus, no memorial was erected because the Israelites were far from home.

This pile of rocks was significant to Israel in two ways. It served to remind them of their miraculous crossing, and it marked that they were now home. Just as we don't decorate our hotel room with mementos, but save the treasures to display at home, the Israelites indicated their arrival into the promised land, their new home, with this monument.

> On that day I will gather you together
>   and bring you home again.
>   I will give you a good name, a name of distinction,
>   among all the nations of the earth,
> as I restore your fortunes before their very eyes.
>   I, the Lord, have spoken! (Zephaniah 3:20)

What physical reminders do you treasure? What memories do they provoke?

Lord, may I always remember the great things you have done for me and for others. Amen.

March 15 ✠ Joshua 7–8

God was prepared to destroy the Israelites over the disobedience of one man. Achan had kept plunder that belonged to God, and because of his sin, God allowed the Israelites to suffer defeat. Thirty-six fighting men were killed due to the sin of one man.

We are interconnected with each other, although we often want to believe that our actions affect no one but ourselves. What we do makes a difference—*always*—for good or for bad. That's an incredible thought.

Every decision I make or don't make reaches beyond me with a powerful impact. If I strive to remember this truth, what difference might it make in how I live my life?

People who conceal their sins will not prosper, but if they confess and turn from them, they will receive mercy. (Proverbs 28:13)

How have your actions in the past week affected others?

Lord, may I remember that all I do or say affects others. May I care so much for all your creation that I seek to do no harm. Amen

March 16 ✠ Joshua 9–10

"So the Israelites examined their food, but they did not consult the Lord" (Joshua 9:14). We put our faith in what we see. If we can see it, we believe it. Thomas reacted this way upon hearing that Jesus had appeared to others after his death.

But what we see isn't always the truth. A bank robbery made the national news because of who the robbers were. Dubbed the "Barbie bandits," the two young women looked more like college coeds than bank robbers. They were not who they appeared to be.

The Israelites looked at the Gibeonites and thought they saw travelers from far away. They made a decision based on what they saw, without consulting God. They trusted their own judgment instead of trusting God's judgment. Put this way, it seems incredible that we would rank ourselves, the created, higher than God, the Creator.

This is what the Sovereign Lord,
*   the Holy One of Israel, says:*
"Only in returning to me
*   and resting in me will you be saved.*
In quietness and confidence is your strength.
*   But you would have none of it.*

You said, 'No, we will get our help from Egypt.
    They will give us swift horses for riding into battle.'
But the only swiftness you are going to see
    is the swiftness of your enemies chasing you!" (Isaiah 30:15-16)

How can you strive to trust God's judgment rather than people's perceptions?

God of truth, why do I ever think I know better than you? May I seek your guidance in all things, even when the solution seems obvious. Amen.

March 17 ✠ Joshua 11–13

"But Moses gave no allotment of land to the tribe of Levi, for the Lord, the God of Israel, had promised that he himself would be their allotment" (Joshua 13:33). Life is often financially challenging. Most people I know feel that there is more month than money. But when we choose to surrender to God, he becomes our allotment. God says to us, "I am sufficient. I am all you need."

When I embrace God as my allotment, all else becomes secondary. My priorities and motivations change. When I put God first, I feel confident that he will take care of me. I may still suffer hardships, but if I keep my eyes on Christ, I have all I need.

For you have been given not only the privilege of trusting in Christ but also the privilege of suffering for him. (Philippians 1:29)

How much faith does it take to accept God as your sole "allotment"?

Lord, I want you to be my allotment. I want my primary aim to be to please you. May my focus be on you and you only as I go through each day. Amen.

March 18 ✠ Joshua 14–16

Caleb waited forty-five years to see the promise of God fulfilled regarding the land he was to possess. That's a long time to wait. In Caleb's case, it was more than half his life because he was forty years old when God promised the gift.

Could I be this patient, or would I grumble that God forgot me or I heard him incorrectly or he changed his mind? God is faithful, but we have a hard time accepting that we must wait to see him work. We live in an "instant" society, but God does not necessarily operate on our timetable!

But if we look forward to something we don't yet have, we must wait patiently and confidently. (Romans 8:25)

How do you struggle to be patient as you wait for God's timing?

Lord, grant me patience to wait on your timing and to trust your faithfulness. Amen.

March 19 ✠ Joshua 17–19

The descendants of Manasseh who did not receive land on the east side of the Jordan River sound like the Israelite spies Moses sent to scout out Canaan while the people waited to enter the promised land. Like those earlier spies, they give Joshua excuses for why they cannot conquer the land God gives them.

How easy it is to forget the power of God and his blessings for us. During the week before I read these chapters, I felt "in sync" with God. My daily devotional times were meaningful, and I had my own day of spiritual retreat that renewed and strengthened me. On Sunday morning, as I reflected on the previous days, I was excited by my awareness of God.

Then on that same Sunday, in the afternoon, I got angry and upset because I could not get something to work on my computer. I ranted and stormed around the house and made everyone miserable. Just like those descendants of Manasseh, I forgot to turn to God. I allowed things of the world to govern my behavior instead of seeing things through God's eyes. Of course, God may not have chosen to fix my computer, but by focusing on him, I know I would have viewed the situation differently.

I am the Lord, the God of all the peoples of the world. Is anything too hard for me? (Jeremiah 32:27)

When have you failed to go to God?

Lord, why do I struggle to do things by myself when you are there, able to do anything? Help me to trust you with all of my life and to rest in your presence because you are almighty. Amen.

March 20 ✤ Joshua 20–21

Joshua 20 and 21 read like a conclusion. The Israelites have conquered the land, and all that remains is to parcel out towns for the Levites.

Ending a project is not always easy. We give so much time and effort that it is sometimes hard to let go of a project once we accomplish our purpose. Joshua 21:44 says the Lord gave the people rest on every side. Part of ending well is taking the rest that should come at the end of a project. Even when another project looms, a time of rest is important.

God rested after creating the earth. He gives us a day every week to rest. Part of the way he cares for us is to provide us the opportunity to stop and catch our breath.

The apostles returned to Jesus from their ministry tour and told him all they had done and taught. Then Jesus said, "Let's go off by ourselves to a quiet place and rest awhile." (Mark 6:30-31)

In what ways do you make time to rest?

Lord, help me to realize that rest is important. You rested, and we should too. May I rest in you and find the peace that only you can provide. Amen.

March 21 ✠ Joshua 22–24

Joshua told the Israelites not to associate with the people remaining in the promised land. Because of his great concern that the Israelites would be led astray, he told them not even to mention the names of these people's gods.

Some sins tempt us so strongly that the only way to avoid them is not to think of them at all. What sin tempts you just by the mention of it?

Joshua urged the Israelites to cling tightly to God. Sometimes that's the only thing we can do when temptations threaten to lead us astray.

This High Priest of ours understands our weaknesses, for he faced all of the same testings we do, yet he did not sin. So let us come boldly to the throne of our gracious God. There we will receive his mercy, and we will find grace to help us when we need it most. (Hebrews 4:15-16)

How do you resist daily temptation?

Lord, I need your help to resist temptation. I need to cling to you and rely on your help because I cannot do it alone. Amen.

March 22 ✠ Judges 1–2

In school, a score of 95 on an exam generally earns a grade of A, but in our spiritual lives, a 95 is not good enough. The Israelites mostly conquered the land God gave them, but they did not completely drive out those who already lived there. They did not follow God's instructions completely. If I follow most, but not all, of God's instructions, have I obeyed him?

In the medical community, there is concern about drug-resistant strains of illness that are becoming more prevalent. These stronger germs are often the result of people who take most, but not all, of their medicine. When sick people begin feeling better, their incentive for taking medicine disappears, so they forget a dose here and there until they finally give up completely. Less than 100 percent obedience to medical instructions may have severe consequences.

In *My Utmost for His Highest*, Oswald Chambers says God desires our complete surrender.[4] The Israelites discovered that anything less than complete obedience was disobedience. It's no different for us. Whenever we fail to surrender completely, we find it easier to resist God's call for us, and finally we fall away completely.

A final word: Be strong in the Lord and in his mighty power. Put on all of God's armor so that you will be able to stand firm against all strategies of the devil. (Ephesians 6:10-11)

How often do you give God only partial obedience?

God, make me strong. May I surrender completely to you and not be satisfied with partial obedience. Amen.

March 23 ✚ Judges 3–5

After the death of Joshua, the Israelites strayed from God, following instead the gods of the people around them. Despite the miracles God performed for their ancestors, despite his leading them into Canaan and giving the land to them, they forgot him. They mixed with the people they failed to remove, and it brought them down.

While we live in the world with all kinds of people, we need the fellowship of other Christians to help us remain strong in our faith. Christ did not select only one helper; he chose twelve apostles, and many others were his faithful followers. When Christ was no longer with them, they supported and encouraged each other, which helped strengthen the early church.

As Christians, we need each other because it's easy to become discouraged and drift away from Christ. The Christian community is much stronger when we all come together.

Two people are better off than one, for they can help each other succeed. If one person falls, the other can reach out and help. But someone who falls alone is in real trouble. Likewise, two people lying close together can keep each other warm. But how can one be warm alone? (Ecclesiastes 4:9-11)

When has the Christian community encouraged you? When have you encouraged other Christians?

Lord, may I not only seek encouragement from other Christians, but may I also offer it in ways that strengthen the whole body of Christ. Amen.

March 24 ✠ Judges 6–7

If Gideon were a dog, he would be the runt of the litter. He was a member of the weakest clan of the tribe of Manasseh, and he apparently was the youngest in his family. He was not terribly brave. The angel of God found him hiding from the Midianites in the winepress. While Gideon obeyed the angel's instructions to build an altar, destroy the altar of Baal, and sacrifice one of his father's bulls, he did it all at night because he feared his family's reaction.

His father's reaction is surprising. After all, Gideon destroyed his father's altar and Asherah pole and killed his bull. Yet when the townspeople want to kill Gideon, his father supports him. And although Gideon earlier feared his family's reaction, when he makes his call to arms, his own clan is the first to respond.

God can do what appears improbable. He can change the hearts of family members through "the least" of the family.

In that day the wolf and the lamb will live together;
*   the leopard will lie down with the baby goat.*
The calf and the yearling will be safe with the lion,
*   and a little child will lead them all. (Isaiah 11:6)*

How has God moved in your life in unexpected ways?

Heavenly Father, help me to trust you even when change seems improbable. May I remember that you are capable of anything. Amen.

March 25 ✠ Judges 8–9

After defeating the Midianites, Gideon deflected attention from himself and pointed to God. He told the people that God, not Gideon or any of his sons, would rule over them. However, in what seems like a contradiction, Gideon asked for gold from the people and made an ephod, which the people began to worship.

Tangible memorials of accomplishments are important. We erect memorials to great people and significant events. We do so in the church. God even commanded us to memorialize certain events.

The gold ephod was supposed to memorialize the victory God gave the Israelites. It was supposed to remind the people of God. However, the ephod itself became the focus, not God.

When we lose sight of God's accomplishments and begin to think of them as our own, we engage in a form of idol worship. Whenever we take our eyes off God, we focus on the wrong thing.

With my great strength and powerful arm I made the earth and all its people and every animal. I can give these things of mine to anyone I choose. (Jeremiah 27:5)

How often do you take ultimate credit for the things you accomplish? How can you genuinely offer that credit to God?

Almighty God, may I never take credit for myself but instead always give you the glory. Amen.

March 26 ✢ Judges 10–11

Why did Jephthah make his vow? He should have known that God was with him because twice before, he was either in the presence of the Lord or the Lord's Spirit was with him. Why then, did he need to make a vow? Did he not fully trust that God would give him the victory?

In the Sermon on the Mount, Jesus says not to make vows, but to simply say, "Yes, I will." If I already believe I do what God wants me to do, then I don't need to bargain with God.

The key is my faith. When I say I trust God and follow where I believe he leads me, how far do I trust him to lead me? Am I able to go with him the entire distance, or do I say, "Lord, I'll go with you partway, but I have other things I need to take care of, and I don't trust you to take care of them for me." Is that what I want to say to my Creator?

Because of our faith, Christ has brought us into this place of undeserved privilege where we now stand, and we confidently and joyfully look forward to sharing God's glory. (Romans 5:2)

What roadblocks keep you from trusting God completely?

Faithful God, may I trust you completely and follow you always. Amen.

March 27 ✢ Judges 12–14

I have always appreciated the wife of Manoah. I wish we knew her name because she is one of the more astute characters in the Old Testament.

When she and her husband realize that they speak with an angel, Manoah exclaims, "We will certainly die, for we have seen God!" His wife's reaction shows her insight because she realizes that

God would not have promised them a son if they were to die from seeing God's angel.

Her comments indicate that she "gets it" and also that she has faith that God will do what he promised. Her commonsense, practical response to her husband's exclamation always makes me chuckle!

The lips of the wise give good advice; the heart of a fool has none to give. (Proverbs 15:7)

When have you recognized God's promises to you and stood firmly on them?

Lord, I ask that you give me the gift of discernment so I may understand and trust your promises to me. Amen.

March 28 ✠ Judges 15–17

Samson was not the most admirable judge of Israel. While other judges were military leaders or prophets, Samson was simply a big strong guy. Any benefit Israel received from his position as judge seemed incidental as he pursued his personal agenda against the Philistines.

But God can use anyone to accomplish his purposes, even a self-focused, brawny guy whose relationship to God seems more the result of his birth than of his active commitment.

Rather than condoning being self-centered and spoiled, this story shows me that even if a person does not have a relationship with God, God can use him. For me to see God's work in the world, I must look everywhere and always be open to how God can act. I also must try to see people the way God sees them.

God knows people's hearts, and he confirmed that he accepts Gentiles by giving them the Holy Spirit, just as he did to us. He made no distinction between us and them, for he cleansed their hearts through faith. (Acts 15:8-9)

When have you limited God's work because of your opinions of the person through whom he chose to move?

Lord, may I not judge others but see them as you see them. Open my eyes so I can see you at work in the world, even in unexpected people and places. Amen.

March 29 ✠ Judges 18–19

If I were writing the section title for Judges 18 and 19, I would call the chapters "Men Behaving Badly." The Israelites don't look much like God's chosen people in these passages. We don't find much that is uplifting or positive.

We, who claim to be God's people, can do horrible things. How we must grieve God by the way we sometimes act. But do we see the horrible things we do?

As part of a Holy Week sermon, I heard a preacher refer to examples of human depravity. One of the examples he shared was that of United States soldiers in Iraq humiliating prisoners. The pictures made international news when they were discovered. Instead of feeling a sense of shame for how his fellow countrymen behaved, I heard a member of the congregation express irritation that the preacher used such a political example.

If we could strip away politics and nationalities and worldly values and see ourselves as God sees us, could we stand to look at ourselves?

. . . these people are stubborn rebels
  who refuse to pay attention to the Lord's instructions.
They tell the seers,
  "Stop seeing visions!"
They tell the prophets,
  "Don't tell us what is right.
Tell us nice things.
  Tell us lies." (Isaiah 30:9-10)

Do you sometimes prefer to remain blind to the uncomfortable truth rather than facing it boldly?

Lord, I don't want to grieve you, and yet I don't always do what I should. I praise you that you still love me, that you are faithful even when I am not. Amen.

March 30 ✠ Judges 20–21

The book of Judges does not inspire us with the Israelites' love of God and obedience to him. They are faithful only when a godly judge leads them. The phrase that is too often repeated is, "In those days Israel had no king; all the people did whatever seemed right in their own eyes."

It appears that they only consulted God when they wanted help out of a jam, never for spiritual or moral guidance. Human behavior has not changed much. Too often we seek God only when we want a miracle. Otherwise, we do whatever seems right in our own eyes.

God desires a relationship with us. We were created to praise him. How it must hurt him when we only seek him in times of trouble, and not in the day-to-day activities of our lives.

Seek the Lord while you can find him. Call on him now while he is near. (Isaiah 55:6)

How long does it take for you to seek God about a particular issue?

Lord, I desire to know your presence always in my life. May I be faithful as I seek to know you better. Amen.

March 31 ✠ Ruth 1–4

The story of Ruth is a love story, but not in the usual way. The centerpiece is Ruth's love for Naomi, her mother-in-law. This love speaks of the nature of Ruth and her loyalty. She is obedient in all things, and Boaz notices her obedience and love.

The fact that she is from Moab, a nation considered an enemy of Israel, is a significant part of the story. In Deuteronomy 23, the Moabites are banned for ten generations from the assembly of the Lord.

The story of Ruth is a good reminder of the sin of making blanket judgments of people groups. When we generalize, our judgment creates an inability to build relationships. Our goal should be to see each person as God sees him or her and let God do the judging.

But the Lord said to Samuel, "Don't judge by his appearance or height, for I have rejected him. The Lord doesn't see things the way you see them. People judge by outward appearance, but the Lord looks at the heart." (1 Samuel 16:7)

What generalizations do you make that are harmful to the kingdom of God?

Lord, help me to remember that others may judge Christians by what they see in me. May my words and actions glorify you. Amen.

April 1 🕆 1 Samuel 1–3

"Now in those days messages from the Lord were very rare, and visions were quite uncommon" (1 Samuel 3:1b). After reading about the behavior of Eli's sons, I don't find it surprising that messages from God were rare. If God sent messages to the priests, probably no one heard or acknowledged them.

Do I live in a way that I am able to hear messages from God? Just as Samuel did not fall into the corrupt and shameful lifestyle of the sons of Eli with whom he worked, I need to behave and think in a different way than the world promotes. To hear messages from God, I must walk with God, just as Samuel did. I must live differently and think differently.

Stop deceiving yourselves. If you think you are wise by this world's standards, you need to become a fool to be truly wise. For the wisdom of this world is foolishness to God. As the Scriptures say, "He traps the wise in the snare of their own cleverness." (1 Corinthians 3:18-19)

How do you hear God amid all the other messages of the world?

God of all wisdom, may I listen to your messages instead of those I hear constantly from the world. May I dare to be different so that I glorify you in all things. Amen.

April 2 ✛ 1 Samuel 4–7

The Philistines recognized that God was greater than the god they worshiped, yet they settled for a god they knew even though it was inferior.

I am often willing to settle for less than what God wants to give me, probably because I am afraid of the unknown. It is more comfortable to stick with what I know than to surrender completely to God and allow him to use me as he wishes.

What blessings do I miss because I settle for the familiar instead of stepping out on faith and trusting God to take care of me?

All these people died still believing what God had promised them. They did not receive what was promised, but they saw it all from a distance and welcomed it. They agreed that they were foreigners and nomads here on earth. (Hebrews 11:13)

When are you tempted to settle for less than the best when it comes to God?

Faithful God, you hold such wonderful blessings for me. I don't want to settle when you want me to soar. May I step out on faith when you call me, even when I cannot see where you are leading me. Amen.

April 3 ✠ 1 Samuel 8–11

Saul was changed when he was anointed as king. First Samuel 10:9 says, "God gave him a new heart."

God can give me a new heart too. Saul followed the direction of Samuel, and I need to trust God and obey his instructions. It is important to stay on the path God has laid out for me.

When I begin to think I have a better way than what God has planned, I get off his path and onto my own. To stay on his path, I must surrender my will to his. I must trust in his timing. I must follow even when I cannot see. It is essential that I stay close to God.

And I will give you a new heart, and I will put a new spirit in you. I will take out your stony, stubborn heart and give you a tender, responsive heart. (Ezekiel 36:26)

In what ways can you surrender daily to God and receive the new heart he has created for you?

Lord, I am hard-hearted and strong-willed. Surrendering to you is not easy for me because I like knowing what to expect. Yet, if I will surrender, I know I can expect fountains of love and a nearer relationship with you. I want that, Lord. Take all of me. I surrender to you. Amen.

April 4 ✠ 1 Samuel 12–14:23

Saul's impatience cost him his dynasty. Although Samuel told Saul to wait for his arrival, Saul got antsy and took on the priestly duty of offering sacrifices to seek God's guidance because he saw his men deserting and the Philistines growing stronger.

The folly of his thinking is evident when Jonathan and his armor bearer defeat the Philistines. Although they were the only two to attack initially, God was with them, and others soon came to fight alongside them.

For me, this story emphasizes that God's timetable is perfect, while mine is imperfect. When I rush ahead of God, not only am I disobedient, but the results are not God's plan. I must resist the urge to do something and instead wait for God's instruction.

Wait patiently for the Lord. Be brave and courageous. Yes, wait patiently for the Lord. (Psalm 27:14)

How often do you rush headlong into what you want to do rather than waiting for God to direct you?

O God, help me to trust in your timing in all things. Amen.

April 5 ✠ 1 Samuel 14:24–16

"People judge by outward appearance, but the Lord looks at the heart" (1 Samuel 16:7b). Reading this verse after reading the story of Saul's disobedience reinforces the truth of its message. Saul's actions of saving the animals, purportedly for sacrifice to God, appeared honorable. If his men had not heard Samuel's command from God, they would have thought Saul's behavior showed reverence to God.

However, it was not what God wanted. He wanted (and still wants) obedience instead of sacrifice. Paul describes it well in 1 Corinthians 13:3: "If I give everything I have to the poor and even sacrificed my body, I could boast about it, but if I didn't love others, I would have gained nothing."

Our obedience should be joyful because it comes out of our great love for God and what he did for us. It's incredible to think of what Jesus endured for me—for us all—and that God gave his only Son as our salvation. Every person I see today, from the homeless person to the person whose arrogance annoys me, is loved by God just as I am.

What sorrow awaits you Pharisees! For you are careful to tithe even the tiniest income from your herb gardens, but you ignore justice and the love of God. You should tithe, yes, but do not neglect the more important things. (Luke 11:42)

How do you let others influence your obedience to God?

Lord, may I be obedient to you regardless of how my obedience looks to those around me. What is important is what you want, not what others think. Amen.

April 6 ✠ 1 Samuel 17–18

The story of David and Goliath is so familiar that it is easy to skim over it quickly. After all, we know it well. But take a moment to think about the match between Goliath and David.

David was the youngest of eight, which means there was a big difference in age between him and his three older brothers, who were in Saul's army. Though Saul's soldiers were seasoned, none of them wished to fight Goliath one on one.

Why was David successful? He did not seek glory for himself and he did not rely on his own skill. He relied on God, and he gave God credit for the victory. Was he afraid? We don't know, but if he was afraid, his fear did not outweigh his faith in God to take care of him.

To the world, he looked like a young man with no hope of wealth (there was not much inheritance for the youngest of eight boys), undesirable skills (he played the harp and wrote music), and a thankless job (tending sheep). But while the world saw these traits, God saw someone with a deep and abiding faith and a strong sense of humility.

We value brains and brawn, but God values a faith-filled and humble spirit. God doesn't need us to be the strongest or the smartest; he just needs us to be faithful.

Then I heard the Lord asking, "Whom should I send as a messenger to this people? Who will go for us?" I said, "Here I am. Send me." (Isaiah 6:8)

When have you felt ill equipped for a job to which God called you? How did it turn out?

Lord, may I remember that if you send me, you will also equip me for the job. Amen.

April 7 ✛ 1 Samuel 19–21

The loving and unselfish friendship between Jonathan and David is truly remarkable. Jonathan understood that God was with David and chose him to be the next king. As the oldest son of Saul, Jonathan would succeed him under a traditional monarchy, but Jonathan was not jealous of David's calling. They loved each other deeply, and Jonathan helped David escape Saul's wrath.

Their relationship with God characterized their friendship. They modeled the highest ideals of friendship in their generosity toward each other.

A friend is always loyal, and a brother is born to help in time of need. (Proverbs 17:17)

What makes your friendships strong?

Lord, thank you for giving us the model of friendship shared by David and Jonathan. May we follow their example in our relationships by loving others and putting their needs ahead of ours. Amen.

April 8 ✛ 1 Samuel 22–24

David's loyalty to Saul, even though Saul wanted to kill him, is amazing. No matter what Saul did, David continued to recognize Saul as God's chosen king of Israel.

David knew he was anointed as king, but he displayed great patience and faith in God's timetable. Surely he was tempted to take matters into his own hands, and he certainly received opportunities to do so. Instead, David was content to wait on the Lord.

Can I be that faithful and patient?

Be still in the presence of the Lord,
*   and wait patiently for him to act.*
Don't worry about evil people who prosper
*   or fret about their wicked schemes.*
Stop being angry!
*   Turn from your rage!*
Do not lose your temper—
*   it only leads to harm.*
For the wicked will be destroyed,
*   but those who trust in the Lord will possess the land.*
(Psalm 37:7-9, a Psalm of David)

Who tries your patience? How can you cultivate contentment in this relationship as you wait for God to work?

Lord, may I be as patient as David was with Saul. Give me a heart of love for others, even when I don't approve of their actions. Amen.

April 9 ✤ 1 Samuel 25–27

David helped Nabal's men, and Nabal returned the favor by insulting David. Perhaps Nabal was afraid David would take advantage of him. By any account, he was not a generous man.

Greed often arises over something minor. We've all seen children suddenly become interested in a previously cast-aside toy because another child wants to play with it. As adults, we don't always act much better. We may find it difficult to give up our "free" time in order to help someone else, even if our potential sacrifice is TV time.

On the other hand, we cannot become closer to God just by doing work for him all the time. We must seek first a relationship with him. If we do that, he will lead us where he wants us to be.

My heart has heard you say, "Come and talk with me." And my heart responds, "Lord, I am coming." (Psalm 27:8)

What keeps you from sacrificing your time for others?

Christ, my Lord and my Friend, may my greatest desire be to know you better every day. Amen.

April 10 ✤ 1 Samuel 28–31

"David was now in great danger because all his men were very bitter about losing their sons and daughters, and they began to talk of stoning him. But David found strength in the Lord his God" (1 Samuel 30:6). The Amalekites carried away David's family along with the families of his men. But David had two problems—the loss of his wives and threats from his men.

When circumstances looked bleak, David found strength in God. He did not despair because he knew God was in control and he sought God's guidance. His faith was the firm foundation that kept him focused even in chaotic times.

The best-equipped army cannot save a king,
*   nor is great strength enough to save a warrior.*
Don't count on your warhorse to give you victory—
*   for all its strength, it cannot save you.*
But the Lord watches over those who fear him,
*   those who rely on his unfailing love. (Psalm 33:16-18)*

How have you clung to God in the past during chaotic circumstances?

Gracious God, may I find my strength in you alone. Amen.

April 11 ✣ 2 Samuel 1–2

Joab and Abner agreed that twelve men from each of their armies would fight hand to hand. They all killed each other. This story disturbs me. It almost seems that the fight serves as entertainment for the two armies, and it certainly seems that these two leaders place little value on the lives of the men in their command. No purpose for this fight is stated in 2 Samuel.

If I lead a group, I bear responsibility for its members. I need to value the members and care for their well-being. Christ gave us a model in how he cared for those who followed him.

Sadly, the behavior of Joab and Abner is not uncommon today. Many leaders fail to show concern for the people they lead.

When he saw the crowds, he had compassion on them because they were confused and helpless, like sheep without a shepherd. (Matthew 9:36)

Do you serve in a leadership position? How do you treat those you lead?

O Lord, may I show the love of Christ to all, especially to those whom I influence. Amen.

April 12 ✣ 2 Samuel 3–5

David was thirty years old when he began to reign. He was anointed as king at a much younger age. Despite the wait, he was faithful to God and did not stray from what God called him to do.

Sometimes God's plans take longer than we want to wait. However, the waiting process may offer a time of preparation for what God calls us to do. If I believe God when he shows me his will, then I also must trust in his timing for the fulfillment of his plan. I may not be able to see how my present circumstances move me toward God's goal, but his plans are always for good.

And we know that God causes everything to work together for the good of those who love God and are called according to his purpose for them. (Romans 8:28)

What do you do in the meantime as you wait for God's timing?

God, grant me patience to trust in your promises to me, even when the timing is not what I expect. Amen.

April 13 ✠ 2 Samuel 6–9

David's behavior embarrassed Michal when the ark was brought into Jerusalem. Instead of rejoicing with him and all the people, she judged David's behavior as inappropriate for a king.

I don't want to be like Michal. I don't want to be more concerned about "appearances" than about worshiping God and praising him with joy.

I suppose the heart of the matter is this—where is my focus? Is my focus on God and God alone, or is my focus on myself and what benefits me? If I keep my eyes on God, and focus on honoring him, I won't have time to think about what will make me look good to others.

Stop deceiving yourselves. If you think you are wise by this world's standards, you need to become a fool to be truly wise. For the wisdom of this world is foolishness to God. (1 Corinthians 3:18-19a)

What hinders you from uninhibited worship of God?

Lord, I want to focus intently on you. I want to live and act to please you, to glorify you and not myself. Consume my thoughts with devotion to you. Amen.

April 14 ✠ 2 Samuel 10–12

God took a relationship that began in adultery and murder and created a child who would succeed David as king. Of all David's wives and children, why did God pick Bathsheba and Solomon? It seems incredible that God chose to honor this union.

It serves as a reminder to me that any time I judge someone, thinking I know God's mind about that person, I am likely to miss the mark. God's ways are not my ways. God's mind is something I cannot comprehend.

It's a lot like my dog, Lightning. He tries to anticipate where I am going so he can beat me there, but he often guesses wrong. When I try to anticipate what I think God will do, I am wrong most of the time. Instead of running ahead of God, like Lightning runs ahead of me, I should follow closely behind God. If I yield to him and let him lead, I will save myself a lot of misdirection.

Have you never heard?
Have you never understood?
The Lord is the everlasting God,
the Creator of all the earth.
He never grows weak or weary.
No one can measure the depths of his understanding.
(Isaiah 40:28)

How quick are you to judge? How has hasty judgment hurt you or another person?

Omnipotent God, your ways are higher than my ways, but they are always good. May I trust you and never assume I can understand your thoughts. Amen.

April 15 ✤ 2 Samuel 13–14

The woman from Tekoa who went to see David spoke comforting words: "Our lives are like water spilled out on the ground, which cannot be gathered up again. But God does not just sweep life away; instead, he devises ways to bring us back when we have been separated from him" (2 Samuel 14:14).

We can't undo what we have done, but God doesn't abandon us. What a beautiful message!

I know that no matter how hard I try, I will fall short, and when I do, my sin is like water spilled on the ground. I can see the spill but I cannot fix it. God, though, shows me that the stain left by sin does not stand between him and me.

He will not constantly accuse us,
*   nor remain angry forever.*
He does not punish us for all our sins;
*   he does not deal harshly with us, as we deserve.*
For his unfailing love toward those who fear him
*   is as great as the height of the heavens above the earth.*
He has removed our sins as far from us
*   as the east is from the west. (Psalm 103:9-12)*

In what ways has God brought you back again and again?

Lord, I need to hear these words of the woman of Tekoa again and again. I want to repent and yet I still sin. Help me Lord, to be strong, but when I am weak, I know you still love me. I praise you! Amen.

April 16 ✤ 2 Samuel 15–16

Even though David and his family were fleeing Jerusalem, he put his trust in God. He had faith that God was in control. His comments in 2 Samuel 15:25-26 show that he accepted God's plan for him.

We are happy to accept good from God, but when hardships come, we complain and rail at God about our plight. If God is in control when things go our way, is he not also in control when we face tribulations?

Even though the fig trees have no blossoms,
*   and there are no grapes on the vines;*
even though the olive crop fails,
*   and the fields lie empty and barren;*
even though the flocks die in the fields,
*   and the cattle barns are empty,*
yet I will rejoice in the Lord!
*   I will be joyful in the God of my salvation! (Habakkuk 3:17-18)*

Is it difficult for you to place your life in God's hands?

Almighty God, I can rest because I know you are in control. May I find peace by believing this with all my heart. Amen.

April 17 ✠ 2 Samuel 17–18

Absalom's rebellion against David was part of the punishment for David's sin regarding Bathsheba and Uriah. David did not question why Absalom rebelled or why he was killed, but he mourned his son and felt grief for his loss.

Maybe we should respond to difficulty not by questioning why, but by trusting God all the more. None of us is exempt from suffering. In the midst of our trials, we can choose to trust God or we can turn away from him. David's trust in God allowed him to remain close to God when times were tough.

Even when I walk
*   through the darkest valley,*
I will not be afraid,
*   for you are close beside me.*
Your rod and your staff
*   protect and comfort me. (Psalm 23:4)*

When are you tempted to question God more than you are inclined to trust God?

O Lord, draw me even closer to you when I am afraid or suffering, for you are greater than my problems. Amen.

April 18 ✠ 2 Samuel 19–20

David knew when to listen to the advice of others and when to make his own decision. In 2 Samuel 19, he does both.

When his mourning for Absalom hurts the morale of his troops, David takes Joab's advice and turns his attention from his loss to the welfare of his troops, congratulating them on their victory. It was the right thing for him to do. As king, he put the needs of the people ahead of his personal grief.

Just a few verses later, David encounters Shimei, who had cursed him and thrown rocks at him as David and his people fled Jerusalem. Shimei comes to David to beg for mercy and ask forgiveness. One of David's chief military officers, Abishai, says Shimei should die because he cursed the king. David wisely ignores that advice and pardons Shimei.

David did not count himself so important as to justify killing a man who cursed him. His response to Shimei shows that David did not have to defend his anointing by God. He knew what God thought of him, and he had no need to address words of men that countered God's guidance.

Fear of the Lord teaches wisdom; humility precedes honor.
(Proverbs 15:33)

How can you focus more on God's thoughts of you than on the way other people perceive you?

Lord, may I seek to please you in all I do. Help me not let pride govern how I treat others. Amen.

April 19 ✠ 2 Samuel 21–22

Although David was a successful king—both militarily and because the people loved him—he did not forget why he was successful. Second Samuel 22 is a song of David that acknowledges God's power and direction in his life. David does what many successful people forget to do—he acknowledges God as the source and provider of his success.

Ego is a powerful force. It can be helpful because without ego, we may not use the talents and gifts God gives us. We may wrongly think we have nothing to offer.

However, ego can become an ugly monster when it grows too big. Self-sufficiency is often the first step toward too much ego. Society values and glorifies those who are self-sufficient, but God values our dependence on him. Vulnerability helps keep our egos in check.

Asking for help breeds humility, but it also breeds relationships. When I ask for help, I reveal my weakness to others. Relationships and humility can only grow when I allow myself to be vulnerable.

Each time he said, "My grace is all you need. My power works best in weakness." So now I am glad to boast about my weaknesses, so that the power of Christ can work through me. That's why I take pleasure in my weaknesses, and in the insults, hardships, persecutions, and troubles that I suffer for Christ. For when I am weak, then I am strong. (2 Corinthians 12:9-10)

What makes humility such a difficult characteristic to achieve?

Lord, may I surrender to you in weakness and humility and allow you to work in me. Amen.

April 20 ✦ 2 Samuel 23-24

David says he won't accept the threshing floor of Araunah as a gift of a place to build an altar. In 2 Samuel 24:24, he says, "I will not present burnt offerings to the Lord that cost me nothing."

When I read the Old Testament, I tend to forget the importance of the word "sacrifice." It's hard to equate the offering of an animal from someone's flock to a gift I give to God. Not being a herdsman, I don't relate easily to the concept of selecting an animal to offer to God.

However, David's words make me think. He says he cannot give something to God unless it costs him something. The king of Israel, who had much, still needed to *feel* the sacrifice of his resources in order to present a gift to God.

Wherever your treasure is, there the desires of your heart will also be. (Matthew 6:21)

When have you truly sacrificed something for God?

O Lord, may I gladly give to you what you have given me, so that my heart is with you alone. Amen.

April 21 ✦ 1 Kings 1-2:25

When Jesus sent his disciples out, he advised them to be shrewd as snakes and harmless as doves. The reading from 1 Kings 1-2:25 is a good illustration of this teaching. First there is Bathsheba's innocence. She sees no harm in giving Abishag to Adonijah to be his wife. Adonijah's plea to her is offered in humility, but with the shrewd reminder that all Israel wanted him as king.

Bathsheba sees nothing wrong with his request and takes it to Solomon. Solomon shrewdly recognizes that granting the request gives Adonijah support to be king because of Abishag's connection to David.

I'm not sure I would have recognized the political maneuvering any better than Bathsheba did. But there is a lesson here. Whenever someone makes a request of you, it is preferable not to respond immediately, especially if you are not certain it is something you want to do or should do. It is best to pray about the request and discern if it is what God wants you to do.

I, Wisdom, live together with good judgment. I know where to discover knowledge and discernment. (Proverbs 8:12)

When are you tempted to rush into a situation without first consulting God?

Lord, may I walk so closely with you that every day your will for me becomes easier for me to understand. Amen.

April 22 ✠ 1 Kings 2:26–4

Solomon carries out the instructions David gives him. He treats Abiathar the priest mercifully, even though Abiathar supported Adonijah as king. Solomon remembers the good he did and his relationship to David.

We don't always want to offer mercy to those who have wronged us, but an understanding of the person, and not just a focus on the hurt we suffered, can help us approach that individual with the right attitude. We must step back, assess the whole situation, and strive to understand how the other person might also hurt.

And do everything with love. (1 Corinthians 16:14)

What helps you see others as God sees them?

Loving Father, help me to see others as you see them and treat them with love and mercy. Amen.

April 23 ✠ 1 Kings 5–7

Solomon built the temple of God before he built himself a palace. David built himself a palace and then thought about building God a temple.

What are my priorities? Do I put God first when planning my day or making decisions about how to spend my time and money? When God is first in my life, my priorities are different than what they might be otherwise. There is nothing more important than knowing the one who created me and saved me.

"So don't worry about these things, saying, 'What will we eat? What will we drink? What will we wear?' These things dominate the thoughts of unbelievers, but your heavenly Father already knows all your needs. Seek the kingdom of God above all else, and live righteously, and he will give you everything you need." (Matthew 6:31-33)

How can you begin each day by seeking God first?

O God, you provide me with everything I need. May I always seek you first. Amen.

April 24 ✠ 1 Kings 8

Solomon's prayer at the dedication of the temple showed his belief that God forgives if his children ask for forgiveness. In every scenario Solomon describes, the process begins with the people turning to God in repentance.

We must seek forgiveness, but when we seek it, God grants it. When we wrestle with our sin, it is not because God makes us feel guilty. It is because Satan uses the sin to make us feel we cannot be who God wants us to be. Forgiveness puts us back in right relationship with God, taking our focus off the sin and placing it on God.

When God our Savior revealed his kindness and love, he saved us, not because of the righteous things we had done, but because of his mercy. He washed away our sins, giving us a new birth and new life through the Holy Spirit. He generously poured out the Spirit upon us through Jesus Christ our Savior. Because of his grace he declared us righteous and gave us confidence that we will inherit eternal life. (Titus 3:4-7)

How often do you ask for God's forgiveness?

Merciful God, may we quickly turn to you when we sin and ask your forgiveness so that we stay in close relationship with you. Amen.

April 25 ✠ 1 Kings 9–11

Though Solomon is still known for his wisdom, he was disobedient when he married. This sin led him to another sin of worshiping foreign gods.

I know I cannot be perfect. However, when I dip my toe into the waters of sin, knowing that my actions are wrong, it's not long before I find my whole self swimming in the pool.

When I think of Solomon's wisdom and remember that he was led astray, I wonder how I can stay on the right path. I believe it's a matter of focus. If I focus intently on God, I will see God. If I focus on many other things (like Solomon focused on his 700 wives and 300 concubines), I will have a much harder time seeing God.

But if you look carefully into the perfect law that sets you free, and if you do what it says and don't forget what you heard, then God will bless you for doing it. (James 1:25)

What distracts you from God each day?

O Lord, keep me focused intently on you and your word. Amen.

April 26 ✚ 1 Kings 12–13

The story of the prophet who foretells the deeds of Josiah is a lesson to me on the importance of the certainty of God's word. If he had any doubt as to whether his message truly came from God, the splitting apart of the altar should have erased those doubts.

So why did Josiah then disobey God and go to eat with the other prophet? Did he think God had changed his mind about eating and drinking in Israel? Or did he decide that particular part of the instruction was not as important as speaking to Jeroboam? Did he believe that following most of God's instructions to him was sufficient?

How often do I do something similar? I follow most, but not all, of God's instructions to me. It's easy to think that if I've obeyed God in the big things, then I'm doing okay.

If you are faithful in little things, you will be faithful in large ones. But if you are dishonest in little things, you won't be honest with greater responsibilities. (Luke 16:10)

What instructions from God do you frequently ignore?

Lord, I want to be faithful in all things. May I never minimize your instructions to me. Amen.

April 27 ✚ 1 Kings 14–15

The author of 1 Kings tells us that David pleased God in all he did, except in the matter of Uriah the Hittite. David's obedience to God is even more significant when you look at the way his descendants lived. God's deep love for David is evident by the way he treats David's descendants.

While Israel did not have an extended family dynasty as rulers, Judah continued to have a descendant of David on the throne, even though the behavior of these leaders was generally negative. God rewarded David's faithfulness to God by being faithful to David's family.

The faithful love of the Lord never ends! His mercies never cease. Great is his faithfulness; his mercies begin afresh each morning. (Lamentations 3:22-23)

How has God been faithful to you?

O Lord, I am thankful for your faithfulness to me. May I never lose hope, for you live in me. Amen.

April 28 ✤ 1 Kings 16–18

The story of the widow who shared her home with Elijah stands in sharp contrast to the "prosperity gospel" we often hear. God provided the widow with just enough flour and oil to get through the drought. She didn't have everything she needed at once, and she had no extra provisions. She always had enough.

We are often more likely to praise God for his blessings when we receive an abundance, but we aren't always as vocal in our praise when we have just enough. Yet God's provision to us is all we need.

The other message from this story is the blessing of generosity. The widow, who is in the process of preparing what she believes is her last meal, makes food for Elijah, then finds sufficient food for herself and her son. Had she been selfish about her meager resources, she may not have received this blessing.

I will be your God throughout your lifetime—until your hair is white with age. I made you, and I will care for you. I will carry you along and save you. (Isaiah 46:4)

When do you feel discontent with what you have? How can you learn to be thankful for "enough"?

Loving Father, may I find peace in knowing that you always provide exactly what I need. Amen.

April 29 ✠ 1 Kings 19–20

Jezebel threatened Elijah's life because he killed the prophets of Baal. The sacrifice "competition" between Elijah and the prophets of Baal must have been an incredibly "high" moment for Elijah. His adrenaline is obvious, for after the sacrifice he tells Ahab that rain is on the way and then outruns Ahab's chariot to Jezreel. Then, after these events, he sleeps.

His mood swing is surprising, though. After the Lord's great victory over Baal, Elijah feels sorry for himself. Even though an angel provides food to sustain him for forty days of travel, he wants only to die. He seems to think he is the only remaining person who is faithful to God.

God responds by showing Elijah both his power, through windstorm, earthquake, and fire, and his tenderness, through the still, small voice. Elijah is unfazed. He wallows so deeply in his pity party that his response doesn't change. God asks him, "What are you doing here?" Elijah doesn't see all that God has done for him. He fails to recognize God's ability to continue to take care of him.

Unfortunately, I understand Elijah's behavior too well. I quickly forget what God has done for me when I feel threatened. I ignore the blessings of God when I get involved in my own pity party.

I am leaving you with a gift—peace of mind and heart. And the peace I give is a gift the world cannot give. So don't be troubled or afraid. (John 14:27)

When have you forgotten God's great blessings and wallowed in self-pity?

Lord, keep me from pity parties by helping me center my thoughts on the love you have given me. Amen.

April 30 ✦ 1 Kings 21–22

Predictions of success are much easier to hear than predictions of failure. Ahab and Jehoshaphat chose to listen to the prophets who prophesied victory instead of the prophet of the Lord, who prophesied defeat. We naturally believe good news more easily than bad news.

Whatever predictions are made, we should seek God's will for our behavior. For me, that means being patient, listening for God's direction through prayer, reading the Bible, talking to people I trust, and observing what is going on around me. I'm not a patient decision-maker, so trusting God's timing is difficult for me.

Be still in the presence of the Lord,
and wait patiently for him to act.
Don't worry about evil people who prosper
or fret about their wicked schemes. (Psalm 37:7)

When are you tempted to listen to ungodly advice because you don't like what God says to you?

O God, whose timing is perfect, may I willingly wait for you. Amen.

May 1 ✦ 2 Kings 1–3

King Ahaziah apparently did not consider asking God for guidance about his injury. He only thought to inquire of the god of another country.

How many times do I seek the guidance of worldly counselors in making my decisions without first going to God? Sometimes I don't ask God because I feel I must make a decision quickly, and I don't trust him to answer me on my timetable. Sometimes I don't ask because I don't want to know God's answer, for I believe it will disappoint me.

However, I cannot claim to yield to God if I don't seek his guidance in all things. When I trust his timing and his response, I am blessed.

As for me, I look to the Lord for help.
I wait confidently for God to save me,
and my God will certainly hear me.
Do not gloat over me, my enemies!
For though I fall, I will rise again.
Though I sit in darkness,
The Lord will be my light. (Micah 7:7-8)

How can you commit to talking with God about your life before you go to anyone else? Why is this important?

All-knowing Father, may I seek your guidance in all things and do what you lead me to do. Amen.

May 2 ✠ 2 Kings 4–5

Elisha and Gehazi seemed to have everything they needed. So when Naaman offered Elisha a gift, Elisha turned him down. Gehazi saw the opportunity to get more for himself, but his greed came with a heavy penalty.

Why am I so consumed with having more of everything? If what I have is sufficient, why do I set my sights on gaining more? When I think about it, it makes no sense. Accumulating things only causes me to spend more time cleaning up and organizing my possessions. If I live more simply, I have more time to spend with God.

Those who love money will never have enough. How meaningless to think that wealth brings true happiness! (Ecclesiastes 5:10)

How do you protect yourself from our culture's obsession with acquiring more material possessions?

Lord, may I be content with what you provide. Amen.

May 3 ✠ 2 Kings 6–8

Elisha moved among all types of people and prophesied not only to Israel and Judah, but to other countries as well. There is much more written in Kings about Elisha than Elijah, and yet the New Testament refers to Elijah more often (twenty-nine times) than to Elisha (one time).

Elisha received a double portion of Elijah's spirit and did incredible things, such as bringing a boy back to life.

In our society, we equate fame with power, but often the most powerful among us are not the most famous. We can be completely unaware of the truly powerful because they may not seek attention for their work.

Make it your goal to live a quiet life, minding your own business and working with your hands, just as we instructed you before. (1 Thessalonians 4:11)

When does the business of others consume you? How can you redirect your focus?

Lord, may I seek to follow you and win your approval, not the approval or attention of others around me. Amen.

May 4 ✠ 2 Kings 9–10

Jehu did a great job of wiping out Baal's worshipers and their temple, pleasing God in the process. But we are also told that he continued to allow worship of the golden calves Jeroboam had made.

There is commitment, and then there is devotion. I define commitment as being a strong supporter and devotion as wholehearted focus on someone or something other than oneself. Jehu was committed but not devoted.

Which one am I? Do I say "yes" when God calls me to do something, or do I say "yes, but . . . "?

Thank God! Once you were slaves of sin, but now you wholeheartedly obey this teaching we have given you. Now you are free from your slavery to sin, and you have become slaves to righteous living. (Romans 6:17-18)

When have you offered God merely half-hearted devotion?

Wonderful Father, may I be wholly devoted to you. Amen.

May 5 ✤ 2 Kings 11–13

"No accounting of this money was required from the construction supervisors, because they were honest and trustworthy men" (2 Kings 12:15). When you think about how many people worked on the temple construction, these words speak highly of them. Did their honesty result from the fact they worked on the temple of God, or were they simply honest men?

The people had become corrupt from their worship of Baal, so surely finding honest and trustworthy men to supervise the work was no easy task. Earlier, Elijah lamented that there were no true worshipers of God other than himself; apparently, such people existed but were not public in their expressions of faith. However, the construction of the temple gave them the chance to express their faith by using their craft to glorify God.

Work with enthusiasm, as though you were working for the Lord rather than for people. (Ephesians 6:7)

What is the value of a trustworthy worker, both for worldly pursuits and for the kingdom of God?

Lord, may I use all my abilities to glorify you in all I do. Amen.

May 6 ✠ 2 Kings 14–15

As bad as Jeroboam II was, God used him to fulfill the promise he made to a prophet. It is easy for me to feel special and overly good about myself when I feel that God has used me. Reading about Jeroboam II brings me back to the reality of my situation.

I am a sinner. Nothing I do makes me worthy of God using me. God doesn't use me because I'm worthy. God uses me because he's God, who can do all things. He created me, just as he created Jeroboam II, and because he creates all people, good and bad, God can use us to accomplish his purposes.

I should rejoice when God uses me, but I should also remember that it is not because I am a good person or worthy of being used. God uses me, and anyone else he chooses, because we are vessels he created to fulfill his purposes.

Remember, dear brothers and sisters, that few of you were wise in the world's eyes or powerful or wealthy when God called you. Instead, God chose things the world considers foolish in order to shame those who think they are wise. And he chose things that are powerless to shame those who are powerful. God chose things despised by the world, things counted as nothing at all, and used them to bring to nothing what the world considers important. As a result, no one can ever boast in the presence of God. (1 Corinthians 1:26-29)

How can you remember that everything you have or do is from God?

O Lord, may I never think more of myself than I ought, but in humility rejoice that you chose me. Amen.

May 7 ✠ 2 Kings 16–17

When the Israelites were exiled and other people were brought into their land, the new settlers learned how to worship God. However, their hearts were not devoted to God. They viewed God as one of many gods. They worshiped with a sense of obligation based on where they lived, not because they had a special relationship with God.

It is not difficult for me to worship God. I live in a country where I can freely go to church, and I've grown up around people who go to church. But I don't want my worship of God to be like that of the settlers in Israel—a matter of convenience because of where I live. I want my worship of God to be out of my love for him and for what he has done in saving me and giving me the promise of eternal life with him.

For it is by believing in your heart that you are made right with God, and it is by confessing with your mouth that you are saved. (Romans 10:10)

How many gods do you worship each day?

O God, may my worship of you be sincere and single-minded. Amen.

May 8 ✠ 2 Kings 18–20

Hezekiah is lauded in 2 Kings 18:5-6 as faithful to God. His trust in God made him incomparable to any other kings of Judah. While he was king, Israel was carried into exile. God's intervention kept Judah from following behind.

Hezekiah turned to God in times of crisis, but he also apparently sought God's direction in all things, which is why he was so highly praised. For faith to endure in crisis, one must strengthen it in the ordinary times of life. Trust in God should always come before trust in my own abilities.

I will praise the Lord at all times.
    I will constantly speak his praises.
I will boast only in the Lord;
    let all who are helpless take heart. (Psalm 34:1-2)

On most ordinary days, how frequently do you think of God?

O God, you are ever faithful. May I trust in you and praise you, especially on ordinary days. Amen.

May 9 ✤ 2 Kings 21–23

King Josiah did much to rid Judah of pagan gods and practices, so the evil of his succeeding sons is surprising. Surely, growing up in Josiah's household, they would have learned the ways of God.

I suppose it was a case of peer pressure. Judah stood on tenuous ground politically, so looking to other nations for help meant exposure to the gods of other nations. This example shows that just because I am in the world, my behavior should not be of the world. If I am truly God's, I am called to live differently. I am called to strive for a higher standard.

Conform to the world or conform to God. It's an either/or decision.

Don't copy the behavior and customs of this world, but let God transform you into a new person by changing the way you think. Then you will learn to know God's will for you, which is good and pleasing and perfect. (Romans 12:2)

When have you been tempted to try to balance between the world and God? How easily were you able to do this?

O Lord, make me strong in my faith so I conform to you. Amen.

May 10 ✤ 2 Kings 24–25

These two chapters are not easy reading. We can summarize them in three words: actions have consequences.

Through 1 and 2 Kings, God has told of his displeasure with the people. They repeatedly refused to follow him, and when the threatened punishment arrived, it was severe.

It's easier to read about forgiveness than punishment, and yet, sometimes punishment is the wake-up call that what we are doing isn't what we should do. Actions have consequences, and often punishment results from bad choices we make.

God gave the people of Judah many chances to change course. They were unresponsive, and God allowed the nation to fall.

For the Lord disciplines those he loves, and he punishes each one he accepts as his child. (Hebrews 12:6)

How has God disciplined you?

Lord, I thank you for loving me and teaching me your ways. Amen.

May 11 ✠ 1 Chronicles 1–2

I don't want to be remembered the way Achan was remembered (1 Chronicles 2:7). While most of the genealogy lists family ties, Achan is forever memorialized as the one who brought disaster on Israel by taking plunder that was meant for God.

Have I been guilty of the same act? When I withhold my talents from God, sharing them inappropriately or not using them at all, then I fail to give to God what he gave me to use for his glory. Maybe I don't give God my best attention, instead using my best energy for worldly pursuits and leaving God only my leftover time for a quick prayer as my head hits the pillow at night.

Christ said, "Seek the kingdom of God above all else . . . ." What do I seek above all else?

They even did more than we had hoped, for their first action was to give themselves to the Lord and to us, just as God wanted them to do. (2 Corinthians 8:5)

Have you withheld from God what is rightfully his?

O God, may I put you first in all things and give you the best of what I have to give—my time, my talent, my gifts, and especially my love. Amen.

May 12 ✢ 1 Chronicles 3–5

Reuben, Gad, and Manasseh settled east of the Jordan River. These three tribes are described as having many skilled warriors. First Chronicles 5:20 tells how they cried out to God during a battle. God answered their prayer because they trusted in him. It's such a simple statement, and yet we often complicate faith because it seems too easy simply to ask and believe.

It is awesome to consider how long ago this battle occurred and think about how many people have cried out to God for help because of their faith in him. It makes me pause and ponder the eternal nature of God. While I know in my head that he created the world and has been here forever, thinking about how many people have cried out to him for help is overwhelming. It makes me realize my own insignificance, and yet to God, I am significant and he loves me.

We also know that the Son did not come to help angels; he came to help the descendants of Abraham. (Hebrews 2:16)

How do you complicate faith?

Eternal God, I am humbled and awed by the thought that with all the people who call to you, you hear each one of us as if we were the only one. Thank you for loving not only me, but all creation. Amen.

May 13 ✢ 1 Chronicles 6–7

In the genealogy of Chronicles, there is an interesting reference to Sheerah, a daughter of Ephraim. First Chronicles 7:24 says she built several towns. I don't remember reading this elsewhere in the Bible. Two of her brothers were killed trying to steal livestock.

It's a significant contrast among siblings. In all the genealogies, little is pointed out about the listed names. Even Samuel is not identified as the one who anointed Saul and David as kings of Israel. Generation after generation is listed before we read an observation about an individual. If my family's genealogy were listed, what would be significant, if anything, about my family members? What is significant about me?

And now I entrust you to God and the message of his grace that is able to build you up and give you an inheritance with all those he has set apart for himself. (Acts 20:32)

What is significant about the members of your family? What is significant about you?

Lord, I am thankful that I am significant to you. When I read all the names listed in 1 Chronicles and realize how many more people you love, I am humbled that you love even me. Amen.

May 14 ✣ 1 Chronicles 8–10

The Lord was with Phinehas, the man in charge of the gatekeepers. If Chronicles were written today, I would like to have this said about me with regard to the performance of my work. Sometimes it's difficult to find space for God within the workday. How do you act if God is with you in your work?

Many of us work under stressful situations. It isn't easy to be in the world but not of the world when work is harried and hurried. A song, a Bible verse, or a brief prayer can help to calm our souls when work seems chaotic.

Finding a spot of refuge in the workday is helpful. God is already with us in our work situations. We simply need to acknowledge his presence and lean on him.

The ropes of death entangled me;
*   floods of destruction swept over me.*

The grave wrapped its ropes around me;
  death laid a trap in my path.
But in my distress I cried out to the Lord,
  yes, I prayed to my God for help.
He heard me from his sanctuary;
  my cry to him reached his ears. (Psalm 18:4-6)

As you go about your daily work, how do you know that God is with you?

O God, you are with me in my workplace. May I place my work in your loving hands and seek your guidance during my workday. Amen.

May 15 ✥ 1 Chronicles 11–13

David was beloved by many Israelites. I don't recall reading an account where David is bossy to the men who fight for him. He honored their accomplishments, as illustrated by how he treated the water drawn from the well at Bethlehem.

He did not take for granted the sacrifices his men made to follow him into battle. He was one of them, recognized as their leader, but he never acted as though he were better than they were. He viewed his kingship as a responsibility, not as something to use to get others to respect him.

I should practice David's humility any time I serve in a position of leadership. Because he did not demand the respect of his men, they revered him. He led with a heart of love for those who supported him.

Don't let anyone think less of you because you are young. Be an example to all believers in what you say, in the way you live, in your love, your faith, and your purity. (1 Timothy 4:12)

Do you know anyone who leads like David led?

Lord, may I lead as one who seeks to please you so that I am an example to others. Amen.

May 16 ✤ 1 Chronicles 14–16

David's love for God is especially evident in 1 Chronicles 15 and 16, when the ark of the covenant is brought into Jerusalem. The people made detailed plans to move the ark, and everything they did was in order to praise God. David's dance as the ark moves into Jerusalem reflected genuine joy in the presence of God. His song of thanksgiving reminds me of his creativity.

It's easy to get caught up in all the battles David led and forget that he was a musician and a poet. He used his creativity to worship God.

Let all that I am praise the Lord;
with my whole heart, I will praise his holy name.
Let all that I am praise the Lord;
may I never forget the good things he does for me. (Psalm 103:1-2)

Do you use the talents God gave you to worship him, or are you so busy being practical that you forget to praise God and use these gifts to glorify him?

O Lord, may I praise you with joy as David did. May I use the talents you gave me to worship you. Amen.

May 17 ✤ 1 Chronicles 17–20

When God promised David that he would be the father of an eternal dynasty, David's response showed why God chose to honor him. David was humble, gracious, and worshipful. He acknowledged his insignificance next to God's significance, and never in his prayer did he speak of his own accomplishments or faithfulness to God.

In everything that happened to David, he recognized God's hand. He remembered that God was in control and that all glory belonged to God. If David, who was considered Israel's greatest king, can remember that all he had came from God alone, I should always be mindful that I accomplish nothing on my own. God alone equips me.

But my life is worth nothing to me unless I use it for finishing the work assigned me by the Lord Jesus—the work of telling others the Good News about the wonderful grace of God. (Acts 20:24)

How are you humbled by God?

Almighty God, may I never fail to remember that all I am is because of you. I depend on you for everything. Amen.

May 18 ✤ 1 Chronicles 21–23

David's act of taking a census shows that pride can creep into anyone's life, even someone with a humble spirit.

Having been blessed with much, David wanted to know how many people lived under his command. Instead of trusting God for strength and power, he wanted to rely on the world's definition of these terms. Because David put his trust in numbers of people, God's punishment was to take the people away. David needed to remember that his strength came from God, not the size of his nation.

Like David, I need to remember that the way the world measures strength and power is not the way God measures them. Money, fame, and political influence mean a lot in the world, but God is greater than these. If I trust him for my strength, I have more than the world could ever provide.

Worldly power is fleeting and temporary, but God's power is unshakable.

I know that the Lord is always with me.
I will not be shaken, for he is right beside me. (Psalm 16:8)

When are you tempted to judge your life by the world's standards?

Almighty God, may I always trust you for my strength. Amen.

May 19 ✠ 1 Chronicles 24–26

David's desire to build a temple is evident in his meticulous preparations to help Solomon. David assigns the duties to the Levites. The assignment alone must have been a big project since 38,000 Levite men were at least thirty years old.

While assigning duties prior to building the temple might seem out of order, doing so meant that Solomon could focus on construction alone, knowing that when the temple was complete, worship in the Temple could commence without delay.

Many involved in church building projects could learn from the way David prioritized the construction process. Often the building is the focus, instead of the worship of God that the building enhances. The people make the church, whether or not a building exists.

When we bless the cup at the Lord's Table, aren't we sharing in the blood of Christ? And when we break the bread, aren't we sharing in the body of Christ? And though we are many, we all eat from one loaf of bread, showing that we are one body. (1 Corinthians 10:16-17)

In what ways do you view the church as a body rather than a building?

Lord, may we live in unity with each other, remembering that the church is your body, not a building. Amen.

May 20 ✠ 1 Chronicles 27–29

David led the people of Israel in giving money for the construction of the temple. He gave his own personal collection of gold and silver—not some, not a gift of whatever was needed, but *all.* He held back nothing. When you read his prayer in 1 Chronicles 29:10-19, you understand why.

David acknowledged that all he had came from God. It's a beautiful prayer. His words in verse 15, "We are here only for a moment," show me how impractical it is to hold on so tightly to what God gives me. I'm not here for long, so why should I not be generous with God's blessings to me?

If someone has enough money to live well and sees a brother or sister in need but shows no compassion—how can God's love be in that person? (1 John 3:17)

When have you been able to give freely, not holding anything back?

O Lord, may I not cling to possessions, but only to you. Amen.

May 21 ✠ 2 Chronicles 1–3

When Solomon wrote a letter to King Hiram of Tyre, he grew enthusiastic about God. He did not merely describe the building project and what they needed for it. He got carried away describing the One for whom the temple was built.

Do my life and conversation display enthusiasm for who God is and what he does, or do I fail to live with the joy that is manifested in such enthusiasm? Am I as excited about God as Solomon was when he wrote the letter?

Even more than Solomon, we should be enthusiastic about what God has done for us. For we are those for whom Christ died. We are saved by grace, not by any meritorious service on our part, but because Christ loved us enough to take on our sin. How can I keep quiet about this greatest gift of all?

And then I heard every creature in heaven and on earth and under the earth and in the sea. They sang: "Blessing and honor and glory and power belong to the one sitting on the throne and to the Lamb forever and ever." (Revelation 5:13)

When have you expressed your excitement about God?

O Lord, my heart bursts with joy when I ponder what you have done for me. Make me an enthusiastic messenger to others. Amen.

May 22 ✤ 2 Chronicles 4–6

When Solomon dedicates the temple, he includes not only the Israelites as recipients of God's mercy when they pray, but also foreigners who acknowledge God and pray to him. Even in Solomon's day, God's love was not limited to Israel. Anyone who turned to God and worshiped him was accepted.

Grace is such a difficult concept to grasp. I'm all about grace toward me, but I am often not as eager for the extension of grace to another. It's hard to view everyone I meet as having the same potential to receive God's grace. I still want to put conditions and limits on God's grace because my human mind cannot comprehend a God who loves everyone the same.

For no one is abandoned
by the Lord forever.
Though he brings grief, he also shows compassion
because of the greatness of his unfailing love.
For he does not enjoy hurting people
or causing them sorrow. (Lamentations 3:31-33)

When does God's grace surprise you?

Merciful God, thank you for not dispensing mercy the way I would. I am grateful that your love is not limited. Amen.

May 23 ✤ 2 Chronicles 7–9

When the temple was dedicated, the presence of the Lord filled the temple and the priests could not enter it. How did it feel to be there?

How does one experience that and then turn away from God? Even when we are awed and changed by an experience of God, we still succumb to behaviors we know are wrong.

In Revelation, John tries to worship an angel. Even after the angel corrects him once, he does it again. John, a faithful disciple, succumbed to the same sin even after correction and seeing the glorious sights described in Revelation.

I am comforted to think that the greatest followers of Christ still sinned. It isn't an excuse for my behavior, but it does remind me of why I cannot achieve salvation on my own.

But God showed his great love for us by sending Christ to die for us while we were still sinners. (Romans 5:8)

How is your faith encouraged by the stories you read in Scripture?

Gracious God, thank you for your great love for us. May I never forget that forgiveness is available if I will turn to you. Amen.

May 24 ✤ 2 Chronicles 10–13

"But when Rehoboam was firmly established and strong, he abandoned the Law of the Lord . . ." (2 Chronicles 12:1a). Rehoboam forgot the source of his strength when he got comfortable. Many of us do this. We call to God when we need help, but we lose sight of him when life goes smoothly. When we lose sight of him, we also forget who got us to a comfortable position in the first place.

God is not the "In Case of Emergency" God. He is God of all our lives—smooth and rough, afflicted and comfortable. When life is good, we should thank God, and when life is difficult, we should also thank God. Steadfastness in difficulty strengthens us.

But if you look carefully into the perfect law that sets you free, and if you do what it says and don't forget what you heard, then God will bless you for doing it. (James 1:25)

When are you tempted to use God as a last resort?

O Lord, may I be faithful to you always. May I never think that my own abilities accomplish anything in my life, but give you glory for all success. Amen.

May 25 ✠ 2 Chronicles 14–17

Asa followed God for a long time during his reign as king of Judah. He even made a law that ordered people to worship God. Yet, after reigning for thirty-five years, he turned to human help instead of seeking God's help. With all the blessings he had received, and the length of time he ruled by seeking to please God, I wonder why he wavered.

I suppose I tend to think that the longer I follow God, the closer I will be to him and the more I will trust him. Maybe Asa followed God but did not seek a deeper relationship with him. Maybe he thought his earlier faith would sustain him for the rest of his life. Whatever happened, the end of Asa's life differed greatly from its beginning.

His story reminds me that a relationship with God is an ongoing process, as is any relationship. I have to work at it, or it can fade over time.

As for me, my life has already been poured out as an offering to God. The time of my death is near. I have fought the good fight, I have finished the race, and I have remained faithful. And now the prize awaits me—the crown of righteousness, which the Lord, the righteous Judge, will give me on the day of his return. And the prize is not just for me but for all who eagerly look forward to his appearing. (2 Timothy 4:6-8)

Why is a relationship with God a lifelong process rather than a one-time decision?

Lord, may I remain faithful to you all my life. May I always seek to draw closer to you all my days. Amen.

May 26 ✠ 2 Chronicles 18–20

Jehoshaphat's cry to God in 2 Chronicles 20:12b is often my cry: "We do not know what to do, but we are looking to you for help." How wonderful it is to be able to cry those words to God and know he hears them.

Even greater is the comfort of knowing he is at my side, with me in whatever I experience and whatever I do, no matter how mundane or ordinary.

> *I can never escape from your Spirit!*
> *I can never get away from your presence!*
> *If I go up to heaven, you are there;*
> *if I go down to the grave, you are there.*
> *If I ride the wings of the morning,*
> *if I dwell by the farthest oceans,*
> *even there your hand will guide me,*
> *and your strength will support me. (Psalm 139:7-10)*

How does it feel to know that you can never escape God?

O Lord, how wonderful it is to know that I always have you with me. I may not know what to do, but you do, God, and you will help me if I cry to you. Amen.

May 27 ✠ 2 Chronicles 21–24

The importance of a single person is often overlooked, but Jehoiada the priest was so significant that after his death, the leaders of Judah decided to abandon God's temple and return to idol worship. All the work done to repair and restore the temple under Jehoiada's leadership was moot, as the temple again became insignificant.

For good or for evil, one person can make a tremendous difference. It makes me think about the impact of each action I take.

Dear friends, I warn you as "temporary residents and foreigners" to keep away from worldly desires that wage war against your very souls. Be careful to live properly among your unbelieving neighbors. Then even if they accuse you of doing wrong, they will see your honorable behavior, and they will give honor to God when he judges the world. (1 Peter 2:11-12)

Who might you influence today?

Lord, may my words and deeds bring glory to you. May I be diligent in living so as to honor you, because I never know who is watching and listening to me. Amen.

May 28 ✠ 2 Chronicles 25–27

When Amaziah paid 7500 pounds of silver to hire troops from Israel, a man of God told him to send the troops home, for God would not be with him in battle. When Amaziah asked about the silver already paid, the man of God told him not to worry about it. "The Lord is able to give you much more than this!" (2 Chronicles 25:9b).

When we make business decisions, we are told not to factor in any money already spent on equipment being considered for replacement. We cannot recover these "sunk costs," as they are called, and therefore we should make the decision without considering them.

In my faith, there are also sunk costs. Amaziah experiences them in this passage. Jesus talks about them in Luke 9:62: "Anyone who puts a hand to the plow and then looks back is not fit for the kingdom of God." So how are we to live?

When God calls us, we can trust that he will provide much more than we give up. He will not only take care of us, but he will also take care of those sunk costs if we only put our hands to the plow and trust him with *all* our lives.

The temptations in your life are no different from what others experience. And God is faithful. He will not allow the temptation to be more than you can stand. When you are tempted, he will show you a way out so that you can endure. (1 Corinthians 10:13)

How difficult is it to trust God with all the details, including finances?

O Lord, may I turn to you and not look back, trusting you with all those things that tempt me to withhold myself from you. Amen.

May 29 ✠ 2 Chronicles 28–30

When I read 2 Chronicles 28–30, I wonder why the priests were so unprepared to offer the sacrifices ordered by Hezekiah and the people celebrating Passover. Were they afraid that Hezekiah might try to trick them, or had they become lax during Ahaz's reign? Maybe they didn't expect that many people to celebrate Passover.

I hope I am not a stumbling block for others who wish to celebrate what God has done. I suppose that is part of being in the world but not of the world. If I am embarrassed by or unwilling to rejoice in the blessings of God, then maybe I have conformed too much to the world, which does not hold Christianity in high regard.

If anyone is ashamed of me and my message in these adulterous and sinful days, the Son of Man will be ashamed of that person when he returns in the glory of his Father with the holy angels. (Mark 8:38)

How can you be prepared to serve God at any time?

Lord, reveal to me the ways I conform myself to the world, and help me to break free from them. I don't want to be as unprepared as the priests and Levites of Hezekiah's day. Strengthen me for serving you boldly, in all ways and at all times. Amen.

May 30 ✠ 2 Chronicles 31–33

Manasseh truly repented. Unlike many of the previous kings of Judah, who continued in their sin even when punished, Manasseh saw that he needed to change, and he actually changed. Given a second chance at being king, he rid the country of foreign gods and idols.

He listened and became a new man. Among the accounts of the kings of Judah, Manasseh's story is unique in Chronicles.

Manasseh embodied repentance. There is a difference between asking forgiveness and repenting. I often ask forgiveness, but it's a lot harder to repent, truly and completely to turn away from things I do that cause me to lose sight of God. It takes humility, discipline, and strength, all gifts from God, to repent.

Don't you see how wonderfully kind, tolerant, and patient God is with you? Does this mean nothing to you? Can't you see that his kindness is intended to turn you from your sin? (Romans 2:4)

How often do you recognize your need for repentance?

Gracious God, open my eyes so I see where repentance is needed in my life, and give me the strength to turn away, once and for all, from the things that continue to stand between me and you. Amen.

May 31 ✠ 2 Chronicles 34–36

If Josiah had consulted with God before facing King Neco of Egypt, might Judah have avoided her eventual destruction? I would like to think so, because I enjoy a happy ending. Instead, what we get is exile, with only the faintest glimpse of restoration.

The ending of Chronicles tells me that while a nation that follows God isn't built in a day, it also isn't destroyed in a day. Because both growth and decline are usually gradual, it is easy to get lulled into thinking individual events do not make a difference—for good or bad. I can become desensitized to my behavior when I don't see immediate consequences.

The story of Judah's decline and fall reminds us that seemingly insignificant choices are more important than they appear because individual choices become part of the total fabric of our lives. Through numerous individual decisions, we strengthen or weaken that fabric.

I will show you what it's like when someone comes to me, listens to my teaching, and then follows it. It is like a person building a house who digs deep and lays the foundation on solid rock. When the floodwaters rise and break against the house, it stands firm because it is well built. But anyone who hears and doesn't obey is like a person who builds a house without a foundation. When the floods sweep down against that house, it will collapse into a heap of ruins. (Luke 6:47-49)

On what foundation is your spiritual house built?

O Lord, may I consider all my actions and choose those that draw me closer to you. Amen.

June 1 ✤ Ezra 1-2

If we seek God's direction, we must remember that God doesn't always work through believers. Cyrus of Persia is a powerful example. He allowed the people to return to Judah and rebuild the temple, but there's no indication that he believed in God himself. However, God used him to bless the people.

I need to be aware of and seek God's direction for my life not only in settings where fellow believers surround me, but in every situation and every day.

Then a despised Samaritan came along, and when he saw the man, he felt compassion for him. Going over to him, the Samaritan soothed his wounds with olive oil and wine and bandaged them. Then he put the man on his own donkey and took him to an inn, where he took care of him. (Luke 10:33-34)

When has God surprised you by working through an unexpected person or situation?

Open my eyes, Lord, that I may see you at work in unexpected places and in unexpected people. Amen.

June 2 ✠ Ezra 3-5

How frustrated the Jews must have felt in their efforts to build the temple and resettle the land after exile. It seems that with every new ruler in Persia, the Jews' enemies sought to stop construction.

Seeking to follow God's will is frequently difficult. Just because we know what God wants us to do doesn't mean we will find a clear, uncluttered path on which to accomplish it. Perseverance may be one of the biggest lessons we learn as Christians because it strengthens our "faith muscles" when we meet and endure resistance.

The Jews likely second-guessed whether God wanted them to return and rebuild. I imagine that on more than one occasion, some said, "I told you so" when another letter arrived and advised them to stop building. To maintain focus in the face of lengthy and continuing opposition required tremendous faith and single-mindedness.

But even if you suffer for doing what is right, God will reward you for it. So don't worry or be afraid of their threats. Instead, you must worship Christ as Lord of your life. And if someone asks about your Christian hope, always be ready to explain it. (1 Peter 3:14-15)

How can you know which way is God's way?

Lord, help me to persevere when the way is full of twists and turns. Like the Jews who returned, give me vision to see your goals, even if they are not accomplished in my lifetime on earth. Amen.

June 3 ✠ Ezra 6–7

The king of Persia recognized Ezra as a man of wisdom and entrusted him with leading exiled Jews back to Judah, supplying the temple with articles for service, and teaching the Jews the laws of God. Ezra could have been proud, but in Ezra 7:27-28, he praises God for acting through the king and for showing his love to Ezra. He realizes that he is God's instrument.

When others recognize me, how quickly do I praise God? When Tim Tebow, quarterback at the University of Florida, won the Heisman Trophy in 2007, he thanked God. His humility and his recognition that God gave him the talent testified to his faith. He shared that the priorities of his life were God first, family second, academics third, and football fourth. Because of this statement, he received even more recognition. How he handled the honor he received was an example for us to follow.

I will tell of the Lord's unfailing love.
   I will praise the Lord for all he has done.
I will rejoice in his great goodness to Israel,
   which he has granted according to his mercy and love. (Isaiah 63:7)

When are you tempted to take all the praise for your accomplishments?

Gracious God, may I never fail to praise you for all the blessings you rain down on me. My very life is a gift from you. Amen.

June 4 ✠ Ezra 8–9

After the journey to Jerusalem, Ezra and the returning exiles rested for three days. I don't know how long the journey took, but it is interesting that they did not immediately take the articles to the temple. Such behavior is foreign to how we live today. In our society, we would expect Ezra to deliver the articles as soon as he arrived in Jerusalem, or at least by the next day. No one would wait three days.

We often take vacations in this manner. We take off from work and leave that day or the next, frantically packing. Then, when we return home, it's back to work the next day. Thus, we often undo the benefits of vacation by not allowing ourselves time to prepare for or recover from the journey.

In addition to needing rest to revive ourselves physically, we also need to rest with Christ. If we are always moving, it's hard for us to hear his messages to us.

The apostles returned to Jesus from their ministry tour and told him all they had done and taught. Then Jesus said, "Let's go off by ourselves to a quiet place and rest awhile." (Mark 6:30-31a)

How can you claim the benefits of true rest in your hectic life?

Lord, forgive me for feeling that I must spend my entire life in a race to get things done. May I take time to rest so I can enjoy your presence and have more strength and energy to praise you and serve you. Amen.

June 5 ✠ Ezra 10

Ezra 10 acknowledges a sin committed by many of the returning exiles: marriage to pagan wives. Having to divorce their wives and send them and their children away was surely not easy. Looking back at Ezra 9:1, the crux of the matter was that the priests and Levites had taken up the "detestable practices" of those they married. They allowed their wives to lead them astray.

It sounds harsh, but my faith cannot depend on another family member. I am responsible for living out my relationship with God regardless of how others in my family view my faith. I am to be an example, seeking to emulate Christ in all I do and in my relationships with family, but ultimately, my chief influence is to live as a faithful follower of Christ, love my family, pray for them, and share my faith with them by example and by words.

Do all that you can to live in peace with everyone. (Romans 12:18)

When do loved ones distract you from your focus on God?

Father God, may I seek always to please you and to love those with whom I live. May I be strong in my love for you, even when others around me do not share my faith. Amen.

June 6 ❁ Nehemiah 1–3

Nehemiah had a comfortable job as cupbearer for the king of Persia. He had regular access to the king of a giant empire who knew him by name. His position could have made him reluctant to return to Jerusalem with the earlier exiles, but upon hearing of their difficulties, he wanted to go to his homeland.

Nehemiah was unsure how the king would respond to his desire to leave. That's understandable. The king could have been angry, calling Nehemiah disloyal. Nehemiah's request could have hindered the work in Jerusalem if it angered the king.

But Nehemiah did not approach the king hastily. For days he fasted and prayed to God. He heard about the situation in the autumn, but did not approach the king until spring. Nehemiah spent about half a year seeking God's guidance before going to see the king. It is easy to miss this point when reading the story.

We want God's assurance and answers to our prayers to come quicker than our order at a fast food restaurant! We are so conditioned to instant—instant oatmeal, instant messaging, instant results—that the thought of seeking clarity for six months before acting is hard to comprehend. If we want to obey God, we must be willing to accept his timetable, not ours.

For the Lord God is our sun and our shield.
He gives us grace and glory.

The Lord will withhold no good thing
  from those who do what is right.
O Lord of Heaven's Armies,
  what joy for those who trust in you. (Psalm 84:11-12)

What actions do you take to discern God's will in a particular situation?

Perfect God, may I trust in you and patiently wait for your guidance. Amen.

June 7 ✠ Nehemiah 4–6

It's good that Nehemiah spent so much time in prayer discerning God's will before going back to Jerusalem. Once the wall was under construction, he faced great opposition, and many tried to discourage him from rebuilding the wall. Without his lengthy preparation before leaving Susa, he might have given up. Because of the time spent in prayer, though, he was certain he was doing God's will and able to persevere throughout the process.

We have to be sure that our course is in accordance with God's plan, for people will seek to discourage us. We should never stop listening to God!

For I know that as you pray for me and the Spirit of Jesus Christ helps me, this will lead to my deliverance. For I fully expect and hope that I will never be ashamed, but that I will continue to be bold for Christ, as I have been in the past. And I trust that my life will bring honor to Christ, whether I live or die. (Philippians 1:19-20)

When are you tempted to go your own way regardless of God's direction?

O Lord, may I never tire of going to you in prayer. May I seek your direction in all things and wait for your instructions always. Amen.

June 8 ✤ Nehemiah 7–8

The Israelites had a great celebration because they had heard God's words and understood them. At first reading, this sounds like a simple reason for celebration, yet, when I study familiar passages and learn something new, I am excited by fresh insight. I can understand why the people celebrated.

Can you imagine our world if we celebrated our ability to understand the word of God? I can imagine that as Ezra read, murmurs arose through the crowd, and heads began to nod as they realized they understood what they heard. They probably clapped and cheered at certain points.

It makes me excited to think about how much God has for me to learn about him, not only throughout my whole life, but *this* day. That is why we call the Bible the *living* word of God; the same words can say something different to us each time we read them.

How sweet your words taste to me;
they are sweeter than honey.
Your commandments give me understanding;
no wonder I hate every false way of life.
Your word is a lamp to guide my feet
and a light for my path. (Psalm 119:103-105)

What new things is God teaching you today?

O Lord, may your joy truly be my strength! Amen.

June 9 ✤ Nehemiah 9–10

In Nehemiah 9, the people react in humility when the story of their predecessors is recounted to them. All the blessings of God were told, as well as how the people then turned away from God. Those who hear this tale in chapter 9 commit themselves to follow God and obey his commands. They acknowledge where they are and vow to follow the Lord. Their obedience is not conditional on God improving their situation.

Their approach is better than that of their ancestors, who often made their obedience conditional on some action of God. Even today, I can catch myself "bargaining" with God to get me out of a situation (that I probably got into because of my disobedience). Instead, I should acknowledge my sin, repent, and humbly ask God for help.

O God, you know how foolish I am;
my sins cannot be hidden from you. (Psalm 69:5)

What stories of the faith humble you?

Gracious God, I am a sinner saved by your grace. May I acknowledge when I fail and humbly seek your forgiveness. Amen.

June 10 ✠ Nehemiah 11–12

The Israelites were thankful for the opportunity to worship the way their ancestors did during the time of King David. They did not take for granted the gift of gathering together to worship and praise God in the temple. They joyfully provided for the Levites and the priests because they appreciated them.

Do I take for granted the gift of being able to congregate with fellow Christians to praise and worship God? Am I excited to go to church each week, or do I see it more as an obligation than a gift?

Reading about the Israelites who returned from exile and worked so hard to build a place to worship God makes me more grateful for my own church and church family.

I was glad when they said to me,
"Let us go to the house of the Lord." (Psalm 122:1)

What does worship mean to you?

Lord, help me recall the joy of the Israelites when they were able to worship in the temple again. I need to appreciate the blessing of being part of your body at my church. Amen.

June 11 ✠ Nehemiah 13

How quickly the people fell back into their old, sinful behaviors when Nehemiah returned to Babylon! He had been in Jerusalem twelve years, but the people could not remain faithful in his absence.

Following God requires diligence. It is easy to slip into old habits because we see them lived out in the world around us. The Israelites adapted to the behavior of their neighbors. We often do the same thing. A behavior may not appear harmful, so we rationalize that it is acceptable.

We have to be strong to remain faithful to God.

Don't copy the behavior and customs of this world, but let God transform you into a new person by changing the way you think. Then you will learn to know God's will for you, which is good and pleasing and perfect. (Romans 12:2)

How do you determine which behaviors are godly and which are harmful?

O Lord, give me strength to stand strong for you, even when the world does not understand my decision. Amen.

June 12 ✠ Esther 1-3

Esther willingly listened to the advice of others who knew more than she did. Consequently, she was chosen to be queen among all the young women.

Proverbs 12:15 says, "Fools think their own way is right, but the wise listen to others." Though she was young, Esther showed wisdom by heeding Mordecai's advice to keep secret her nationality, and she listened to the advice of the king's eunuchs about how to behave in the presence of the king.

Wise counsel can make us wise when we listen and follow it. When we accept instruction, we also gain the support of those who teach us. An arrogant person has few friends because he won't seek help, and he discounts the wisdom of others.

People who despise advice are asking for trouble; those who respect a command will succeed. (Proverbs 13:13)

When has the advice of others helped you in your spiritual journey?

Lord, grant me the humility to recognize my limitations of knowledge and ability. Give me the wisdom to learn from others. Keep me open to hear you through the voices of others. Amen.

June 13 ✠ Esther 4–7

The story of Esther is the story of Haman's ego. Without his overwhelming desire for honor and recognition, there would be no story. Haman was so consumed with the need for honor that when only one man did not bow to him, he made it his mission to take revenge on Mordecai.

There was no humility in Haman. He went home after dining with the king and queen and bragged to his family and friends about what he had attained. Even so, nothing satisfied him. His hatred of Mordecai was greater than his enjoyment of the recognition he received from the king and queen.

Do I recognize my blessings, or do I focus on problems? Haman's inability to be satisfied cost him his life.

Haughty eyes, a proud heart, and evil actions are all sin. (Proverbs 21:4)

When does pride take hold of you?

Lord, open my eyes to all the blessings you have given me. Grant me a grateful heart and a humble spirit. Amen.

June 14 ✥ Esther 8–10

For the Jews living in Persia, Purim must have been a sign that God was with them even though they did not live in their homeland. The final message, where the Jews fight their enemies, was important for a persecuted people to hear. It gave them hope for the future.

Although God is never mentioned in the book of Esther, his influence is felt all through the book. Sometimes we find it difficult to sense God's presence because of circumstances or even our environment. The book of Esther reminds us that he is always present. We may need to slow the pace of our lives to listen to him. As in the story of Esther, God may not speak directly to us, choosing instead to speak to others around us.

Then Jacob awoke from his sleep and said, "Surely the Lord is in this place, and I wasn't even aware of it!" (Genesis 28:16)

When has God spoken to you through others?

All-present God, may I know your presence in all the moments of my life. You are as close as my own heart. Amen.

June 15 ✥ Job 1–4

When I feel worried and anxious, Job 4:3-6 reminds me that God is in control. Reverence for God should give me confidence. Living with integrity should give me hope. Troubles are part of life, but God reigns.

Many of us take for granted our blessings. But even if we suffer as Job did, God is still God, and we are not separated from him or his love.

Even now we go hungry and thirsty, and we don't have enough clothes to keep warm. We are often beaten and have no home. We work wearily with our own hands to earn our living. We bless those who curse us. We are patient with those who abuse us. We appeal gently when evil things are said about us. Yet we are treated like the world's garbage, like everybody's trash—right up to the present moment. (1 Corinthians 4:11-13)

How has God made himself evident even in your most difficult times?

Lord, we are not exempt from suffering. Your own Son, who was perfect, suffered. But we are never separated from you. Thank you for always being with us. Amen.

June 16 ✤ Job 5–8

Job asks a question we all ask at one time or another: "Is not all of human life a struggle?" (Job 7:1a). Even if we do all that God asks of us, life is still not carefree. Troubles will come, no matter how strong our faith.

The difference is how we view our troubles. If our faith is strong, we can see hope even in great despair. Job says, "At least I can take comfort in this: Despite the pain, I have not denied the words of the Holy One" (6:10).

Life isn't fair, but God is constant and loves us unconditionally. Praise God!

The Lord is close to the brokenhearted,
he rescues those whose spirits are crushed. (Psalm 34:18)

How does your faith alter your perception of suffering?

O God, sometimes all I can do is cling to you. I am thankful that I can always do that. Amen.

June 17 ✠ Job 9–12

"People who are at ease mock those in trouble. They give a push to people who are stumbling" (Job 12:5). Job's friends weren't the first to do it, and they certainly aren't the last. It's easy to look at those in troubled situations and analyze what got them there. It gives us an excuse not to help. When we can tie a person's situation to his behavior, we can depersonalize the situation and take compassion out of the analysis. In fact, analysis and compassion do not easily live together.

We may not *mock* those in trouble, but when we analyze them, it has the same effect. Truthfully, even if we know the message of Job, we still fall into the trap of looking for a behavior to blame for someone's misfortune.

When I see the homeless person and analyze how her actions may have caused her to end up homeless, I mock her from my position of ease. When I laugh at the plight of a public figure whose personal life is plastered all over the news, I give a push to someone who is stumbling.

Do not judge others, and you will not be judged. For you will be treated as you treat others. The standard you use in judging is the standard by which you will be judged. (Matthew 7:1-2)

How do you react to those in difficult situations?

O Lord, may I look on others with compassion and not judgment. Give me eyes that love instead of eyes that analyze. Amen.

June 18 ✠ Job 13–16

Job's fourth speech sounds as if he believes this life is all there is (Job 14:10-12). It's hard for me to imagine what it must be like to believe that way, having grown up in the church and always hearing about heaven and eternal life. Therefore, the words of Job in Job 14:7-9 inspire me, as he describes how a tree will sprout even after being cut down.

When I watch a beautiful sunrise, the birds on my feeder, and the flowers of summer, maybe I don't feel strongly the need to know that there is more to life than my days on earth. But when illness comes, troubles abound, and death takes away a loved one, then I find great comfort in knowing that beyond this life is a place where there is no more illness, no more pain, no more trouble.

I tell you the truth, those who listen to my message and believe in God who sent me have eternal life. They will never be condemned for their sins, but they have already passed from death into life. (John 5:24)

What convinces you that there is more than this life?

Everlasting Father, may I find comfort in knowing that I am always in your presence, now and forevermore. Amen.

June 19 ✠ Job 17–20

While yesterday's passage painted a picture of hopelessness, devoid of the promise of eternal life, Job 19:25-27 gives us hope for life eternal with God. Job's railing at God is contrasted with his deep and abiding faith: "I know that my Redeemer lives." Job still sees God as his redeemer, while at the same time seeing God as the perpetrator of his misery.

I write these words as I watch a beautiful sunrise. Maybe Job uttered his hopeful words while watching such a sunrise. A sunrise is always a sign of hope for me, because no matter how bad things were the previous night, the fact that the sun rises the next day reminds me that God is unchanging and always in control.

Sing to the Lord, all you godly ones!
Praise his holy name.

For his anger lasts only a moment,
but his favor lasts a lifetime!
Weeping may last through the night,
but joy comes with the morning. (Psalm 30:4-5)

When have you been able to praise God even in the depths of despair?

Lord, help me to see in the world around me the signs of your steadfastness, so that even in times of trials and suffering, I can remember that you are in control. Amen.

June 20 ✠ Job 21–24

Job, even in his misery, knows that God has not forgotten him, although in Job 23:8-9 he says he cannot find God anywhere he looks. Verse 10 says, "But he knows where I am going." Job is confident in his faithfulness. Even though Job cannot find God or experience a reprieve from his suffering, he continues to hope and be faithful. Job 23:8-12 shows us both the frustration and confidence of Job.

When I consider what Job experienced and realize that he still maintained his faith in God, I am ashamed for how I waver in putting my whole trust in the Lord. Too quickly I become discouraged and turn away from God, the only one who is always faithful.

But I will keep on hoping for your help; I will praise you more and more. (Psalm 71:14)

How does continually praising God in tough times draw you closer to him?

O Lord, may I be confident in your faithfulness and love to me. Even when I cannot see you in my circumstances, may I remember that you are always with me. Amen.

127

June 21 ✤ Job 25–29

Job 28 speaks of the ability of people to do many things, except discover wisdom. God is the source of wisdom, for he created everything and understands how it all fits together. For me to seek wisdom apart from God is futile. While I may learn many things "in the world" from others, true understanding comes from God alone.

I can never have the complete mind of God, but I pray that I can learn to see things and especially people as God sees them. I believe the truly wise have the gift of seeing others more as God sees them. Thus, they are better able to love all people.

For the Lord grants wisdom! From his mouth come knowledge and understanding. (Proverbs 2:6)

How can you grow wise in the ways of God?

O God, may I only seek wisdom through you, because you are the source of all wisdom. Amen.

June 22 ✤ Job 30–33

Job's friends quit arguing with him because Job was unwavering in declaring his innocence. I don't know if they were tired of trying to convince Job or if they had begun to believe him.

In any case, Elihu wasn't satisfied. He apparently had not heard enough wisdom from either Job or his friends. It is often difficult for me to sit quietly when I feel strongly about something. My listening ability is also impaired because I am so busy thinking about how I feel and what I want to say that I may miss another person who makes the same point I want to make.

I try to remember that I have two ears and one mouth, so I must listen twice as much as I talk. However, like Elihu, I am often full of pent-up words.

Fools vent their anger, but the wise quietly hold it back.
(Proverbs 29:11)

When have you failed to listen carefully to the words of others?

O Lord, may I not rush to give my opinion. Instead, help me wait and listen to others so that when I do speak, my words are the right ones for the situation. Amen.

June 23 ✠ Job 34–37

"God's voice is glorious in the thunder. We can't even imagine the greatness of his power" (Job 37:5). As I read Elihu's entire response to Job, I wondered if I would find anything to cling to. So much of his diatribe is harsh and angry, and knowing that God soon responds, I wasn't excited to read four chapters of nothing but Elihu!

But the above verse is powerful. Even if I had no personal relationship with God, thinking about the world he created is mind-boggling. The countless varieties of plants, flowers, animals, the sun, moon, stars, and all the vastness of space—it is impossible to imagine the greatness of his power.

Then combine the Creator of the universe with the God who knows the number of hairs on my head and my every thought, and I am truly humbled by it all!

The Lord merely spoke,
and the heavens were created.
He breathed the word,
and all the stars were born. (Psalm 33:6)

How easily do you comprehend that God, the creator of the universe, is your personal Lord and Savior?

Lord, thank you for showing me your truth, even in the argument of one who doesn't understand you fully. I also do not understand you fully. May I be humble as I approach you, remembering your majesty even as I pray to you as my dearest friend. Amen.

June 24 ✠ Job 38–40

Finally, the words of Job's so-called friends end. God's response is a series of questions to Job, challenging him in his knowledge of God. Job 40:8 strikes me as something I do, if not directly, then indirectly by my disobedience and lack of faith: "Will you discredit my justice and condemn me just to prove you are right?"

Do I do this when I question God's actions (or perceived inactions) toward people? Do I do this when I intervene in situations that God already has under control? If I am not listening to God, I can do a "good" thing, but not necessarily what I am supposed to do. Am I so steadfast in my beliefs that I harm the beliefs of others?

Just as God questioned Job, I need to question what I do and believe to be sure that it is in accordance with God.

Have you never heard?
  Have you never understood?
The Lord is the everlasting God,
  the Creator of all the earth.
He never grows weak or weary.
  No one can measure the depths of his understanding.
(Isaiah 40:28)

In what ways have you harmed the cause of God by your actions?

Lord, help me to be tolerable and tolerant, lovable and loving, careful and caring in all I do, so that I don't harm your cause. Amen.

June 25 ✠ Job 41–42

"Who has given me anything that I need to pay back? Everything under heaven is mine" (Job 41:11). Sometimes I want to think, "God owes me this because I did something for him." When responding to Job, God reminds him that everything already belongs to God, so God doesn't owe us anything. As I make decisions about how to spend money, I need to remember this. My financial resources are actually God's, and I should use them in a way that glorifies him.

Watching the birds in my back yard or the baby rabbit in my front yard, I am reminded that I get the most pleasure from what I don't possess—nature, friends, family.

I will send you the seasonal rains. The land will then yield its crops, and the trees of the field will produce their fruit. Your threshing season will overlap with the grape harvest, and your grape harvest will overlap with the season of planting grain. You will eat your fill and live securely in your own land. (Leviticus 26:4-5)

What good gifts has God given to you?

Lord, thank you for all good gifts. Amen.

June 26 ✦ Psalms 1–9

Psalm 4:5 speaks to me of the importance of acting out of love instead of obligation. It is better if I do less and do it with a loving spirit than it is to do many things and resent doing them. While serving the Lord is a good thing, it is only good if I am in the right spirit.

Acting out of love refreshes both the recipient of my service and me. Acting out of obligation not only drains me, but the recipient often senses that my actions are not performed in a spirit of love. God would rather have our love than our service.

It is easy to act out of love when we have joy within us. When we have a relationship with God, we receive the blessing of that joy. Like the psalmist, we can sleep peacefully and we can serve joyfully!

One of the teachers of religious law was standing there listening to the debate. He realized that Jesus had answered well, so he asked, "Of all the commandments, which is the most important?" Jesus replied, "The most important commandment is this: 'Listen, O Israel! The Lord our God is the one and only Lord. And you must love the Lord your God with all your heart, all your soul, all your mind, and all your strength.'" (Mark 12:28-30)

When have you ministered to others out of pure love and joy rather than obligation?

Lord, help me to remember that you alone are the source of joy and peace. May I find both in you. Amen.

June 27 ✤ Psalms 10–17

Psalm 11 is not familiar to me, but I appreciate the strength David showed in the face of danger. While others urged him to run and hide, he rose above and saw the big picture—that God is in charge. In a sermon I heard the week before reading this psalm, our minister said worship is our opportunity to get higher up so we can see the big picture.

We can't live all of life up high because we must attend to details. Sometimes, though, we focus so hard on details that we bring ourselves down and become anxious, worried, or fearful. Our anxiousness may cause us to act in inappropriate ways.

David's priorities are obvious from the first line of the psalm. Instead of listing the things that are going wrong in his life, he announces that he trusts in the Lord. While many of life's details can cause despair, if we acknowledge God first, the events that bring worry seem less significant because we view them from a higher place.

> *You will keep in perfect peace*
> *all who trust in you,*
> *all whose thoughts are fixed on you!*
> *Trust in the Lord always,*
> *for the Lord God is the eternal Rock. (Isaiah 26:3-4)*

How can you keep your focus on God's perspective?

Faithful Father, I want to see things from your perspective and trust in you for all things. Banish worry from my life and give me peace and joy as I lean on you. Amen.

June 28 ✠ Psalms 18–22

We relate to God imperfectly because he is perfect and we are not. Psalm 18:25-26 tells us how we will see God, which depends on how we seek to live for him.

God is always faithful, but if my desire is to live a faithful life, I will see his faithfulness all the more. In my effort to develop an attribute of God, I will come to know more and more of that attribute and gain greater insight into how the Lord exemplifies it.

However, if I turn away from God, deliberately leading a wicked life, he may seem hostile to me. While in fact he continues to be faithful, pure, and true, I won't realize that because I don't want to see his goodness in contrast to my wickedness. I may justify my behavior by viewing God as hostile, for how can I fight him when he offers me love and forgiveness?

The Lord isn't really being slow about his promise, as some people think. No, he is being patient for your sake. He does not want anyone to be destroyed, but wants everyone to repent. (2 Peter 3:9)

How does it feel to know that God is patient with you?

Merciful God, may I grow more like you every day. I want to imitate you and know you better. Amen.

June 29 ✠ Psalms 23–30

Psalm 29 does not describe the Lord as my companion, but instead praises him for his majesty. It's a contrast to Psalm 27:8, where God says, "Come and talk with me." As described in Psalm 29, God is so large and awesome that the wilderness quakes upon hearing his voice.

The same God whose voice shatters the cedars of Lebanon also knows when a sparrow falls to the ground. He is both our Creator and our closest companion. How amazing that he hears my innermost thoughts but also has the power to create the world!

I am the Lord, and I do not change. That is why you descendants of Jacob are not already destroyed. (Malachi 3:6)

What does it mean that the magnificent God loves you personally?

O Lord, great is your faithfulness! I am amazed that you, who are God, love me and know me completely! Amen.

June 30 ✤ Psalms 31–35

Psalm 34 has been my favorite psalm since my teenage years. At that time, verse 18 spoke to me, as heartbreak seemed a regular part of my life (not an uncommon teenage experience). Through the years, as I return to this psalm, other verses have been meaningful to me. Today verse 19 got my attention: "The righteous person faces many troubles, but the Lord comes to the rescue each time."

Notice it doesn't say the righteous will have an easy time of it because God is with them. It says the righteous will face *many* troubles. However, the troubles of the righteous are different than those of the wicked. Because the righteous have faith in God, they will experience rescue from their troubles.

That rescue comes in the form of the peace of the Holy Spirit and a focus on God instead of despair and hopelessness. No matter how difficult the trial, the righteous are assured that God is with them. Amen!

Each one will be like a shelter from the wind
 and a refuge from the storm,

like streams of water in the desert
    and the shadow of a great rock in a parched land. (Isaiah 32:2)

How has God proved faithful to rescue you, no matter what your circumstances are?

O Lord, thank you for being with me whether I face many troubles or rejoice in your greatness. Amen.

July 1 ✠ Psalms 36–39

When I read Psalm 36:2, I fear that the psalmist is describing me. I don't believe I am wicked, but I do sin. I don't want to be blind to my sin. Blind conceit scares me, and if I judge myself by comparing myself with others, it is easy to think more highly of myself than I should.

That's why it is so important to stay focused on Jesus. It's almost like I need to wear spiritual blinders so that instead of comparing myself to people, I only see Jesus and compare my behavior to his. When I do that, I am humbled rather than conceited because I realize how imperfect I really am.

Thankfully this psalm doesn't end with the description of the wicked. Verse 5 refreshes my spirit: "Your unfailing love, O Lord, is as vast as the heavens; your faithfulness reaches beyond the clouds."

This is why I can still have hope! It's not the end of the story when I recognize my sin. God's unfailing love lifts me from my sin, feeding me from the abundance of his own house and letting me drink from his river of delights!

And may you have the power to understand, as all God's people should, how wide, how long, how high, and how deep his love is. May you experience the love of Christ, though it is too great to understand fully. Then you will be made complete with all the fullness of life and power that comes from God. (Ephesians 3:18-19)

What sins has God shown you, and how did you react?

O Lord, I praise you for showing me my sin and also for showing me your amazing, unfailing love. Your awesome love is breathtaking to me, and I fall at your feet! Amen.

July 2 ✛ Psalms 40–45

"If I tried to recite all your wonderful deeds, I would never come to the end of them" (Psalm 40:5b). When I walk alone in the mornings, I pray, using the acrostic I first learned in a book by Rick Warren: P—praise and thanksgiving, R—repentance, A—ask, Y—yield to God.[5] Many mornings, before I move to "R," I cover a lot of distance while going through "P." Seeing a full moon, hearing the birds wake, or just enjoying the stillness of the pre-dawn darkness, I often find that I share the plight of the psalmist. I feel like a child reading her list to Santa, staying so long that she must be pulled out of his lap so the next child can sit there.

On days when I am not feeling spunky at 5:30 A.M., beginning my prayer with praise and thanksgiving lifts my spirits and helps me remember my blessings.

Beginning my day and my prayer by thinking of God's wonderful deeds puts joy in my heart for the rest of the day. Even if my day does not go well, I can praise God again the next morning!

Always be full of joy in the Lord. I say it again—rejoice!
(Philippians 4:4)

How easily do you praise God each day?

O Marvelous Lord, may I never tire of praising you! Amen.

July 3 ✛ Psalms 46–51

"Be still, and know that I am God" (Psalm 46:10a). This is one of my favorite verses and also one of my biggest challenges. I can work all day doing physical labor while on a mission trip easier than I can still my mind and contemplate God. Before writing this meditation, I read the verse and tried to practice it. Sitting outside at first light, I tried to empty my mind and think about the verse. Then I noticed an empty bird feeder and got up to fill it, thinking that after that, I would be still. Then the day's activities entered my mind and I began planning how I would spend the day. Again, stillness eluded me.

I want to tell my mind what you sometimes tell a small child: "Can't you be still for just a few minutes?" How can I expect to hear God over the TV, the radio, or even the constant hum of activity in my head? Unlike Peter (who had trouble being still himself), I don't hear God thundering, "This is my beloved son. Listen to him."

Our society values activity, but God values our devotion. We have to change our priorities to God's priorities if we want to hear God. We have to be still.

This is what the Sovereign Lord,
  the Holy One of Israel, says:
"Only in returning to me
  and resting in me will you be saved.
In quietness and confidence is your strength.
  But you would have none of it." (Isaiah 30:15)

When are you truly able to "be still and know"?

Lord, may I rest in you and be refreshed in your presence. The world is a dry and desolate place, but in you are springs of life. Amen.

July 4 ✤ Psalms 52–59

The preface to Psalm 59 says David wrote it about the time Saul sent soldiers to his house to kill him. David lived with the threat of being killed by Saul's men and had many close calls, but he remained faithful to God. I wonder if one of the keys to his faithfulness was how he started his day: "But as for me, I will sing about your power. Each morning I will sing with joy about your unfailing love" (Psalm 59:16a).

Thinking these thoughts and singing praises to God is a good way to start the day. Instead of hitting the floor thinking of all I need to do and the challenges the day holds, I should begin by singing of God's power and his unfailing love. When I remember that no matter what happens in my day, God is in control and he loves me unfailingly, I approach my day with confidence.

But Jesus deserves far more glory than Moses, just as a person who builds a house deserves more praise than the house itself. For every house has a builder, but the one who built everything is God. (Hebrews 3:3-4)

How can you start your mornings with God on your mind and heart?

O Lord, may I begin every morning singing praises to you. Amen.

July 5 ✦ Psalms 60–66

In *My Utmost for His Highest*, Oswald Chambers says that if we fret and worry, it's a sign of wickedness.[6] Worry is a sin because it shows that we don't trust God.

Psalm 62:5 says, "Let all that I am wait quietly before God, for my hope is in him." I can't wait quietly if I am anxious. Being anxious is an all-or-nothing emotion. Either I am anxious or I am waiting quietly. I must trust God totally. I cannot trust God partially, because partial trust is actually no trust. All that I am must trust God. He is my *only* hope.

My hope is built on nothing less than Jesus' blood and righteousness.
I dare not trust the sweetest frame, but wholly lean on Jesus' name.
On Christ the solid rock I stand,
all other ground is sinking sand;
all other ground is sinking sand. (Edward Mote)[7]

When do worries threaten to overcome you? How can you give them to God?

Lord, I want to give my anxiety to you and repent of that sin in my life. I want all that I am to wait quietly before you, knowing that in you alone is my hope. Amen.

July 6 ✠ Psalms 67–71

Most of us don't want to be called foolish, but in Psalm 69:5, David, God's chosen king of Israel, calls himself foolish: "O God, you know how foolish I am; my sins cannot be hidden from you."

David not only calls himself foolish; he also acknowledges that he is a sinner. Neither description is appealing to those of us living in the self-esteem generation! We've been told to be assertive, self-confident, and self-sufficient. But what is foolish to the world is wisdom to God. How can I ever abandon myself completely to God if I am concerned about looking foolish to others?

I don't want to be abandoned to others, abandoned to the world's standards. The world's standards are ever changing, and people aren't perfect. God doesn't change, and his standards are perfect. I would rather look foolish to an imperfect world than to our perfect God!

That's why I take pleasure in my weaknesses, and in the insults, hardships, persecutions, and troubles that I suffer for Christ. For when I am weak, then I am strong. (2 Corinthians 12:10)

How can you fully abandon yourself to God?

Lord, keep my focus on you and not on the world. I abandon myself to you, O Lord, today and always. Amen.

July 7 ✠ Psalms 72–77

Last night, I tried to do too many things at once. Although I did not ask for help, I became resentful when none of my family rushed in to assist me. It was a true Martha moment! This morning, I read Psalm 73 and realized my bitterness.

Psalm 73 speaks of envying the proud and all who prosper despite their wickedness. The psalmist envies them because they seem to lead such trouble-free lives, while he struggles with troubles despite leading a faithful life.

Verse 21 says, "Then I realized that my heart was bitter, and I was all torn up inside." When I read that verse, it cut me to the core! My bitterness was not directed at the proud, wealthy, or wicked, but instead at my own family. Bitterness is such an evil sin because it takes our focus off God, harms our relationships with others, and causes us to wallow in self-pity. Ouch!

For the word of God is alive and powerful. It is sharper than the sharpest two-edged sword, cutting between soul and spirit, between joint and marrow. It exposes our innermost thoughts and desires. (Hebrews 4:12)

When has bitterness hindered your ministry?

Lord, I want and need to repent of bitterness. Remove it from my heart. Replace it with humility and with the joy that comes from being led by your counsel. Your word is not always easy to hear, but I want to learn from it. Amen.

July 8 ✠ Psalms 78–80

Psalm 78 recounts how God took the Israelites from Egypt to the promised land. We considered the sin of worry several days ago; verses 19 and 20 illustrate why worry is a sin. Although the people had seen God cause water to come from a rock, they didn't believe he could give them bread and meat. Verse 22 says, "for they did not believe God or trust him to care for them."

I think about some of the trivial things I worry about. If God could feed a whole nation, surely he can handle my worries. If God could save Daniel from the lions, certainly he can get me through the situations in which I find myself.

Some people think they should only ask God for help with the big issues in their lives, but Jesus talked about proving faithfulness in small ways in the parable of the talents. How can we trust God with the big issues if we don't trust him with the small ones?

Do not despise these small beginnings, for the Lord rejoices to see the work begin. (Zechariah 4:10a)

When do you usually pray to God? Do you trust God's care for all the issues in your life?

Lord, may I trust you to care for me in both the big and small issues in my life. Amen.

July 9 ✠ Psalms 81–87

Every now and then, I catch glimpses of what it must be like to live in God's house. Psalm 84 reminds me of what I have to look forward to. I long to live in God's house, always singing his praises. Sometimes in worship I experience this on a small scale, but I know it will be grander and more glorious to live in his courts all the time.

If I am open and receptive to what is around me, I get a sneak peek of what life will be like in the courts of the Lord. When I think of the joy I will experience there, I do not fear death. I know the journey from life on earth to life in God's house will be the best journey I'll ever make!

The high and lofty one who lives in eternity,
*   the Holy One, says this:*
"I live in the high and holy place
*   with those whose spirits are contrite and humble.*

I restore the crushed spirit of the humble
and revive the courage of those with repentant hearts."
(Isaiah 57:15)

When have you felt closest to God?

O Lord, I love you and long to sing your praises always! Amen.

July 10 ✠ Psalms 88–91

Psalm 90 is a prayer of Moses, so I found the opening verse particularly meaningful: "Lord, through all the generations you have been our home."

During much of Moses' life, the Israelites were nomadic people. Moses did not have a place to identify as his home, so he thought of God as home. What a peaceful and wonderful way to think of God!

Seeing the destruction of Hurricane Katrina reminded me that many of the things I consider important in my life are not permanent. In fact, none of the things in my life are permanent except God. Health, friends, family, possessions, and even our minds can be taken from us, but God cannot. He truly is our home.

"On that day I will gather you together
and bring you home again.
I will give you a good name, a name of distinction,
among all the nations of the earth,
as I restore your fortunes before their very eyes.
I, the LORD, have spoken!" (Zephaniah 3:20)

What does it mean to you that God is your home?

God, you are my home. I dwell in you without fear of losing you, for you are eternal and almighty. Amen.

July 11 ✠ Psalms 92–100

"You thrill me, Lord, with all you have done for me! I sing for joy because of what you have done" (Psalm 92:4). I love the use of the word "thrill." It's not a word I often read in the Bible, but it fits here. What God does for me should thrill me. Maybe I should feel about God the way I feel on a ride at the fair: excitement, anticipation, breathlessness, a bit of fear. How would my faith be if I felt this way about God?

Maybe a thrilling faith is what allows the psalmist to declare, "Even in old age they will still produce fruit; they will remain vital and green" (Psalm 92:14).

What a great vision of old age—a strong tree still producing fruit!

Always be joyful. (1 Thessalonians 5:16)

How does God thrill you today?

Awesome God, when I see a beautiful sunrise or hear the birds sing, I am thrilled because I think of all the amazing things you have done for me and for us all. You surround us with things that remind us of your love for us. May I never cease to see your world with wonder. Amen.

July 12 ✠ Psalms 101–105

I sit on my patio as I write these words. At 6:45 A.M., the sky is golden with the sunrise. A chickadee sings just over my head in a maple tree, and other birds come and go at my bird feeder. When I read Psalm 104:24, I smiled and related to the psalmist's praise: "O Lord, what a variety of things you have made! In wisdom you have made them all. The earth is full of your creatures."

Nature helps me praise God. As I hear birds sing, I feel my own heart sing praise to God.

The chickadee is such a tiny bird, but God gave it a song bigger than its body and a distinctive black cap. He paid so much attention to the detail of creating this little bird. Imagine the time he put into creating me! Just as he gives the chickadee its own distinctiveness, he also blesses me with gifts that are uniquely mine. Praise God!

But now, O Jacob, listen to the Lord who created you.
O Israel, the one who formed you says,
"Do not be afraid, for I have ransomed you.
I have called you by name; you are mine." (Isaiah 43:1)

What do you see in the created world that draws you closer to the Creator?

Creator God, how you must love me! When I look at the tiny feet and feathers and the color and design of the birds, I am in awe that you would spend so much time to make me as you have. Thank you for loving me and giving me life! Amen.

July 13 ✠ Psalms 106–107

"Has the Lord redeemed you? Then speak out! Tell others he has redeemed you from your enemies" (Psalm 107:2).

I find it easier to be redeemed than to tell others about it. I suppose that indicates that I am still concerned about what the world thinks of me instead of being totally focused on what God thinks of me. How difficult it is to be in the world but not of the world!

Being bold enough to declare to others what the Lord has done for me is also offering praise to God. If I speak out, not only do I share God with others, but he hears my praise and is pleased.

David retorted to Michal, "I was dancing before the Lord, who chose me above your father and all his family! He appointed me as the leader of

Israel, the people of the Lord, so I celebrate before the Lord. Yes, and I am willing to look even more foolish than this, even to be humiliated in my own eyes!" (2 Samuel 6:21-22a)

When have you boldly proclaimed what God has done for you?

Lord, help me to embrace, not just accept, looking foolish in the eyes of the world, because I love you and want to declare to others that you have redeemed me. You gave your son for me; I can let go of my pride for you. Amen.

July 14 ✥ Psalms 108–118

I can say I trust God and that I know he is in control, but do I fear receiving bad news? Psalm 112 speaks to our attitude if we are truly abandoned to God: "They do not fear bad news; they confidently trust the Lord to care for them" (Psalm 112:7).

Waiting for the results of a medical test, college admissions letter, job offer, or other news is never pleasant. But if I trust God to take care of me, then I can never receive bad news that will be stronger than the good news that Christ died for me and loves me unconditionally. Even if I am disappointed in the news, I know God's plans for me are good.

The Lord is good,
a strong refuge when trouble comes.
He is close to those who trust him. (Nahum 1:7)

What is your biggest fear? How can you hand it over to God?

Lord, when I am tempted to fear, may I lean on you and feel your comforting arms around me. Amen.

July 15 ✠ Psalm 119

Reading Psalm 119 in one sitting, I realized that it is a psalm of praise for the commands of God. The psalmist cannot say enough about God's regulations. It's interesting to think about, because when I praise God, it's usually because of his mercy, his miracles, his creation of nature, or his blessings—but not his *rules*.

When we start talking about God's rules, most of us get squirmy if we think of having to follow those rules ourselves. Talk usually turns to God's forgiveness when we don't follow the rules. Yet the psalmist says, "I have rejoiced in your laws as much as riches" (Psalm 119:14).

But those who obey God's word truly show how completely they love him. That is how we know we are living in him. (1 John 2:5)

How does God love and protect you through his commands?

Lord, may I also praise you for your commands and be obedient to them because I love you. Amen.

July 16 ✠ Psalms 120–131

I like the prayerful quality of Psalm 131. It calms and quiets me as I read it. It fills me with peace.

A weaned child who no longer cries for his mother's milk has enough maturity to understand that his mother no longer feeds him, but he has no fear because he understands that she will still take care of him. This analogy reminds me to be confident that God is with me all the time and will always protect me and care for me, even if I don't see physical evidence of him. I don't have to receive the "milk" of signs and wonders to know that I am beloved of God.

You will live in joy and peace.
The mountains and hills will burst into song,
and the trees of the field will clap their hands. (Isaiah 55:12)

What gives you assurance that God cares for you?

Heavenly Father, may I always find peace as I trust in your care for me. Amen.

July 17 ✠ Psalms 132–138

Psalm 133 praises harmony. In music, there is unison, where all sing the same note, and there is harmony, where people sing different parts but it blends together into something beautiful.

Unison is simple and often appropriate if there is a strong message to deliver. The impact of a large number of voices singing the same notes is powerful. However, if all we ever heard were songs sung in unison, music (and life) would get boring.

Harmony is not always easy to sing. When I used to sing in choir, I found it difficult to sing my notes correctly if I didn't know the song well and stood next to someone whose notes were different from mine. Other times, I knew my notes well, but could not hear how the notes blended together, so I could only trust the choir director that the whole chorus sounded beautiful.

I think it's often that way with our churches. Each of us may feel that we sing from completely different sheets of music. To our ears, the music we make sounds like chaos rather than music. But God, our Choir Director, sees that it blends together into something beautiful to those who most need to hear it.

Live in harmony with each other. Don't be too proud to enjoy the company of ordinary people. And don't think you know it all! (Romans 12:16)

How easily do you find it to live in harmony with others, even as they differ from you?

O Lord, may I appreciate the differences of fellow Christians and celebrate the harmony we bring to worship you. Amen.

July 18 ✠ Psalms 139–143

"Let me hear of your unfailing love each morning, for I am trusting you. Show me where to walk, for I give myself to you" (Psalm 143:8).

I look forward to my first cup of coffee each morning. The aroma of it brewing fills me with anticipation, and makes the first taste something to savor. Many times, I enjoy my coffee outside as the world wakes up.

Mornings are magical to me. The coffee and my devotional time combine to make mornings my favorite time of day. What a blessing it is to hear of God's unfailing love each morning.

Every day I pray to God, "Lord, today I lay down my life for you." Every day is a gift God gives me, and instead of saving the best for last, he gives me the best first—in the morning! Because of this incredible gift, I cry out, "Show me where to walk, for I give myself to you."

The Sovereign Lord has given me his words of wisdom,
so that I know how to comfort the weary.
Morning by morning he wakens me
and opens my understanding to his will.
The Sovereign Lord has spoken to me,
and I have listened.
I have not rebelled or turned away. (Isaiah 50:4-5)

How do you approach each new day?

Lord of each new day, I thank you for the promise of morning. Your gift of the day is a blessing to me. May I use the gift to honor and glorify you with my life. Amen.

July 19 ✠ Psalms 144–150

"He takes no pleasure in the strength of a horse or in human might. No, the Lord's delight is in those who fear him, those who put their hope in his unfailing love" (Psalm 147:10-11).

We come by it honestly enough—the perceived need for power, strength, or superiority. Nations don't behave much different from children in that regard. We want to know who has the biggest, the most, the strongest, the fastest (fill in the blank)—and on and on. The only difference is what comes next. For children it could be swing set, toys, or Disney World. For nations, it could be army, land, support, or missiles. As adults, we are not immune. We could fill in our own blanks with house, jewelry, 401(k), computer.

God doesn't think that way. He values people who love him and trust him, not the things they own. A tornado can destroy the biggest house. Thieves can steal our jewelry. On a national level, one-upmanship can always be one-upped.

When our faith is in worldly things, we can never have peace, either world peace or inner peace. Things, people, and circumstances will always fail us.

But God will never fail us. If we put our whole trust in his unfailing love, we can have inner peace, even in a world torn by conflict and greed.

"I am leaving you with a gift—peace of mind and heart. And the peace I give is a gift the world cannot give. So don't be troubled or afraid." (John 14:27)

How can you seek God's gifts rather than the gifts of the world?

Lord, forgive me when I seek peace and comfort in possessions instead of you. You are my strong tower, the only strength I need. Amen.

July 20 ✤ Proverbs 1–3

"Don't be impressed with your own wisdom" (Proverbs 3:7a). I returned yesterday from a spiritual growth conference feeling full of new spiritual direction and knowledge. Then I read the verse above this morning. God's timing is amazing!

I was already impressing myself with what I learned and considering how I could share it with others. Sharing the experience was not the problem, but my motivation for sharing was. I wanted to impress others with my spirituality, which, of course, showed how unspiritual I was!

Because of the privilege and authority God has given me, I give each of you this warning: Don't think you are better than you really are. Be honest in your evaluation of yourselves, measuring yourselves by the faith God has given us. (Romans 12:3)

When are you tempted to share God's blessings with a prideful spirit?

Lord, may I share the gifts you have given me with a spirit of humility, remembering that they come solely from you and are nothing I have earned or am entitled to. Amen.

July 21 ✤ Proverbs 4–7

So much of Proverbs talks of the consequences of adultery. It contradicts our society's view of such behavior. Adultery is so commonplace in movies and television that it appears acceptable and even expected. The real-life instances of adultery by politicians, actors, and even ministers and priests make it appear that this "sin" isn't much of a sin. What is our response as those who seek to be faithful to God's commands? Does our willingness to forgive such behavior appear to be an acceptance of it? How do we balance love with accountability?

I recently taught a Sunday school lesson about Jeremiah. He was ridiculed for much of his prophecy because he called on the people to renew their covenant relationship with God by upholding their end of the agreement. He challenged the people to obey the commandments they were taught, and because of that, he was derided.

Does fear of ridicule prevent me from speaking out against behavior that, while accepted by our society, goes against God's commandments? How do I respond as a Christian, holding others (and myself) accountable for their actions but still showing the love of Christ?

Carefully determine what pleases the Lord. Take no part in the worthless deeds of evil and darkness; instead, expose them. (Ephesians 5:10-11)

How can we hold others and ourselves accountable to the standards of God and also show and accept the love of Christ?

Lord, show me how you want me to live in this world. It is not always easy to know what to do, but may I turn to you for guidance before I open my mouth. Amen.

July 22 ✤ Proverbs 8–11

"The blessing of the Lord makes a person rich, and he adds no sorrow with it" (Proverbs 10:22). I noticed this particular proverb today, probably because of the most recent sermon I heard. Our pastor spoke of how following Christ doesn't mean an easy life. I observed in this proverb that the *blessing* of the Lord makes a person rich. It doesn't say that believing in God guarantees worldly wealth.

Many times I feel rich because I have seen a beautiful sunrise, smelled sweet flowers, heard the birds sing, or experienced some other element of God's creation. I can enjoy these blessings without a penny in my pocket and still have an abundance of riches!

This verse doesn't say that we won't experience difficulty. The difference is that, with God's blessing as the source of our wealth, we see hard times from a different perspective. We have hope in eternal life, so we view suffering differently.

Then God looked over all he had made, and he saw that it was very good! And evening passed and morning came, marking the sixth day. (Genesis 1:31)

How can you cling to the knowledge of all God has given you, even when you feel poor by the world's standards?

O God, you created all life and all things beautiful. May I never feel poor as I recall the many ways you bless me. Amen.

July 23 ❖ Proverbs 12–15

"The wise don't make a show of their knowledge, but fools broadcast their foolishness" (Proverbs 12:23). Because I teach Sunday school, I tend to talk a lot in my Sunday school class on the Sundays when I don't teach. I confess that I often gain satisfaction by sharing my knowledge. This proverb hits home with me! When I am quick to share my thoughts, I may misinterpret the discussion or stifle someone else's ability to speak out. Consequently, I end up looking foolish.

I have to remember that I am not the repository of knowledge, that I have much to learn, and that by listening more and talking less, I can learn from others.

Understand this, my dear brothers and sisters: You must all be quick to listen, slow to speak, and slow to get angry. (James 1:19)

When has your knowledge of God surpassed your love for God as evidenced by your compassion toward others?

Lord, bridle my tongue that I may not trample your wisdom by my feeble words. May I be slow to speak and quick to hear. Amen.

$\mathcal{July}$ 24 ✠ Proverbs 16–19

"A truly wise person uses few words; a person with understanding is even-tempered" (Proverbs 17:27). Last night I lost my temper because I ended up doing something someone else was supposed to do. I wasn't angry with the person who failed to handle his responsibility. Instead, I was angry with another person who did not come to my aid when I took on the task. This morning I read a story in *Having a Mary Heart in a Martha World,* by Joanna Weaver, about a man who pulled a wagon up a hill.[8] What began as an easy task became difficult as he added the burdens of others to the wagon.

I realized that I had taken on the burden of another person. My anger was not only misdirected, but it also clouded my understanding of the best way to handle the situation.

The Lord replied, "Is it right for you to be angry about this?"
(Jonah 4:4)

How can you contain your anger rather than unleashing it on others?

Lord, help me to step back and gain an understanding of the situation before I get angry. Give me the discernment to know what you want me to do. Amen.

$\mathcal{July}$ 25 ✠ Proverbs 20–22

"The Lord directs our steps, so why try to understand everything along the way?" (Proverbs 20:24). I have read many self-help books in my adult life. I have tried to be more effective, better organized, more flexible, a better leader, purpose-driven, and beautiful! This simple proverb reminds me that I don't have to understand everything that happens because God is in control. While it's not wrong for me to try to understand myself, I must look inward and see myself accurately if I want to know how to be more like Christ.

This proverb invites me to less stress and greater joy. Instead of worrying, I can spend time discerning God's direction and seeing God's hand in the events and circumstances around me. This verse offers freedom and comfort. It calls me to rest in God. It's a call I need to hear.

You will keep in perfect peace
  all who trust in you,
  all whose thoughts are fixed on you! (Isaiah 26:3)

When are you tempted to seek help from everyone but God?

Lord, may I rest and let you drive, confident that you know the way and will get me there safely. Amen.

July 26 ✣ Proverbs 23–26

"Putting confidence in an unreliable person in times of trouble is like chewing with a broken tooth or walking on a lame foot" (Proverbs 25:19). People will disappoint. It's not an easy lesson for me to learn because I want those I love to be reliable in all things. I must remind myself that they are not perfect, just as I am not perfect, so they may not meet my expectations of them.

I often read in business books that people will rise to one's level of expectation, and often they do. However, when they don't, I need to determine if I have set my expectations too high. Or maybe I asked them to do something on a day they don't feel well or face difficulties in their lives. Or maybe, as the proverb says, they are generally unreliable.

I also need to look at how I respond to the expectations of others. Am I reliable, or do I disappoint? Is what I am asked to do reasonable and in line with what I can and will do? If not, I am responsible to let people know up front.

Obey your spiritual leaders, and do what they say. Their work is to watch over your souls, and they are accountable to God. Give them reason to do this with joy and not with sorrow. That would certainly not be for your benefit. (Hebrews 13:17)

In what ways can you temper your expectations of others to be more reasonable? In what ways can others do this for you?

Lord, help me to be reasonable. Remind me that meeting your expectations of me is most important. Make me more patient with others, just as you are patient with me. Amen.

July 27 ✠ Proverbs 27–31

"Fire tests the purity of silver and gold, but a person is tested by being praised" (Proverbs 27:21). I was surprised by the final words of this proverb. I would have expected to see words like adversity, sorrow, defeat or poverty. I did not expect to read "being praised."

We think of testing as a negative experience—something painful or uncomfortable that we must endure in order to reach a certain goal: pass the course, find the disease, get the license, make the team. But this verse says we are tested by being praised.

How do I handle success? This proverb says that is the biggest test I face. When things are going well and I am winning in life, then I am tested. We think of Job as an example of one who was tested, but maybe the better examples are found in Kings and Chronicles. Asa followed God at first, but as he grew in power, he made alliances with other nations instead of relying on God.

When I am successful and receive praise, do I credit God? Or do I treat success as something I have earned on my own?

For everything comes from him and exists by his power and is intended for his glory. All glory to him forever! Amen. (Romans 11:36)

How often does pride threaten your relationship with God?

Lord, may I remember always that all I am and all I do are because of your blessings. Do not let me become proud. Instead, help me to always give you the glory. Amen.

July 28 ✠ Ecclesiastes 1–4

Ecclesiastes 3:1-8 is a well-known passage of Scripture. In less poetic terms, it says that life is not all sunshine and roses, nor is it supposed to be.

Verse 11 speaks to our expectation of all good and no bad in our lives: "Yet God has made everything beautiful for its own time." He has planted eternity in the human heart, but even so, people cannot see the whole scope of God's work from beginning to end.

If everything is beautiful for its own time, then beauty lives even in tragedy and suffering. How often in my brief time on earth have I been able to look back at a difficult period or event and see the good that actually resulted from it? When I think about eternity, I realize that the things that cause me to ask, "Why, God?" may also be beautiful for their own time. My limited vision cannot see how a circumstance will unfold, but God is in control and has a plan. I can trust him to carry out his plan.

I should also remember this when I feel my efforts are small and feeble. If I do what pleases God, then my actions are not small and feeble. They are part of a plan I may not grasp, but I know it is good because it is God's plan. God's plans are beautiful for their own time!

"For I know the plans I have for you," says the Lord. "They are plans for good and not for disaster, to give you a future and a hope." (Jeremiah 29:11)

When have you found it easy to trust God's plans? When have you found this difficult?

Lord, help me to trust that your plans are always beautiful. Amen.

July 29 ✠ Ecclesiastes 5–8

"Control your temper, for anger labels you a fool" (Ecclesiastes 7:9). No matter how righteous the cause, we don't look wise when we lose our tempers. I have struggled with this my whole life. I can blame it on fatigue or emotion or stress, but the end result is that I don't look wise when I lose my temper.

When I lose my temper, I also lose my influence for positive change. And when I lose my temper, people remember that I was angry, but they may not remember what I was angry about. If I seek to be a catalyst for change, I have to control my temper.

Since God chose you to be the holy people he loves, you must clothe your-selves with tenderhearted mercy, kindness, humility, gentleness, and patience. Make allowance for each other's faults, and forgive anyone who offends you. Remember, the Lord forgave you, so you must forgive others. (Colossians 3:12-13)

What does your temper say about God?

Lord, help me to control my temper, and clothe me with kindness. Amen.

July 30 ✠ Ecclesiastes 9-12

"Whatever you do, do well. For when you go to the grave, there will be no work or planning or knowledge or wisdom" (Ecclesiastes 9:10). I know this verse serves as a warning that death is the end of everything, but thinking of death with heaven in mind makes dying seem more positive.

"Whatever you do, do well." This sentence alone is great advice. It doesn't say to do *everything* well, but to do *whatever* you do well. When I read that, it reminds me that I should think before doing. My tendency is to do too much, which makes it impossible to do everything well.

I must be prayerful about what I do, letting God guide me to what he wants me to do. Then my doing it well will glorify him.

He will feed his flock like a shepherd.
He will carry the lambs in his arms,

holding them close to his heart.
   He will gently lead the mother sheep with their young.
(Isaiah 40:11)

How can you discern when to act for God and when to rest?

Lord, guide me in all I do. You lead me gently. You don't ask me to exhaust myself for you. May I allow you to guide me and find rest close to your heart. Amen.

July 31 ✤ Song of Songs 1–8

Song of Songs reminds me that God blesses love. The exchanges between the man and woman in this book of the Bible compose a sensual love song.

Many people think being a faithful Christian means that life is dour, boring, and miserable. Song of Songs shows us that God wants us to be alive, to love each other, and to share in exciting and fulfilling relationships.

And Nehemiah continued, "Go and celebrate with a feast of rich foods and sweet drinks . . . ." (Nehemiah 8:10a)

How do Christians sometimes forget to live the abundant life that God gave us?

Lord, may I celebrate life with joy, loving, living, eating, and drinking with laughter in my spirit! You created me to praise you and to be joyful always. Amen.

August 1 ✤ Isaiah 1–4

When I read Isaiah 3:16-24, I feel compelled to look at myself closely to see if I have any arrogance or haughtiness is in me. I struggle with these attitudes. I need a constant reminder to focus on Jesus as my example instead of comparing myself with other people.

I don't want to rely on material possessions or my own abilities. I want to rely totally on God because I truly am nothing without him.

"Stop acting so proud and haughty! Don't speak with such arrogance! For the Lord is a God who knows what you have done; he will judge your actions." (1 Samuel 2:3)

Is arrogance a problem for you? How can you tame it?

Lord, keep my eyes on you today. Don't let me be tempted to rely on anyone or anything but you. Thank you for your constant love. Amen.

August 2 ✠ Isaiah 5–9

In my NLT Bible, Isaiah 8:11-27 is titled "A Call to Trust the Lord." Verse 11 begins, "The Lord has given me a strong warning not to think like everyone else does." Verse 17 says, "I will wait for the Lord, who has turned away from the descendants of Jacob. I will put my hope in him."

Isaiah's words in verse 17 make no sense in a worldly way of thinking. He himself was a descendant of Jacob. God was turning away from his land and his people. However, Isaiah had a view that was longer and higher than that of his neighbors. He saw that even if God did turn away from his land and people, God was still his *only* hope. No matter how bad things look, God is always our only hope.

When we put our whole trust in God, we are not thinking like everyone else does. Our viewpoint is different. Our focus is different. Our motivation is different. When we view life from an eternal perspective, things look different than when we view them from a worldly perspective.

So we have stopped evaluating others from a human point of view. At one time we thought of Christ merely from a human point of view. How differently we know him now! This means that anyone who belongs to Christ has become a new person. The old life is gone; a new life has begun! (2 Corinthians 5:16-17)

What does it take for you to see life from God's perspective?

Lord, it is challenging to be different than what our world admires, but you call us to be your people, obedient to you. Give me the conviction to stand firm in my faith even when others don't understand. Amen.

August 3 ✠ Isaiah 10–14

Isaiah 11 is a wonderful promise of God's ultimate goal for creation. It is a vivid mental picture of the world returning to God's original plan. While I may not observe it in my lifetime here on earth, I catch glimpses of it when I carefully watch the world around me. God desires a world at peace, and we should strive for it.

It's easy to say that one person cannot make a difference, but when one person speaks or acts, others who agree may follow, and eventually form a group large enough to effect change. How could Christians change our world if we lay aside what divides us and unite behind a shared goal?

Imitate God, therefore, in everything you do, because you are his dear children. Live a life filled with love, following the example of Christ. He loved us and offered himself as a sacrifice for us, a pleasing aroma to God. (Ephesians 5:1-2)

What steps can you take to move your little corner of the world toward God's ultimate goal for all creation?

Lord, may I show love to everyone and work to bring your vision for our world to reality. Amen.

August 4 ✤ Isaiah 15–21

In Isaiah 17, beginning with verse 10, Isaiah describes the normal activity of planting. When we plant, we do so with the expectation of enjoying the harvest. Isaiah tells the people that while they may see their crops blossom and sprout, they will not reap a harvest from them.

I like things to happen in the expected fashion. I want to harvest what I plant, I want to see my financial plans go as expected, I want my career to move in the normal progression. But life is not always predictable. If I live as though I expect my plans to succeed always, I will be disappointed.

Even though the fig trees have no blossoms,
and there are no grapes on the vines;
even though the olive crop fails,
and the fields lie empty and barren;
even though the flocks die in the fields,
and the cattle barns are empty,
yet I will rejoice in the Lord!
I will be joyful in the God of my salvation! (Habakkuk 3:17-18)

When your plans fail, do you lose faith in God?

O Lord, may I remember that whatever happens, you are the God of my salvation. Amen.

August 5 ✤ Isaiah 22–26

"You will keep in perfect peace all who trust in you, all whose thoughts are fixed on you! Trust in the Lord always, for the Lord God is the eternal Rock" (Isaiah 26:3-4). When doubt and worry threaten to creep into my thoughts, I need to keep my thoughts fixed on God. If I bring my thoughts back to him, I can live at peace because I trust him with my life and all my circumstances.

I cannot always control what happens to me and around me, but I can control how I react. If I trust God and am at peace because of my trust in him, then I can remain calm despite the chaos around me.

Therefore, since we have been made right in God's sight by faith, we have peace with God because of what Jesus Christ our Lord has done for us. Because of our faith, Christ has brought us into this place of undeserved privilege where we now stand, and we confidently and joyfully look forward to sharing God's glory. (Romans 5:1-2)

What do your reactions to circumstances say about your relationship with God?

Lord, keep my thoughts fixed on you and not on my circumstances. Amen.

August 6 ✠ Isaiah 27–31

When I rely on anyone or anything else other than God, I turn my back on him and show contempt for his power and love. Isaiah's message to Judah is strong in Isaiah 30:1-5. Instead of turning to God for help, the people of Judah sought help from Egypt. A seen ally was more valuable to them than God, the unseen all-powerful ally.

I have been guilty of similar behavior. I tell myself that God cannot or will not help me with the daily events of life, so I only turn to him when I am in crisis. But he is interested in every detail of my life. He wants me to turn to him first, even with the small stuff.

Then Jesus said, "Come to me, all of you who are weary and carry heavy burdens, and I will give you rest. Take my yoke upon you. Let me teach you, because I am humble and gentle at heart, and you will find rest for your souls. For my yoke is easy to bear, and the burden I give you is light." (Matthew 11:28-30)

Why is our desire to cling to God so strong in times of crisis? How can we cultivate a relationship with God that we enjoy daily?

Lord, you stand ready to take my burdens. May I give them all to you—big and small—and find rest and peace in you alone. Amen.

August 7 ✠ Isaiah 32–37

In the face of a tremendous threat from Assyria, Hezekiah did something that would seem ridiculous to one who did not believe in God. He prayed. He sought no alliance with another country. Instead, when his frightened officials reported to him what the Assyrians had said, Hezekiah went to the temple and called for Isaiah to pray for the people. What Isaiah prophesied, Hezekiah believed. So when circumstances gave Judah a reprieve from attack, Hezekiah prayed to God in thankfulness and praise. He gave credit to God for something that many would have explained away as coincidence.

If we will simply look, we will see God's actions in many ways. Events that others call lucky, coincidental, or strategic don't always appear that way to those who follow God's guidance in their lives and acknowledge God as the source of their ability and success.

Rejoice in our confident hope. Be patient in trouble, and keep on praying. (Romans 12:12)

How often do you turn to God first?

Lord, may my first thought in trouble be to turn to you in prayer. Amen.

August 8 ✠ Isaiah 38–42

Isaiah 40 contains many verses familiar to me, thanks, in large part, to Handel's *Messiah*. Isaiah 40:11 shows us a picture of God's immanence, his nearness to us: "He will feed his flock like a shepherd. He will carry the lambs in his arms, holding them close to his heart. He will gently lead the mother sheep with their young."

Isaiah 40:15c presents a picture of the transcendence of God: "He picks up the whole earth as though it were a grain of sand."

The God who is so mighty and powerful that the earth is like a grain of sand to him is the same God who holds me close to his heart. How incredible is that? Just thinking about God in this way makes me feel amazingly loved and humbled. What could be better than to be one of God's lambs?

I am the good shepherd; I know my own sheep, and they know me, just as my Father knows me and I know the Father. So I sacrifice my life for the sheep. (John 10:14-15)

Can you envision yourself as a beloved lamb of God?

Lord, I am awed and humbled that you, the God who created all things and rules over all things, love me as a lamb, holding me close to your heart. I want to stay in that place always. Give me ears to hear your voice and the desire to follow it. Amen.

August 9 ✦ Isaiah 43–46

The Israelites had to change their thinking over the period of their exile. Initially, they had to realize that the temple and the promised land were not talismans that protected them from harm regardless of how they behaved. That was a huge shift in their understanding of their relationship to God. The thought that their restoration would come from the hand of one who did not know God, Cyrus of Persia, was truly radical.

We sometimes get our own brand of tunnel vision. It's difficult for us to love our enemies or anyone who is not like us. It is even more difficult for us to imagine God using such a person to carry out his purposes. We can be rather territorial in our faith, much as the Israelites were.

God created all people. He can use them for his purposes whether or not they acknowledge him. As believers, we should always be alert for God's movement in the world—however and through whomever it happens.

"But Lord," exclaimed Ananias, "I've heard many people talk about the terrible things this man has done to the believers in Jerusalem! And he is authorized by the leading priests to arrest everyone who calls upon your name."

But the Lord said, "Go, for Saul is my chosen instrument to take my message to the Gentiles and to kings, as well as to the people of Israel." (Acts 9:13-15)

How has God surprised you today?

Lord, thank you for your incomprehensible plan for us. Give us vision to see your work in places where we may not think to look for it. Amen.

August 10 ✠ Isaiah 47–51

"I, yes, I, am the one who comforts you. So why are you afraid of mere humans, who wither like the grass and disappear?" (Isaiah 51:12). As I read today's passage, I reflected on my busy and stressful week. We have traveled out of town (on our so-called vacation) looking for housing for a son who us beginning graduate school, and the other son leaves tomorrow to begin his freshman year at college. I'm not only catching up on laundry from our trip, but I'm also washing clothes to go to college tomorrow. Between the older son moving things home from his college apartment (and dumping them in the den) and the younger son accumulating what he needs to take to college (and staging it in another room), our house looks like robbers have ransacked it.

Add to the mix the emotion associated with these life changes, and while I am not afraid, I am experiencing an unsettling time.

This verse is welcome reading for me today. God is there to comfort me when I'm afraid, when I'm stressed, when my life feels as though it's been shaken like one of those snow globes.

All praise to God, the Father of our Lord Jesus Christ. God is our merciful Father and the source of all comfort. He comforts us in all our troubles so that we can comfort others. When they are troubled, we will be able to give them the same comfort God has given us. (2 Corinthians 1:3-4)

When has God comforted you?

Lord, I am thankful for your comfort. You give me all I need if I will only turn to you to receive it. Amen.

August 11 ✠ Isaiah 52–57

Isaiah 55 poses a question I need to ask myself: Why spend your money on food that does not satisfy? For much of our lives, we focus on acquiring things. I look at the community where I live and realize that it has grown around the shopping areas. The newspaper is full of ads, and our Sunday paper mostly contains sales circulars for area stores.

Yet Isaiah says "wine" and "milk" are available without money. Isaiah used these items because they represented the best, the richest, the most desired. Instead of feasting on God's word, which is available for no money, we spend money on things that do not satisfy.

Most of us have too much stuff, and it's not the stuff that makes us happy. It's the relationships—with God, with each other—that provide the joy in our lives.

Yes, he humbled you by letting you go hungry and then feeding you with manna, a food previously unknown to you and your ancestors. He did it to teach you that people do not live by bread alone; rather, we live by every word that comes from the mouth of the Lord. (Deuteronomy 8:3)

How can you determine to feast on the word of God?

Lord, you tell me, "Listen to me, and you will eat what is good." I am listening. Let me feast on your word. Amen.

August 12 ✠ Isaiah 58–63

In my Bible, the heading given for Isaiah 58 is "True and False Worship." Isaiah attacks the practices of the people and instructs them in what God calls worship. He addresses fasting first.

I practiced fasting during Lent a couple of years ago. I gave up lunch on Fridays. It was supposed to be a worshipful practice, but instead, I was more irritable on Friday afternoons, and the only benefit I seemed focused on was whether I lost any weight as a result. Such fasting does not honor God.

Isaiah's description of right fasting focuses on blessing others. The way I approached fasting didn't bless anyone. Isaiah says to turn our time and resources toward others who need them. Isaiah's message to me is to discover what I cling to most tightly and give that up for the benefit of others.

But Samuel replied,
"What is more pleasing to the Lord:
*   your burnt offerings and sacrifices*
*   or your obedience to his voice?*
Listen! Obedience is better than sacrifice,
*   and submission is better than offering the fat of rams."*
(1 Samuel 15:22)

What do you need to give up?

Lord, open my grip on that to which I cling. Give me a generous heart so I will share with others. Amen.

August 13 ✠ Isaiah 64–66

The Lord says, "I was ready to respond, but no one asked for help.
  I was ready to be found, but no one was looking for me.
I said, 'Here I am, here I am!'
  to a nation that did not call on my name." (Isaiah 65:1)

Sometimes we think our needs are too trivial to take to God. We feel we must wait and use him like a wild card in a game. This verse from Isaiah portrays a God who wants us to choose him, much like a child wants to be picked for a team to play a playground game. God wants us to turn to him, to ask him for help, to pray without ceasing. He does not try to be hidden from us, but makes himself visible, if we will just open our eyes and look.

Are you seeking him? Are you asking for help in the everyday issues of life? Faith is a lot like exercise. If we don't exert ourselves physically with some regularity, we can't summon the energy for a sprint or a marathon. If we don't practice our faith regularly in small ways, it is harder to summon it for the critical events in our lives.

Sometimes I hear Christians say, "God helps those who help themselves." But what God says is that he helps those who turn to him for help.

"Look! I stand at the door and knock. If you hear my voice and open the door, I will come in, and we will share a meal together as friends." (Revelation 3:20)

How often do you turn to God for help?

Loving Father, may I turn to you and ask with the faith of a child, knowing that you love for me to seek you out at all times. Amen.

August 14 ✦ Jeremiah 1–3

The Bible is full of people who protested when God called them. While some like Isaiah say, "Here I am; send me," many give God excuses for why he has made a poor selection. Jeremiah's excuse is his age. Although God tells him that before Jeremiah was born, he was set apart as a prophet, Jeremiah balks at his call.

If we stop and think about it, it makes no sense to offer excuses to God about why we are inadequate to answer his call. After all, he made each one of us. He knows exactly what we are capable of because he gave us the ability.

By his divine power, God has given us everything we need for living a godly life. We have received all of this by coming to know him, the one who called us to himself by means of his marvelous glory and excellence. (2 Peter 1:3)

What is God calling you to do? Are you listening for his call? Are you offering your own protest?

Lord, I want to follow you faithfully, wherever you lead. I want to do whatever you want me to do. I don't want to fight you. Speak, for your servant is listening. Amen.

August 15 ✦ Jeremiah 4–6

We tend to perceive God as vengeful when we read the Old Testament, but reading Jeremiah 4, I see that God offers the people of Judah the chance to turn away from their destructive behavior. Jeremiah 4:3b-4 says,

Plow up the hard ground of your hearts!
  Do not waste your good seed among thorns.
O people of Judah and Jerusalem,
  surrender your pride and power.
Change your hearts before the Lord,
  or my anger will burn like an unquenchable fire
  because of all your sins.

I like a song that talks about wanting to be love but wanting to stay safe. I cannot have a soft heart and live safely. For me to be loving to others, I have to take risks. When I play it safe, I am guilty of not surrendering to God.

"Love your enemies! Do good to them. Lend to them without expecting to be repaid. Then your reward from heaven will be very great, and you will truly be acting as children of the Most High, for he is kind to those who are unthankful and wicked. You must be compassionate, just as your Father is compassionate." (Luke 6:35-36)

What chances has God given you to turn back to him?

Lord, soften my heart to serve you in whatever way you choose to use me. Take away my pride and replace it with such love for you that your way is all I see. Amen.

August 16 ✠ Jeremiah 7–10

I know, Lord, that our lives are not our own.
  We are not able to plan our own course.
So correct me, Lord, but please be gentle.
  Do not correct me in anger, for I would die. (Jeremiah 10:23-24)

I am a planner, so verse 23 makes me pause and wonder if I am allowing God's plans to guide my life or attempting to plan my life by myself. If I attempt to plan without God, my plans are bound to be frustrated and unfulfilling.

If I allow God to move me in his direction, I can be at peace, even when his direction takes me down an unfamiliar path. Peace comes from knowing that God is in control. Of course, sadness and disappointment will come, but knowing that God has planned my course gives me peace, even when that course is twisting and bumpy.

Guide my steps by your word, so I will not be overcome by evil. (Psalm 119:133)

How often do your plans for yourself overshadow any plans God may have for you?

Loving Father, may I listen for your direction always and follow you. Make me obedient and holy. Amen.

August 17 ✠ Jeremiah 11–14

Pride is a dangerous thing. God condemns the pride of Judah in Jeremiah 13. When Jeremiah digs up the rotting loincloth, God compares the cloth with how he will rot away the pride of Judah.

I struggle with the sin of pride. Whenever I receive a compliment or am recognized for an honor, I am in danger of letting pride get ahead of God. I am tempted to think my own efforts earned me the recognition, instead of acknowledging that God's ability allowed it.

His mighty arm has done tremendous things! He has scattered the proud and haughty ones. He has brought down princes from their thrones and exalted the humble. (Luke 1:51-52)

When does pride threaten to overcome your witness?

Lord of all things, may I remember that you alone are worthy of praise. I am your vessel and only able to act as you fill me. Amen.

August 18 ✠ Jeremiah 15–18

Jeremiah contrasts those who trust people with those who trust God in Jeremiah 17:5-8. He uses trees and shrubs to paint a visual picture of the differences in the lives of people depending on where their hope lies.

Where I live, we have suffered a drought this summer, so this image is real and timely for me. As I walk through our neighborhood, I see dead or dying shrubs. However, in the same yard, I see trees that are still green and alive. Because the roots of the trees run deeper than those of the shrubs, they can survive a longer period without rain.

In whom do I put my trust? If I put it in people, I will be disappointed because people are imperfect. They make mistakes. Their knowledge is limited, and they become distracted by many things. I even disappoint myself for the same reasons.

Yet, if my trust is in God, I can stand strong regardless of what happens. Even in the droughts of my life, God is with me.

By standing firm, you will win your souls. (Luke 21:19)

What is the object of your trust?

Lord, keep me firmly planted in your word. Amen.

August 19 ✠ Jeremiah 19–22

Jeremiah suffered to follow his calling to serve God. Several places in the book of Jeremiah record his complaint about how he is treated for being faithful to God. Jeremiah 20:7-18 is one of those places.

Am I willing to suffer the ridicule and misery Jeremiah endured for the sake of following God where he leads me? If God calls me to speak out, even when my words are not well received, will I do it? Am I able to stand up and condemn wrong behavior even when other Christians accept it as tolerable?

If I am devoted to God, I should answer yes. For Jeremiah to endure, he had to be totally devoted to God. Otherwise, he would have given up completely.

The proud hold me in utter contempt, but I do not turn away from your instructions. (Psalm 119:51)

When has it been especially difficult for you to stand up for God? How did you cope?

Lord, may I desire complete obedience to you, so that I am strong in upholding your will. Amen.

August 20 ✠ Jeremiah 23–25

Jeremiah condemned the false prophets, who told the people everything would be okay. Jeremiah said they filled the people with false hopes.

I wonder if I am listening to false prophets instead of modern-day Jeremiahs. Maybe there are warning signs to look for, such as only preaching good news and not preaching repentance—the "I'm okay, you're okay" philosophy. Maybe I can observe if the prophet stands to gain from his prophecy. Do the prophet's words ring true to the Bible or not?

I think about how the movie *The Secret* caused such a stir. People embraced it as part of their spiritual lives. It seems to me that it espouses a selfish aim—you can be successful and prosperous by thinking the right thoughts. The book of Job contradicts that philosophy!

Beware of false prophets who come disguised as harmless sheep but are really vicious wolves. You can identify them by their fruit, that is, by the way they act. Can you pick grapes from thornbushes, or figs from thistles? A good tree produces good fruit, and a bad tree produces bad fruit. (Matthew 7:15-17)

How do you know when God speaks?

O God, grant me wisdom and discernment so that I test what I hear to see if it is from you. Amen.

August 21 ✠ Jeremiah 26–28

When I read Jeremiah 26–28, I am humbled by Jeremiah's faith and his devotion to God. In these three chapters, his life is at risk and he wears an ox yoke. He apparently wore it for months, not days, because chapter 28 refers to late summer the same year, when a false prophet broke the yoke Jeremiah wore.

How would I react if God called me to place my life in danger and to wear something that would draw such negative attention to myself? Am I so devoted to God that I can truly lay aside my life for him? It could mean physical death, but it could also mean laying aside any behavior that shows I think more highly of myself than I do of God. Oswald Chambers, in *My Utmost for His Highest*, writes that our devotion to God means that we are not conscious of ourselves at all.[9]

And if you do not carry your own cross and follow me, you cannot be my disciple. (Luke 14:27)

How devoted are you to God?

Lord, remove any obstacle that stands between me and you. I want to be completely devoted to you. Amen.

August 22 ✠ Jeremiah 29–31

Jeremiah's letter to the exiles in chapter 29 contains a familiar passage of Scripture: "For I know the plans I have for you . . . ." In the verses prior to this passage, Jeremiah tells the exiles to get on with their lives. Their temptation is to wait passively for God to act, but Jeremiah says to be active.

In my life, I need to find a balance between doing so much that I shut out the ability to hear God and sitting still all the time listening for him to speak. When I want to hear God speak and give me direction, I would prefer not to move until I hear him. Jeremiah says my listening should be active, not passive. However, I should not be so active that I'm consumed with busyness, but instead continue to move while I listen for God. His plans will be carried out, and they are always good!

So if you sinful people know how to give good gifts to your children, how much more will your heavenly Father give good gifts to those who ask him. (Matthew 7:11)

How do you balance your listening to God with your acting for God?

Loving Father, I know I can trust you to care for me. May I balance my listening with my activity so that I hear your voice and move where you want me to go. Amen.

August 23 ✠ Jeremiah 32–33

Jeremiah's prophecy about King Zedekiah landed him in jail. But while in jail, he continued to prophesy—and not only about the restoration of Judah. His willingness to continue to speak out, prophesying faithfully, even when the news was not well received, causes me to examine my faithfulness and devotion.

Would I be willing to suffer jail to speak out in a way that God leads me to speak? And if I were so bold, would that boldness carry over once I was imprisoned? God may not use me in such dramatic fashion, but am I also willing for God to use me in a menial way? Can I accept doing his will with no notice of myself at all? That may be the more difficult question to answer because I love to be recognized for a "job well done."

God chose things despised by the world, things counted as nothing at all, and used them to bring to nothing what the world considers important. As a result, no one can ever boast in the presence of God. (1 Corinthians 1:28-29)

How dangerous is your faith in God?

Lord, may I be so devoted to you that I don't care whether anyone in this world recognizes me. I only want to be obedient to you. Amen.

August 24 ✠ Jeremiah 34–36

The Recabites were faithful to instructions passed down from one of their ancestors. Their faithfulness was contrasted with the unfaithfulness of Judah in following the laws of God.

I confess that I am often more faithful to the "laws" of this world than I am to what God tells me. In fact, this morning I had an excellent example of that behavior. Someone was angry with me and blamed me for something that happened to them, and instead of turning the other cheek, I defended myself. Our world teaches us to defend ourselves when attacked, but Jesus teaches us to turn the other cheek.

Our dedication to Christ makes us look like fools, but you claim to be so wise in Christ! We are weak, but you are so powerful! You are honored, but we are ridiculed. (1 Corinthians 4:10)

When are you tempted to react to others as the world expects you to react rather than following a more godly way?

Lord, change my hearing and understanding so that your wisdom seems wiser to me than the "wisdom" the world teaches me. Amen.

August 25 ✠ Jeremiah 37–40

When Babylon took over Judah, Jeremiah was given the choice of going to Babylon with the exiles or staying behind in Judah with the poor. Jeremiah chose to stay behind. I wonder why he chose as he did. The leaders of Judah knew him, and the exiles were the people to whom he had prophesied. Did God instruct him to stay in Jerusalem?

With all the leadership in Judah carried to exile, Jerusalem would have been an unsettled place. That Jeremiah remained in harsh living conditions seems to fit with the way he lived as a prophet prior to the fall of Jerusalem.

Can anything ever separate us from Christ's love? Does it mean he no longer loves us if we have trouble or calamity, or are persecuted, or hungry, or destitute, or in danger, or threatened with death? (As the Scriptures say, "For your sake we are killed every day; we are being slaughtered like sheep.") No, despite all these things, overwhelming victory is ours through Christ, who loved us. (Romans 8:35-37)

Do you truly believe God is with you wherever you go?

Lord, wherever I am, there you are. I thank you that even in the most desolate places of my life, I am not alone. Amen.

August 26 ✠ Jeremiah 41–44

Even after the exile, those Judahites who remained in Judah had not learned that God was in control. Against God's orders, they went to Egypt and worshiped the gods they had worshiped before the fall of Judah. Am I that hardheaded? How does my behavior mimic that of the remnant of Judah?

Self-examination is not fun, but when I read of the waywardness of the people of Judah, I feel compelled to look for similar behavior in myself. Human nature hasn't changed in all these years, so, hopefully, I can learn from their mistakes.

But the people refused to listen, and Manasseh led them to do even more evil than the pagan nations that the Lord had destroyed when the people of Israel entered the land. (2 Kings 21:9)

What can you learn from past followers of God?

Lord, may I listen and learn from the examples in the Bible. Amen.

August 27 ✠ Jeremiah 45–48

Baruch was Jeremiah's faithful scribe. After all the messages Jeremiah received for Judah, in chapter 45 God has a message just for Baruch. Baruch has grown weary of his troubles. He apparently desires recognition for himself, because God's message asks Baruch, "Are you seeking great things for yourself?"

I can relate to Baruch. Although I have not suffered as he and Jeremiah did, when I do something for God, I look for an accolade to acknowledge my "sacrifice." All I've done is obey, which is what I'm supposed to do. God's response to Baruch puts things into perspective: "I will give you your life as a reward wherever you go."

Baruch did what he was called to do. If I obey what God calls me to do, I have my reward—the joy of being obedient. Because I love him, my reward is the opportunity to serve him.

If you love only those who love you, what reward is there for that? Even corrupt tax collectors do that much. If you are kind only to your friends, how are you different from anyone else? Even pagans do that. (Matthew 5:46-47)

How can you serve God with no expectation of something in return?

Lord, may I be so in love with you that I view obedience to you as a privilege. Amen.

August 28 ✠ Jeremiah 49–50

In the final chapters of Jeremiah, the prophet predicts the destruction of Judah's neighbors. I find it interesting that hope is given to Moab, Ammon, and Elam. Sometimes when reading the Old Testament, it seems there is no good message for any nation other than Israel. With everything that the entire region suffered, did God seek cooperation for the rebuilding effort?

I may say that God loves all people, even those who don't believe in him and who seek to destroy his word, but do I treat others as children of God and my brothers and sisters? We often act as badly as Israel did, relying on being the "chosen people" of God. Can we embrace each person we encounter as a child of God, loved by him as much as we are?

So God created human beings in his own image. In the image of God he created them; male and female he created them. (Genesis 1:27)

In what ways do you see others as less than God created them?

O Lord, help me to see each person through your eyes. May I love all people, even the unlovable, because each one is my sibling because you are my Father. Amen

August 29 ✠ Jeremiah 51–52

Amid the prophecies of destruction and revenge in the final chapters of Jeremiah is a hymn of praise to God.

Jeremiah 51:15-19 speaks of God's power over all things. I read from Genesis 1 this morning. Afterward, I read these words from Jeremiah: "With his own understanding he stretched out the heavens" (Jeremiah 51:15b).

God created our world simply by his understanding. He thought it, and it came to be! How utterly amazing to think about! Each flower, each creature, and even me—created by God and alive because of his thoughts.

179

You saw me before I was born.
    Every day of my life was recorded in your book.
Every moment was laid out
    before a single day had passed.
How precious are your thoughts about me, O God.
    They cannot be numbered! (Psalm 139:16-17)

What does it mean to you that God thought of you so deeply before you were even born?

O Lord, I cannot begin even to comprehend what all you have done. And you love me! Thank you! Amen.

August 30 ✣ Lamentations 1-2

In Lamentations, the terrible despair of the people who lived apart from God for so long takes hold. There is no railing at God here—only the acknowledgment of sin and brokenness. In Lamentations 1:18, the writer says God is right in his treatment of Jerusalem.

It's never easy to admit a mistake. I prefer to blame others than to accept responsibility; I often make excuses to justify my actions. I don't want to face consequences when I mess up. It is humbling to say, "The Lord is right," but it is necessary in order for us to change. Without our admission of failure, we have no hope of moving forward.

Thank God for his amazing grace that he still loves us even amid the consequences of our mistakes.

For everyone has sinned; we all fall short of God's glorious standard. Yet God, with undeserved kindness, declares that we are righteous. He did this through Christ Jesus when he freed us from the penalty for our sins. (Romans 3:23-24)

Where do you turn in times of deepest despair?

O God, thank you for your infinite love and mercy. I can never cease to praise you for your wonderful gift of everlasting life. Amen.

August 31 ✠ Lamentations 3–5

"The faithful love of the Lord never ends! His mercies never cease. Great is his faithfulness; his mercies begin afresh each morning" (Lamentations 3:22-23). I love the morning. I enjoy being up before anyone else and watching the world wake up. I especially like the morning when the previous day was difficult; the new day offers an opportunity for a new beginning. I can wipe the slate clean and begin again.

The author of Lamentations says God's mercies begin afresh each morning. What a wonderful thought to read at the dawn of a new day! Whatever I've done, whatever happened yesterday, is past. I cannot take it back. But even better, God's mercy wipes the slate clean so I can face this day with hope and anticipation!

For his anger lasts only a moment,
but his favor lasts a lifetime!
Weeping may last through the night,
but joy comes with the morning. (Psalm 30:5)

Amid the lamentations we read of God's new mercies. How does God make his mercies new to you each day?

O Lord, great is your faithfulness! Amen.

September 1 ✠ Ezekiel 1–4

" . . . and he felt the hand of the Lord take hold of him" (Ezekiel 1:3b). When I first read this verse, I thought it would be nice to know with such certainty that I was moving where God wanted me to move. However, as I read further, I realized that Ezekiel wasn't thrilled that the hand of God gripped him: "I went in bitterness and turmoil, but the Lord's hold on me was strong" (Ezekiel 3:14b).

His words remind me that not all experiences of obedience are pleasant. When I surrender to God, I don't merely sign on for the euphoria of an Easter or Pentecost experience. I also get Gethsemane and the cross. But if Christ is living in me, I still have joy in knowing that I have an eternal relationship with him.

So be happy when you are insulted for being a Christian, for then the glorious Spirit of God rests upon you. If you suffer, however, it must not be for murder, stealing, making trouble, or prying into other people's affairs. But it is no shame to suffer for being a Christian. Praise God for the privilege of being called by his name! (1 Peter 4:14-16)

When have you resented God for allowing you to endure a particular trial?

Lord, may the trials I endure because of my obedience to you bring me joy because I suffer for the privilege of belonging to you. Amen.

September 2 ✠ Ezekiel 5–9

God took Ezekiel to different places in Jerusalem to show him how the people worshiped anything but God. They had fallen far from the experience of the exodus, when they depended totally on God for food, direction, and salvation. Of course, even then, they had questioned God's wisdom and disobeyed.

If God were to show me "detestable practices" today, what would they be? Where am I guilty of putting things ahead of God? Is God truly at the center of my life, or do I push him to one side and put something else at the center? Do work, money, pleasure, possessions, or family come ahead of God? Do I bow down to pride, ego, conceit, jealousy, or self-pity?

No one can serve two masters. For you will hate one and love the other; you will be devoted to one and despise the other. You cannot serve both God and money. (Luke 16:13)

What competes with God for your devotion and worship?

O Lord, turn my heart away from anything that causes me to stray from you. I want to depend on you alone. Amen.

September 3 ✠ Ezekiel 10–13

Why do we believe we can hide our evil thoughts and activities from God? God created us, and he knows us inside and out. In Ezekiel 11:5, God tells Ezekiel to say to Israel's leaders, "I know what you are saying, for I know every thought that comes into your minds."

Because I cannot hide my thoughts or actions from God, I must rely on his grace. It is the only way I can have a relationship with him. Without grace, I could not lift my eyes up to God, but the grace I received through Jesus' sacrifice makes it possible for me to live joyfully in God's presence.

So don't make judgments about anyone ahead of time—before the Lord returns. For he will bring our darkest secrets to light and will reveal our private motives. Then God will give to each one whatever praise is due. (1 Corinthians 4:5)

How does it feel to know that God sees all of you, inside and out, and loves you more than you can fathom?

Gracious God, I am thankful that nothing is hidden from you. You know my every thought, and yet you love me anyway. Amen.

September 4 ✠ Ezekiel 14–16

In Ezekiel 14:1-11, the prophet says the people have set up idols in their hearts. What idol dwells in my heart? Is it wealth, work, leisure, TV, family, fame, myself, food, or something else? What consumes my thoughts? What determines my behavior? What do I consider before making a decision? How I answer these questions can give me a clue as to what is in control of my life.

It's a lot easier to dismiss idols when Ezekiel refers to statues that are worshiped rather than what resides in my heart. Is God filling my heart, or is he only able to occupy a corner of it? What do I need to clean out to make room for God?

"All right then," Joshua said, "destroy the idols among you and turn your hearts to the Lord, the God of Israel." The people said to Joshua, "We will serve the Lord our God. We will obey him alone." (Joshua 24:23-24)

How can you identify and address the idols in your heart?

O Lord, examine my heart and show me anything living there that pulls me away from you. Amen.

September 5 ✠ Ezekiel 17–19

As I read the story about the two eagles in Ezekiel 17, I thought of how fickle some people are in their faith. They cannot be satisfied with knowing Jesus as their Lord and Savior, so they turn to the current spiritual fad. Instead of experiencing the joy that comes from a deepening relationship with Christ, they look for "inner peace" through other means.

We who are Christians often fail to make our faith joyous and appealing. God is the same yesterday, today, and tomorrow. He loves us infinitely and never leaves us. Why don't we proclaim that to others? Why do we seek peace anywhere other than in him?

Shout with joy to the Lord, all the earth! Worship the Lord with gladness. Come before him, singing with joy. (Psalm 100:1)

How tempted are you to explore spiritual fads? When you wander, how does God bring you back to his joy?

O wonderful Lord, may my joy in you be so evident in my life that others notice and turn to you because of it. Amen.

September 6 ✠ Ezekiel 20-21

While I often berate myself over things I've done wrong, sometimes I forget my errors. Ezekiel prophesied that Judah did not expect an attack from Babylon because they had a treaty. But the Judahites had rebelled and therefore violated the treaty.

I find that I sometimes need to pray to God to show me my sin. While I commit some sins that I am acutely aware of, other sins are such a part of my life that if I depend on myself, I will not be conscious of them. I need to quiet myself before God and listen to him to see the sin in my life that he wants me to see.

But I confess my sins; I am deeply sorry for what I have done.
(Psalm 38:18)

How often do you take time to confess your sins to God? How often do you unintentionally leave some out?

O Perfect Lord, show me my sin so I can change and draw closer to you. Amen.

September 7 ✠ Ezekiel 22-24

I find some things about the prophets incredible, and the way Ezekiel is commanded to act at the death of his wife is one of them. God refers to her as Ezekiel's dearest treasure and tells Ezekiel that she will die. I cannot imagine not being able to display any emotion in such a situation.

When I think I am at a certain point of growth in my devotion to God, I read a story like this and realize how far I have to go. I can say all day long that God is first in my life, but Ezekiel's example makes me question if it is really true.

Have you never heard?
  Have you never understood?
The Lord is the everlasting God,
  the Creator of all the earth.
He never grows weak or weary.
  No one can measure the depths of his understanding.
(Isaiah 40:28)

To what depths will you go assure that God holds first place in your life?

Lord, although there is much about you I cannot understand, I know that you love me and that whatever plans you have for me are good, even when I don't see how things will ultimately work out. Amen.

September 8 ✠ Ezekiel 25–28

The wealthy city of Tyre was the trading center of the region. Ezekiel prophesied harshly about Tyre, a prominent city that once was an ally of King David. The destruction was prophesied to be so complete that even the dust of the city would be dumped into the sea. It's hard to imagine a more complete destruction than that.

The description of Tyre reminds me of one of our modern cities that is a hub of commerce. It is easy to get caught up in prosperity and forget that God is the reason for our existence and blessing. Arrogance can spread throughout a community and country until those living there feel as though they are immune from judgment.

O Jerusalem, Jerusalem, the city that kills the prophets and stones God's messengers! How often I have wanted to gather your children together as a hen protects her chicks beneath her wings, but you wouldn't let me. And now, look, your house is abandoned and desolate.
(Matthew 23:37-38)

When do you fail to let God gather you under his wings, preferring to do things your own way?

Lord, make me aware of my complacency in following your ways. Give me strength to be the voice crying out in the wilderness. Amen.

September 9 ✤ Ezekiel 29–32

Ezekiel prophesied the fall of Egypt. He said Egypt would never regain its prominence as a world power, even after its restoration, because of its arrogance.

Arrogance often accompanies power. It is easy to be blinded to the source of all power and mistakenly assume that power is of one's own making. Even if a person in power attempts to maintain the right perspective, others surrounding him or her can be a snare. It's hard to focus on God as the source of power when others tell you how great you are.

In the thirty-ninth year of his reign, Asa developed a serious foot disease. Yet even with the severity of his disease, he did not seek the Lord's help but turned only to his physicians. So he died in the forty-first year of his reign. (2 Chronicles 16:12-13)

When do you let the compliments of others divert your focus from God and onto yourself?

Lord, may I remain faithful to you both in times of trouble and in times of prosperity. Amen.

September 10 ✤ Ezekiel 33–36

Ezekiel spoke harsh words for those who were supposed to lead the people. In Ezekiel 34:1-6, the leaders are described as brutal shepherds who take for themselves and have no concern for the welfare of the sheep.

It is easy to dismiss these verses by saying that I am not a minister, so they don't apply to me. Yet, at a church leaders' retreat a couple of years ago, our pastor read these words to us as we prepared to serve in leadership roles in our church. I remember feeling humbled when I realized that how I fulfill my responsibilities at church could have an impact that I may never see or know—for good or bad. It would be easier to bask in the honor of leadership if not for these words in Ezekiel.

Never be in a hurry about appointing a church leader. Do not share in the sins of others. Keep yourself pure. (1 Timothy 5:22)

How seriously do you take your commitment to lead others in the name of Christ?

Lord, may I hold your words to the leaders of Judah before me as I seek to serve in leadership roles. May these words keep me from becoming complacent and thinking that what I do or don't do doesn't really matter. Amen.

September 11 ✣ Ezekiel 37–39

One of the best-known parts of Ezekiel is his vision of the valley of dry bones. It's hard to read Ezekiel 37 without "dem bones, dem bones, dem *dry* bones"[10] playing in my head!

God's message to the Jews is that despite the spiritual dryness caused by the exile, there will be new life—a restoration that not only revives the nation, but also unites the two kingdoms again.

For me, the story of the dry bones reminds me that even in my walk with Christ, I can experience "dry spells" when I don't sense God's presence and activity. I may be too caught up in the ways of the world to acknowledge God or to rest in his presence.

I am thankful that God gives us stories like this one that assure us there is always the chance for renewal.

The instructions of the Lord are perfect,
reviving the soul.

188

The decrees of the Lord are trustworthy,
  making wise the simple. (Psalm 19:7)

In what ways do your "dry bones" need to come alive again? How can you trust God to revitalize your spiritual life?

Lord, thank you for your refreshing words to me. Amen.

September 12 ✦ Ezekiel 40–42

Ezekiel 40–42 is not the most interesting reading for me, but I am impressed at Ezekiel's detail in recording the dimensions of the temple.

I hear people say, "God does not want me to bother him with the trivial things in my life." They believe they should only go to God with big issues. When I read the detailed description of the temple that God revealed to Ezekiel, I can believe that God cares deeply about the details. When I go to him with the little things, it strengthens my faith in him for the times when the big things come.

What is the price of two sparrows—one copper coin? But not a single sparrow can fall to the ground without your Father knowing it. And the very hairs on your head are all numbered. (Matthew 10: 29-30)

What little things concern you right now? Would you talk to God about them?

Lord, I am thankful that you are interested in even the smallest details of my life. May I never hesitate to seek your guidance for all things, large and small. Amen.

September 13 ✦ Ezekiel 43–45

The priests who led the people astray to worship idols receive a second chance to serve God in Ezekiel 44:10-15. However, their responsibilities are limited in the new temple because of their sin.

189

Actions have consequences, and while God was gracious to these priests, they were no longer able to serve in a visible role in the temple. They abused their position and missed out on a leadership role.

Some might view their punishment as harsh, but I believe God was merciful to them because they were still allowed to serve him in the temple. God did not abandon them even though they had turned away from him.

If we are unfaithful, he remains faithful, for he cannot deny who he is. (2 Timothy 2:13)

How has God been merciful to you despite your sin?

Lord, may I always be thankful that though I sin, you never cease to show me your great mercy. Amen.

September 14 ✠ Ezekiel 46–48

God's instructions to Ezekiel included the way the people were to enter and exit the temple. In Ezekiel 46:9, God tells Ezekiel that the people should exit from the gateway opposite the one that they entered.

Such a specific instruction must have been significant. I wonder if it was to signify that after being in the presence of God in his temple, the people were holy, different than when they entered. Worship should be that way for us. We should be different people after encountering God's presence. We should leave holy. Leaving the same way we entered means nothing is different about us.

Encountering God in worship should change us, but because we are human, we must return again and again so we can be changed a little more each time. Just as a writer changes and edits a manuscript until it is perfect, so it is with God. We are his manuscript, and for our whole lives we come to him to be shaped into what is ultimately perfection.

That is why we never give up. Though our bodies are dying, our spirits are being renewed every day. (2 Corinthians 4:16)

How does worship renew and change you each week?

Lord, I am thankful that you are changing me. May I always yield to your ways for me so that I can continue to grow into your likeness. Amen.

September 15 ✠ Daniel 1–3

When Daniel and his friends were chosen to participate in the king's training, it would have been easier for them to comply with the rules set forth by the king regarding food than to insist on other food. I am sure the food from the king's table was tempting, especially if the young men had lived through the siege of Jerusalem.

However, the king's food likely included food forbidden by God. Giving in to the king's rules meant not obeying God. Being faithful to God while living in Babylon, especially at the palace, required great discipline. Acquiescing in the matter of diet would have been the first step toward losing faithfulness.

How do I compromise my faith to avoid making waves in the society in which I live?

If you are faithful in little things, you will be faithful in large ones. But if you are dishonest in little things, you won't be honest with greater responsibilities. (Luke 16:10)

Do you find it easier to be faithful to God in the little things or in the big things?

Lord, open my eyes so I can see when I am compromising my faith to conform to the world. Keep my feet from the slippery slope of conformity. Amen.

September 16 ✠ Daniel 4–6

Daniel, who was faithful to God, was also faithful and responsible in his work. Those who were jealous of him found no fault in what he did.

Why was Daniel such a good employee? Because he worked to glorify God, not himself. God placed him in a certain position, and Daniel was faithful where God planted him.

Daniel was also close to God. Three times a day he prayed to God, giving thanks to him. Daniel did not allow the practices and pressures of the world to take priority over his obedience to God.

What can I learn from this? If I seek God's guidance faithfully and regularly and do what he calls me to do, I work to bring glory to God, not to myself. Thus, I should do my work as though I work for God.

Work with enthusiasm, as though you were working for the Lord rather than for people. (Ephesians 6:7)

In what ways can you conduct the work of your daily job(s) to glorify God?

Lord, give me the right perspective on my work. May I remain faithful to you in all I do. Amen.

September 17 ✠ Daniel 7–9

In chapter 9, Daniel prays for his sin and the sin of his people. While his life was good in exile, he discovered Jeremiah's prophecy that Jerusalem would lie desolate for seventy years. The length of time meant that most people who were taken from Jerusalem in exile would die in Babylon and never return to their homeland. I imagine this was a low moment for Daniel as he realized that he would not likely return to Jerusalem.

Despite his faithfulness, he suffered the same fate as the other exiles, whether they were faithful to God or not. God heard Daniel's prayer and sent Gabriel to him. Gabriel told Daniel what would happen in the future, but Daniel's circumstances did not change. But Daniel was also told that he was precious to God. While Daniel would not see the end result, he knew God was in control.

"I will strengthen Judah and save Israel;
    I will restore them because of my compassion.
It will be as though I had never rejected them,
    for I am the Lord their God, who will hear their cries."
(Zechariah 10:6)

How difficult is it for you to trust God when you realize you may never know the outcome of a certain situation?

Faithful God, may I never cease to be thankful that you love me and are always in control, even when I cannot see the end result. Amen.

September 18 ✠ Daniel 10–12

"He will flatter and win over those who have violated the covenant. But the people who know their God will be strong and will resist him" (Daniel 11:32). I like to hear good news. I want to be told that I am smart, witty, attractive, and influential. I beam when my family praises a new dish I've cooked, and I am thrilled when people compliment my children. There is nothing wrong with receiving a compliment, but when I live for praise and flattery, I lose sight of God.

The last chapters of Daniel are apocalyptic, dealing with kingdoms conquering other kingdoms and the rise of ungodly leaders. There is plenty of war and strife, and yet not all power is gained by military might.

Daniel 11:32 says flattery is also a weapon. Flattery is an insidious tool. We may stand strong against an outright, overt threat to our faith, but flattery can take us in. It makes us feel special, needed, and important.

These people are grumblers and complainers, living only to satisfy their desires. They brag loudly about themselves, and they flatter others to get what they want. (Jude 16)

How can you be aware of the way others use flattery to promote themselves? How can you control your own use of flattery?

Lord, keep me from concern about how others perceive me so that flattery does not lead me astray. May I only be concerned about how you see me, and remember that all I am and all I have is a gift from you. Amen.

September 19 ✠ Hosea 1–6

When I read the story of Hosea and Gomer and how God used their situation to portray his relationship to Israel, I rejoice at the depth and steadfastness of God's love for us. What Gomer did was abhorrent, and yet Hosea took her back and loved her despite her unfaithfulness. Gomer got another chance. Praise God—so do I!

We know what real love is because Jesus gave up his life for us. So we also ought to give up our lives for our brothers and sisters. If someone has enough money to live well and sees a brother or sister in need but shows no compassion—how can God's love be in that person? (1 John 3:16-17)

When have you received another chance from God or others? When have you given another chance to someone else?

Gracious and Loving God, you are so faithful to us even though we are unfaithful to you. Thank you for loving us with such a deep love, meeting us where we are and bringing us to redemption. Amen.

September 20 ✠ Hosea 7–14

"Worshiping foreign gods has sapped their strength, but they don't even know it. Their hair is gray, but they don't realize they're old and weak" (Hosea 7:9).

My hair has been gray for years. However, for a long time after I turned gray, in my mind's eye I was still a younger-looking woman with brown hair. It took quite a few years before my mental image caught up with reality. This verse from Hosea makes sense to me.

We often don't see ourselves as we really are, which may result in our being wrong about where we need to change to grow closer to God. One of my regular prayers is, "Lord, show me my sin, so I can change." Thankfully, God has not dumped the whole bushel basket at my feet at once! Instead, he shows me one thing at a time about myself and gives me time to change each one.

Just as I gradually lose my strength or my hair color, God can gradually move me closer to him. To change for the better requires a desire to change and the willingness to see what God has placed before me, much as God opened Hagar's eyes to the well that was near her in the desert.

Dear brothers and sisters, we can't help but thank God for you, because your faith is flourishing and your love for one another is growing. (2 Thessalonians 1:3)

Do you ever wish for instantaneous spiritual change? In what ways are you grateful that God gradually changes you?

Lord, I thank you that you don't give up on me, but continue to woo me to a closer relationship with you. Amen.

September 21 ✠ Joel 1–3

"Rejoice, you people of Jerusalem! Rejoice in the Lord your God! For the rain he sends demonstrates his faithfulness" (Joel 2:23a).

The rain demonstrated God's faithfulness to Israel and Judah because both countries suffered from drought and swarms of locusts. The rainbow was a sign to Noah and continues to remind us of God's promise. God used the stars to show Abraham how numerous his descendants would be.

If we ever begin to doubt God's presence and his love for us, we only need to look at nature. When I watch a hummingbird, I know that God is real. These incredibly tiny, magnificently fast birds delight me as they dart around the yard and chase each other away from the bird feeder I hung up for them.

God is all around us. All we need to do is look at the world he created!

Open my eyes to see the wonderful truths in your instructions. (Psalm 119:18)

How does nature draw you closer to the Creator?

Lord, all around me is evidence of your presence and your love for me. May I never cease to see you every day. Amen.

September 22 ✠ Amos 1–5

"I hate all your show and pretense—the hypocrisy of your religious festivals and solemn assemblies. I will not accept your burnt offerings and grain offerings. I won't even notice all your choice peace offerings. Away with your noisy hymns of praise! I will not listen to the music of your harps. Instead, I want to see a mighty flood of justice, an endless river of righteous living" (Amos 5:21-24).

This is an often-quoted passage from Amos because it calls us all, no matter the generation, to worship God honestly and faithfully. Amos 5:21-24 tells us, as it told Israel, that it's not how formal and fancy your worship services are, it's not about the language you use, it's not about being recognized as "religious" that matters. It's about love and justice and mercy. It's about what is in our hearts, not what we say or do. That's what matters to God.

People may be right in their own eyes,
  but the Lord examines their heart.
The Lord is more pleased when we do what is right and just
  than when we offer him sacrifices. (Proverbs 21:2-3)

How often do you get so caught up in the trappings of worship that you forget the true calling of God—to bring him your love and humble service?

Lord, may my service to you be done out of joy and love, so that it glorifies you and gives you joy. Amen.

September 23 ✠ Amos 6–Obadiah 1

Amos prophesies of a time when there will be a famine, but not in the usual sense. Instead of food, people will crave the words of God, but will not be able to find them (Amos 8:11-13).

We sometimes take God's word for granted. Yet, when troubled times come, we want to hear God's word. Immediately after the terrorist attacks of September 11, 2001, people returned to church. They hungered for God's word. As time passed, attendance again fell away. It seems that we are not as interested in God's word when things seem to be going well.

Oh, how I love your instructions!
  I think about them all day long.
Your commands make me wiser than my enemies,
  for they are my constant guide. (Psalm 119:97-98)

When have you craved God's word? How can you learn to crave it every day?

Lord, may I always cherish your word. May I rejoice in the ability to read my Bible, and may your word be in my thoughts all day long. Amen.

September 24 ✠ Jonah 1–4

Jonah was a selfish person. I wonder why God called him to prophesy to Nineveh. He put an entire ship at risk and then was angry that the people of Nineveh repented after he prophesied to them.

He was angry with God when things didn't go his way. How arrogant to think that God was only interested in granting wishes, like a genie! Yet I know people who don't get what they want and are angry with God about it. I have been that way myself.

How differently Jesus responded in Gethsemane, when the reality of death was at hand. Instead of anger, he said, "thy will be done." Instead of blaming God, he accepted God's will and faced death for our sake.

So why do you keep calling me "Lord, Lord!" when you don't do what I say? (Luke 6:46)

Do you seek God's will only when it benefits you?

Lord, instead of seeking my will, may I seek your will. Give me the strength to say "thy will be done." Amen.

September 25 ✠ Micah 1–7

Micah 6:6-8 includes the familiar words of verse 8: "to do what is right, to love mercy, and to walk humbly with your God." The preceding verses ask if God is pleased with elaborate sacrifices. God doesn't care as much about the sacrifices as he does about our hearts.

I recently served on a committee to select the recipient of an award. One of the criteria for winning the award was community service. Several candidates produced a long list of organizations they had supported with cash donations, but the candidates our committee viewed more favorably were those who *did* something. One crocheted blankets for seriously ill children while another made bracelets for children attending a summer camp.

Micah knew that giving a calf or olive oil means nothing if you aren't living right. When your heart is right, the gift is meaningful.

If I gave everything I have to the poor and even sacrificed my body, I could boast about it, but if I didn't love others, I would have gained nothing. (1 Corinthians 13:3)

How do you give to others in the name of God?

Lord, may my heart and my actions bring joy to you. Amen.

September 26 ✠ Nah 1–Hab 3

"If it seems slow in coming, wait patiently, for it will surely take place. It will not be delayed" (Habakkuk 2:3b). I am not a patient person. I don't know if it is in my nature or if technology has made me unwilling to wait for results. I'm sure I would not have made a good prophet. I expect to see results quickly, and many of God's prophets never knew what became of their words.

God's timetable is not the same as mine. This verse from Habakkuk reminds me of that. Wait for it. It *is* coming, but it is coming when God is ready, not when I want it to come.

Abraham and Sarah grew impatient. They waited for God to provide a son, but then they took matters into their own hands. God blessed Ishmael, but their impatience caused family strife that continues today.

Be still in the presence of the Lord,
*   and wait patiently for him to act.*
Don't worry about evil people who prosper
*   or fret about their wicked schemes. (Psalm 37:7)*

What do you think is the most difficult aspect of waiting for God to work?

Lord, I trust in you. Help me to trust not only your promises but also your timing. Amen.

September 27 ✠ Zeph 1–Hag 2

When Haggai prophesied to the returning exiles about building a new temple, they enthusiastically responded. As they built, Haggai delivered another message from God: "Does anyone remember this house—this temple—in its former splendor? How, in comparison, does it look to you now? It must seem like nothing at all!" (Haggai 2:3).

However, instead of discouraging the people, God's words were meant to build them up, for he went on to tell them that he would fill the temple with glory, and its future glory would be greater than its past glory.

From outward appearances, the new temple did not look as spectacular as the temple Solomon built. But God told the exiles that it's not the building that makes the temple great—it's the presence of God that dwells there.

So anyone who becomes as humble as this little child is the greatest in the kingdom of heaven. (Matthew 18:4)

What makes your temple (the place where God resides) great?

Lord, may the temple of my heart be filled with your presence. Amen.

September 28 ✠ Zechariah 1–7

"Do not despise these small beginnings, for the Lord rejoices to see the work begin" (Zechariah 4:10a).

I want to do great things to glorify God. I look at others whose work has made a large spiritual impact on people's lives and wish to accomplish similar feats. The exiles wanted to glorify God with a grand temple, but they experienced difficulty getting it built.

God's message to the people, delivered by Zechariah, was one of encouragement. God told them not to discount what had been done. God rejoiced in it, so who were the people to despise what pleased God?

I am a planner, and I often devise grand plans only to be frustrated when they don't play out as quickly or elaborately as I had hoped. God's words speak to me as well!

It is like a mustard seed planted in the ground. It is the smallest of all seeds, but it becomes the largest of all garden plants; it grows long branches, and birds can make nests in its shade. (Mark 4:31-32)

What keeps you going when your beginning efforts seem meek?

Lord, when I am tempted to become discouraged about small beginnings, help me to stay the course, remembering that you are rejoicing about the work. Amen.

September 29 ✠ Zechariah 8–14

Zechariah 14:20-21 tells of a time when the harness bells of the horses and cooking pots will be holy to the Lord. Common, ordinary, taken-for-granted articles will be holy to the Lord.

Do we have to wait for that day, or can we make that day happen now? I believe we can treat every part of our lives, every activity in which we engage, as holy to the Lord. Our lives should be wholly devoted to the worship of God, and we should approach each day as an act of worship, even when it is filled with mundane, routine activities.

When we live as an act of worship to God, two things happen. First of all, we make better decisions about our time. When we know that our activities reflect our devotion, we make different choices. Second, when we treat our day as worship, we experience greater joy because our awareness of the presence of God is heightened.

Praise the Lord!
Let all that I am praise the Lord.
*   I will praise the Lord as long as I live.*
*   I will sing praises to my God with my dying breath.*
(Psalm 146:1-2)

How can you make today a day of worship? How can you find God in every aspect of your day?

Lord, help me remember that all I do is either worship or rejection of you. May I choose to worship you today. Amen.

September 30 ✠ Malachi 1–4

Malachi 1:6-14 condemns the people for offering defective sacrifices to God. While we no longer sacrifice animals, I wonder when I have given to God less than I was capable of giving? When have I cheated God by promising to do one thing and then doing something less or not doing anything at all?

I can easily think of grand plans I've had for God that have not come to fruition. I can recall gifts that are less than my best. In Acts, when Ananias and Sapphira sold property, they only gave part of the money but claimed that they gave it all. God struck them dead. I look at myself and consider that I may have done something similar.

So you cannot become my disciple without giving up everything you own. (Luke 14:33)

Why is it sometimes so difficult and frightening to give our best?

Lord, when I don't give you my best, you know it. When I over-promise and under-deliver, you know it. God, who gave your Son for me, I confess that I do not always give my best to you. I am convicted, yet you are merciful. Help me to remember Malachi's words and to offer you my best. Amen.

October 1 ✠ Matthew 1–4

In preparation for his ministry, Jesus was baptized by John the Baptist. As Jesus came out of the water, God declared his love for him. But this confirmation was not the sending forth into ministry. Instead, Jesus was led into the wilderness to fast for forty days and be tempted by Satan.

While a period of retreat and fasting before beginning his ministry makes sense, Matthew's language makes it seem that the primary purpose of the retreat was to endure the devil's temptations. Matthew 4:1 says, "Then Jesus was led by the Spirit into the wilderness to be tempted there by the devil."

From this writing, the temptation is not a by-product but is the main purpose of the trip into the wilderness. Did God want to make sure his Son measured up? Did he want Jesus to experience the temptations we face so he could understand us better? I don't know the motivation, but I do know that I will face temptation my whole life, no matter how closely I follow the Lord.

If God's own Son was not immune from temptation, how much more I can expect to face temptation. Satan has a much better chance of succeeding with me than he did with Jesus!

The temptations in your life are no different from what others experience. And God is faithful. He will not allow the temptation to be more than you can stand. When you are tempted, he will show you a way out so that you can endure. (1 Corinthians 10:13)

When has God provided a way out of temptation for you?

Lord, I ask for strength to resist the temptations placed in my path daily. But Lord, even when I fail, I know that you are full of mercy and I can run to you for grace. Amen.

October 2 ✠ Matthew 5-6

Jesus' teaching about the birds and lilies speaks to me often. I am a person who wants a detailed plan with a clear progression toward accomplishing whatever goal is before me. I don't do well with ambiguity and uncertainty.

So when Jesus tells me not to worry about the details of life, his teaching flies in the face of my compulsion to plan and reveals my lack of trust in God. In the book *Having a Mary Heart in a Martha World*, Joanna Weaver talks about "spiritual junk food," those activities with which we fill our time that take the edge off our desire for more of God.[11] Planning falls into that category for me. If I have the detailed plan, I don't need to depend on God.

But it is God's desire to care for me, and he certainly can do better than I can!

Give all your worries and cares to God, for he cares about you.
(1 Peter 5:7)

When have you found it difficult to trust God with the details of your life, both good and bad?

Lord, why do I hesitate to trust you to take care of all my needs? You created me, and you created this world in which I live. Why should I trust anyone else other than you? Amen.

October 3 ✠ Matthew 7-9

In Matthew 7:21-23, Jesus tells of people who perform miracles in his name but who will not be allowed to enter the kingdom of heaven. Jesus tells those people that he doesn't know them.

I can get busy doing "God's work" only to find that I am not doing what God wants me to do. My problem is that I put serving God ahead of knowing God. When I jump into service for God without knowing what he wants me to do, it's like taking a test without reading the instructions.

I must *listen* more and *do* less. When I listen and discern where God wants my service, I will be able to serve him joyfully and effectively. The important thing is to let God lead.

This is what the Sovereign Lord,
  the Holy One of Israel, says:
"Only in returning to me
  and resting in me will you be saved.
In quietness and confidence is your strength." (Isaiah 30:15a)

How can you incorporate more listening into your relationship with God?

Lord, may my greatest desire be to know you better. Help me to slow down and listen to your voice. Amen.

October 4 ✠ Matthew 10–11

In Matthew 10, Jesus sounds like a militant Messiah. He speaks of persecution and violence and families in discord. For me, the words are difficult to read because I was raised in a Christian family in a nation of religious freedom. Not all who claim Christ are able to love and worship him without risks. In many places around the world, the words of Matthew 10 are closer to reality for some Christians.

While I may not face overt persecution, I still experience challenges to my faith. Christianity is frequently ridiculed, making a mockery of those who don't believe that their strength comes from their own abilities. A recent Emmy award recipient made remarks deriding God, which drew laughter from those in the audience.

Those who turn to God for help are sometimes characterized as weak. I've heard too many times, "God helps those who help themselves." Accepting that belief causes us to water down the power of God. We turn him into an emergency fire alarm, only calling on him when we have tried to help ourselves without success.

Maybe it would be easier to resist overt persecution. What we face is often much more insidious—the creeping kind of persecution that gradually works into our lives until we are embarrassed to share our faith with others or to challenge society's desecration of Christ's teachings.

Let all the world look to me for salvation! For I am God; there is no other. (Isaiah 45:22)

When do you allow the subtle persecution of others to keep you from proclaiming Christ as Lord?

Lord, may I be strong in my faith regardless of what those around me think of you. Amen.

October 5 ✠ Matthew 12

In Matthew 12:33-35, Jesus says our fruit identifies us. A good tree produces good fruit, and a bad tree produces bad fruit. If I think bad thoughts, say bad things, and fill my heart and mind with bad stuff, I cannot produce good fruit. But instead, if I think good thoughts, say good words, and fill my heart and mind with God's word, I produce good fruit.

It's a struggle to feed on good things because what I see and hear in the world around me is often negative. It takes effort and conscious, deliberate practice to fill my mind and heart with God's word. It also can take changing the radio dial or television channel or maybe even turning them off altogether.

What would change in my life if I spent as much time in the word of God as I do in mindless pursuits?

I have hidden your word in my heart,
that I might not sin against you.
I praise you, O Lord;
teach me your decrees. (Psalm 119:11-12)

How can you fill your mind and heart with God today?

Lord, what fills my ears and eyes fills my heart. May I feed on your word instead of the empty words of this world. Amen.

October 6 ✠ Matthew 13–14

When Jesus returned to Nazareth, his hometown, he taught in the synagogue as he had in other places. But because the people there knew him growing up, they discounted his teaching. They could not accept his words because they could not accept him as anything other than what they already knew about him.

I frequently do this with people I know. It's hard to see someone as a physician when you've watched him grow up with your children. It may be difficult to accept and celebrate someone's success or conversion when I know how she has behaved in the past.

I even do it to myself. I get excited about a new challenge in my life, only to begin hearing voices of doubt in my head. I look only at my ability, not the ability of God to work in me.

God doesn't see as we see. His vision is not limited by past performance. He sees possibilities we cannot even imagine. I need to remember this not only when I see others, but also when I look at myself.

This means that anyone who belongs to Christ has become a new person. The old life is gone; a new life has begun! (2 Corinthians 5:17)

What hinders you from becoming everything God intends you to be? How do you hinder others in this way?

Lord, let my eyes see what you see—in others and in myself. Save me from my own limiting vision, and let me see instead the glorious possibilities you have for me and for others. Amen.

October 7 ✠ Matthew 15–17

In Matthew 16:21-23, Jesus tells his disciples that he will suffer, die, and be raised from the dead. Peter takes him aside and reprimands him for saying such things. Jesus' response to Peter shows me that he wrestled with temptation in his life at times other than his forty days in the wilderness. He tells Peter, "You are a dangerous trap to me. You are seeing things merely from a human point of view, not from God's."

Although Jesus knew God's point of view better than we ever can, he was still tempted to fall into the trap of seeing things from a human point of view. However, the human point of view was dangerous to Jesus, as it is to us.

When we see things only from the human point of view, we see limitations, revenge, jealousy, striving for power, and materialism. When we see things from God's point of view, we see possibilities, love, openness, humility, and a desire to share with others.

O Jacob, how can you say the Lord does not see your troubles?
  O Israel, how can you say God ignores your rights?
Have you never heard?
  Have you never understood?
The Lord is the everlasting God,
  the Creator of all the earth.
He never grows weak or weary.
  No one can measure the depths of his understanding.
(Isaiah 40:27-28)

How difficult is it for you to see the world from God's point of view? In what ways can you cultivate this kind of vision?

Lord, help me to see things from your point of view, which is opposite from that of the world, so that I catch a glimpse of your divinity. Amen.

October 8 ✠ Matthew 18-20

Jesus had a different set of "rules" about living than what the world teaches us. At the beginning of chapter 18, he tells his disciples that the greatest is the person who becomes as humble as a little child. Near the end of today's reading, Jesus again talks about greatness and status when the mother of James and John asks for places of privilege for her sons. Jesus says that becoming a servant to others is the way to rise in his kingdom. This contradicts typical advice about how to get ahead in the world.

Jesus also said we are to lose track of how often we forgive others. His formula means those who exploit our willingness to forgive will take advantage of us. There is no way around such treatment if we truly do what Jesus says. The world teaches us not to allow others to take advantage of us.

In the parable of the vineyard workers, Jesus throws out the ideas of tenure and seniority, concepts that drive many of the working arrangements in our world. Instead, he preaches about abundance and generosity, not scarcity and competition.

How closely can I live according to Jesus' rules?

I believe in your commands; now teach me good judgment and knowledge. (Psalm 119:66)

How can you strive each day to live against the system of the world and live toward God's contrasting standards?

Lord, I know your way is right and righteous. Give me the strength to follow your commands. Amen.

October 9 ✠ Matthew 21-22

When I read about Jesus' discussions with the Pharisees and the Sadducees in Matthew 22:15-46, I am reminded that some things are not much different now than they were in Jesus' day. Our churches, both denominations and individual congregations, love rules! Even today, we want to ask, "Lord, what about (fill in the blank)?"

Jesus answered simply and directly, summing up with one command: love God with all your heart, soul, and mind. If we can do this, all the other stuff will take care of itself. This command unites us, whereas many of our church rules divide us.

Dear friends, let us continue to love one another, for love comes from God. Anyone who loves is a child of God and knows God. (1 John 4:7)

How can you let the complete love of God become your top priority each day?

Lord, help me to love you and love others with all my heart, soul, and mind. Amen.

October 10 ✠ Matthew 23–24

Matthew 23:12 is a difficult verse for me to live: "But those who exalt themselves will be humbled and those who humble themselves will be exalted." It is another teaching of Jesus that goes against the teaching of the world. The world tells us to toot our own horns, but Jesus said to be humble. *A Covenant Prayer in the Wesleyan Tradition* includes this line: "Put me to what thou wilt, rank me with whom thou wilt."[12]

Those are hard words for me to say. It takes great humility to say, "rank me with whom thou wilt."

I am not worthy of all the unfailing love and faithfulness you have shown to me, your servant. When I left home and crossed the Jordan River, I owned nothing except a walking stick. Now my household fills two large camps! (Genesis 32:10)

How can you overcome this world's spirit of competition in favor of God's spirit of humility?

Lord, let me honestly and completely pray, "Rank me with whom thou wilt." May my focus be on doing your will so that I have no thought of myself. Amen.

October 11 ✠ Matthew 25–26

I had lunch with a friend recently who said Matthew 25 contained one of her favorite stories—that of the sheep and the goats. Reading the story, I can see why it is one of her favorites, for she lives like a sheep. I began to think of others who fit the description of the sheep in this story. I thought of one of the older ladies in my church who saw a homeless woman sitting on the curb one day and sat beside her to talk. I also thought of a nurse whose great passion is medical mission work.

You know sheep. You may be a sheep, although if you are, you probably would not believe you are. How would our world be different if we resolved to live like the sheep in Matthew 25?

Do not take advantage of foreigners who live among you in your land. Treat them like native-born Israelites, and love them as you love yourself. Remember that you were once foreigners living in the land of Egypt. I am the Lord your God. (Leviticus 19:33-34)

What are the characteristics of a sheep of God? How can you be more aware of the presence of Christ each day?

Lord, I want to be numbered with the sheep. Open my eyes and lead me where you want me to serve you. May I lay aside my own hesitations and do your will, not mine. Amen.

October 12 ✠ Matthew 27–28

When I read Matthew's account of Jesus' resurrection, I wonder about the soldiers who guarded the tomb. They accepted a bribe from priests to say that the disciples stole the body. I wonder what the rest of their lives were like. They witnessed the resurrection of Jesus! They saw firsthand the event that changed our relationship with God. Do you suppose they ever became believers and followers of the Way?

Reflecting on their experience makes me wonder when I have missed out on something earth-shattering because I was afraid, unprepared, or overly concerned with my reputation. Can I live my life less bound by my concern about what others think and more interested in being open to the things God wants to show me?

And may you have the power to understand, as all God's people should, how wide, how long, how high, and how deep his love is. (Ephesians 3:18)

What hinders you from living an abundant life in Christ?

Lord, open my eyes to you today. Don't allow me to be paralyzed by fear or concerned about my reputation. Instead, keep my spirit free and my life open to you, always and in all ways. Amen.

October 13 ✠ Mark 1–3

Jesus, in his allegorical way, tells us that following him will not be comfortable and familiar. When he responds to those who questioned why his behavior differed from that of the Pharisees or John's disciples, he uses examples of a new patch on old clothes and new wine placed in old wineskins. Neither of these is a comfortable fit.

Think of the discomfort illustrated by trying to patch an old garment with a new piece of cloth. The fit is so poor that the new patch leaves a bigger hole than before. To me, this says that once I experience God's grace in my life, turning away from it is worse than not turning to Christ at all. His teaching is so different that it cannot possibly fit into any existing teaching or behavior. It is radical.

Likewise, the wineskin example shows how it is impossible to fit Christ's teachings into the conventional teachings of our world. They are so completely incompatible that we must become "new wineskins" to be able to absorb them.

Don't imagine that I came to bring peace to the earth! I came not to bring peace, but a sword. (Matthew 10:34)

What does it take for you to become a "new wineskin"?

Lord, change me completely so that I only seek to do your will, not my own. Make me a new wineskin and then fill me up with you. Amen.

October 14 ✠ Mark 4–5

I have always been fascinated by the response of the people when Jesus sends demons into a herd of pigs. Mark's account tells us that the people wanted Jesus to leave them alone and go away. Why did they act this way? In many places, Jesus could not get away from the crowds who wanted him to heal, to cast out demons, or to preach. Yet in this place, the townspeople begged him to leave.

Did fear cause this reaction? Did they fear the change that could result from Jesus' power and faith? Was it too unsettling to see the demon-possessed man from the cemetery "fully clothed and perfectly sane" (Mark 5:15)?

Maybe they thought, "If Jesus could change this man, what could he do to me?" Maybe we still think that way. If we are unable to approach Jesus in faith, it *is* unsettling to read his words about commitment to him. Maybe we don't want to be changed. Our familiarity with mediocrity is more comfortable than allowing Jesus to enter us and change us completely.

This means that anyone who belongs to Christ has become a new person. The old life is gone; a new life has begun! (2 Corinthians 5:17)

In what ways do you resist becoming the new person Christ wants you to be?

Lord, forgive me for clinging to my demons instead of releasing them to you. Make me open to you. May I invite you into my heart and allow you to change me completely. Amen.

October 15 ✠ Mark 6–7

Mark tells us that Herod had great respect for John the Baptist, although John condemned his marriage to Herodias. However, Herod was apparently moved more by what made him feel good rather than what he knew was right.

When Herod's stepdaughter danced for him, he made a rash promise to her. His emotion got in the way of good sense, and when she asked for the head of John the Baptist, he let his ego get in the way and didn't back off his promise.

Emotion is a fickle master. When I allow my feelings to govern my behavior, the results are inconsistent and sometimes harmful to others. When I snap at a family member because of a bad day at work, I damage our relationship. Life is much better when I don't allow negative emotions to guide my interaction with others.

As we see in the story of Herod, even the positive emotion he felt as his daughter danced led to negative consequences. I cannot let good feelings control my life. If I govern myself according to what feels good, I will likely make many wrong decisions.

Be my rock of safety
where I can always hide.
Give the order to save me,
for you are my rock and my fortress. (Psalm 71:3)

How can you look beyond your emotions and see what God is telling you?

Lord, may I seek the deep joy and peace that come from knowing you. Let them, not the temporary and changing emotions I feel, guide me. Amen.

October 16 ✠ Mark 8–9

Jesus did not stay where he was not welcome. In Mark 8, he and the disciples leave the area where Jesus fed 4,000 and travel by boat to another area on the Sea of Galilee. When they arrive, Pharisees come to argue with Jesus, demanding that he perform miracles to prove his authority. Instead of complying or resisting, Jesus leaves.

As Christians, we often fail to emulate this behavior of Jesus. Instead, we argue with others, both Christians and non-Christians, about our faith. Our arguments are often over trivial matters. Jesus never forced himself on others. Why do we think we should do something he didn't do?

Jesus loved the Pharisees, even though they challenged him. Maybe that's why he chose the approach he used in this instance. Maybe if we loved others as Jesus did, we would be less willing to engage them in futile arguments about faith. Jesus may not have won every battle, but he won the war. That's what mattered. It should be our goal as well.

Do everything without complaining or arguing, so that no one can criticize you. Live clean, innocent lives as children of God, shining like bright lights in a world full of crooked and perverse people. (Philippians 2:14-15)

How do you let details get in the way of your relationships with others and with God?

Lord, may I remember that what is most important to my faith is that you came to be the sacrifice for my sins, and because of your death I am saved by grace. May I be more willing to proclaim your love than to argue over details. Amen.

October 17 ✤ Mark 10-11

Peter told Jesus that he and the other disciples had given up everything to follow him. In response, Jesus told people what they could expect if they gave up everything to follow him. At first, the deal doesn't sound too bad—a hundred times as many family and possessions than they gave up. Then he throws in the catch—persecution. In our day, we hear many people preach the first part but avoid the second part. I wonder if those who preach a prosperity gospel would retain their followers if they knew the catch.

Jesus never told anyone that things would be easy if they followed him. What he promises is that he will be with us every step of the way. We won't endure suffering alone. He promises peace and rest for our souls, but that does not preclude the possibility of persecution.

However, the peace that comes from knowing Christ allows us to find comfort even in the midst of persecution.

Take my yoke upon you. Let me teach you, because I am humble and gentle at heart, and you will find rest for your souls. (Matthew 11:29)

Are you willing to accept all of Jesus' teachings, or only the ones that make you comfortable?

Jesus, you provide all the prosperity we need—peace, rest, comfort. As we draw closer to you, we find that material items are much less important than we thought. May we always be rich in your blessings. Amen.

October 18 ✤ Mark 12-13

The story of the widow is really a love story. In four short verses, we observe one of the greatest examples of human love in the Bible—

that of an unnamed widow who loves God so much that she wants to give all she can to him. Jesus, on observing her act of love, says she gave everything she had to live on. While she gave everything she had, she was rich spiritually because she had God's love and presence in her life. Nothing she could ever possess would be as glorious as her relationship with God.

I am not in the financial straits of this widow, but I have experienced financial difficulty. Yet, knowing that God loves me and cares for me is greater than any problem I could face. How could I want to cling to anything but Jesus?

You go before me and follow me.
You place your hand of blessing on my head.
Such knowledge is too wonderful for me,
too great for me to understand! (Psalm 139:5-6)

When have you been able to give with the freedom of the widow in this story?

Precious Savior, thank you for always being with me. I never face any situation alone because you are always with me. Amen.

October 19 ✠ Mark 14–16

The woman who poured the jar of expensive perfume on Jesus is remembered for her extravagant, uninhibited, sacrificial act of love. It is no less extravagant than that of the widow who put her two coins in the offering box at the temple. Both are acts of unrestrained love for God.

Contrast these acts with that of Judas. His betrayal came immediately after the woman poured her perfume on Jesus. Instead of incredible love, Judas exhibited the cruelest selfishness—to betray to death the man with whom he spent three years of his life, and for a mere thirty pieces of silver.

Had he become disillusioned with the teachings of Jesus, he could have walked away. Instead, he chose to better himself economically at the expense of the Son of God.

Am I willing to love Jesus extravagantly, or do I hold back, allowing greed and selfishness to limit my ability to respond in love? My selfishness may be about my reputation, my questionable habits and activities, or my unwillingness to let go of what stands between me and an authentic relationship with Jesus.

But the person who loves God is the one whom God recognizes. (1 Corinthians 8:3)

Whose example will you choose to follow—that of the two women or that of someone like Judas?

Lord, break into the alabaster jar of my heart and receive the love I joyfully pour out to you. Let there be no part of me withheld from you. Amen.

October 20 ✷ Luke 1

While the world values education, God values those who trust in him. Zechariah was a priest, so he was expected to have a certain amount of theological education. Yet when Gabriel appeared to him, he questioned the truth of the angel's message.

Mary, on the other hand, a young girl who did not have the benefit of formal theological education, also had a visit from Gabriel. She responded in faith: "I am the Lord's servant. May everything you have said about me come true." Mary put no restrictions on God. She believed him.

We are often inclined to pray with conditions: if God will do what we ask, we'll do something in return. Or we pray as if we aren't sure God is capable of doing what we ask. Maybe we should listen first to the way God speaks to us—through his word, through the words of others, through our circumstances, and through our silence. When we begin to hear God through all these channels, we can exclaim with Zechariah, "Because of God's tender mercy, the morning light from heaven is about to break upon us."

I bow before your holy temple as I worship.
I praise your name for your unfailing love and faithfulness;
for your promises are backed
by all the honor of your name. (Psalm 138:2)

How difficult is it for you to react as Mary did when God leads you?

Lord, may I quiet my head and my heart and listen to you, trusting that your word is always true. Amen.

October 21 ✠ Luke 2–3

John the Baptist called the people to account when they came to be baptized. He warned that they should not feel comfortable just because they were descendants of Abraham.

We are not made holy by those to whom we are related to or because we attend church. We are made holy by confessing that Jesus is Lord of our lives and by accepting with gratitude that he died to take on the wrath of God for us. While we can associate ourselves with many good and holy people, we have to come to Jesus on our own. It's like the difference between hearing someone describe a place and going there yourself. You simply have to be there!

Our actions will show that we belong to the truth, so we will be confident when we stand before God. Even if we feel guilty, God is greater than our feelings, and he knows everything. (1 John 3:19-20)

What makes you feel comfortable in the presence of God? Is it actually keeping you from growing closer to God?

Lord, I surrender all to you out of my immense gratitude that you surrendered all for me. May I eagerly serve you in love wherever you place me. Amen.

October 22 ✤ Luke 4–5

Luke 4 and 5 almost always leave me out of breath when I read them. These two chapters contain a lot of activity. It seems that Jesus is everywhere doing something—healing, preaching, fishing, feasting, calling disciples.

In the midst of the activity, Luke tells us that Jesus often withdrew to the wilderness for prayer. Jesus knew that the most important part of his ministry was staying connected to his Father. If Jesus needed that connection, we are arrogant to think we don't. If the one who was wholly divine had to retreat and spend time in prayer, then we, sinful creatures that we are, need to connect to God even more.

I have known people who are doing much for God but who say they don't have time for contemplation and daily quiet time with God. Our first responsibility is to remain connected to the Vine. If we don't take the time to do that, then we'll quickly find that we cannot produce fruit.

You will show me the way of life,
granting me the joy of your presence,
and the pleasures of living with you forever. (Psalm 16:11)

How can you be more deliberate about spending time with God?

Lord, my connection with you is not always what it should be. Help me to be more focused on time spent with you, so I can be a fruitful disciple. May I follow the example of Jesus, who retreated from his work to be with you. Amen.

October 23 ✤ Luke 6–7

". . . For he is kind to those who are unthankful and wicked" (Luke 6:35c). The passage from which these words come is familiar to me, but I have never focused on this one phrase. It's not easy to think of being kind to those who are unthankful and wicked. But God is.

I don't want to include myself in this definition, but I know I have been unthankful. I have taken for granted the many gifts God has given me, from breath to a new day to family and friends, and especially my salvation. I am also sure I have done things that are wicked when I have hurt others by my words or actions or even my thoughts.

We aren't called to judge who can receive our kindness or compassion. We are to be compassionate to all. Our example is Christ alone.

Get rid of all bitterness, rage, anger, harsh words, and slander, as well as all types of evil behavior. Instead, be kind to each other, tenderhearted, forgiving one another, just as God through Christ has forgiven you. (Ephesians 4:31-32)

How can you remove your tendency to judge others and instead see them with the eyes of Christ?

Lord, your challenge to me is incredible, yet you call me to obedience, and each person I meet is your child. May I love each one of your children so that they see no guile or ulterior motive in me, only the love of Christ. Amen.

October 24 ✚ Luke 8–9

I don't want to dwell long on Luke 9:57-62. In my NLT Bible, this section is titled "The Cost of Following Jesus." But this passage demands my attention in a painful way, like a piece of glass in your foot or a fishhook in your hand. It's not a dull, throbbing pain, but a sharp, stabbing one.

I say I want to follow Jesus wherever he leads, but these verses ask me, "Are you sure?" I wonder how I can know for certain, because avoiding particular places and situations can become so ingrained in me that I fail to see that my actions are not what God wants from me.

How strong is my love for Christ? Is it strong enough for me to put family in second place? My decision to follow must come from such a love of Christ that all else pales in comparison.

I will pursue your commands, for you expand my understanding.
(Psalm 119:32)

What frightens you about the cost of following Jesus? How can you give those fears to God?

Lord, I want to put my hand to the plow and not look back. Give me faith and help me when I struggle to be strong. Amen.

October 25 ✠ Luke 10–11

"Make sure that the light you think you have is not actually darkness" (Luke 11:35). In Luke 10, Jesus condemns certain towns because of their failure to repent. These people had seen the miracles of Jesus and yet continued on their way with no change of heart. Our society places a high value on intellect. We look up to the "enlightened" and look down on those who are not. Enlightenment often manifests itself as tolerance and acceptance of all ideas, faiths, and lifestyles.

I expect the residents of the towns Jesus condemned considered themselves enlightened and, therefore, would not allow themselves to be transformed by a carpenter and his band of fishermen and tax collectors, uneducated men who were not of the religious elite. While enlightenment implies tolerance, it is only a tolerance of those deemed intellectual. Any contact with those not considered enlightened is condescending at best.

If Christ were here today, which communities and people would embrace his teaching? Which would dismiss it? Would I follow him?

Stop deceiving yourselves. If you think you are wise by this world's standards, you need to become a fool to be truly wise. (1 Corinthians 3:18)

How tempted are you to agree with society's standard of enlightenment?

Lord, I want to see people and ideas through your eyes. Give me the simplicity of a child so I may not dismiss those through whom you speak. Keep me from spiritual arrogance. Instead, give me a teachable heart. Amen.

October 26 ✠ Luke 12–13

"Life is not measured by how much you own" (Luke 12:15b). As a follower of Christ, I know that this verse is true, but do I live like I believe it? So much of my time and money says otherwise. I look around me and think how much less complicated my life might be if I didn't have so many things.

Now is a good time of year to focus on possessions because as Christmas approaches, my temptation is to spend a lot of money on gifts instead of being a living treasure to those I love. Can I focus on acts of love for others more than I do on possessions?

And what about when I am asked for gifts I want? Can I think of simple gifts that may speak to the giver and bless both of us? Can I truly be joyful with fewer packages to open?

In that day he will be your sure foundation,
*   providing a rich store of salvation, wisdom, and knowledge.*
*   The fear of the Lord will be your treasure. (Isaiah 33:6)*

How difficult is it to get past the worldly desire for more and find satisfaction in the greatest gift from God?

Lord, help me remember your words—that life is not measured by my possessions. May I learn to live sacrificially and simply. Amen.

October 27 ✠ Luke 14–16

It's not necessarily the "big" sins that tempt me. Instead, I give in to the little things. I eat an extra dessert, I don't send a card when I should, I put off doing something, or I make excuses and justify my lack of action. When Jesus said, "If you are dishonest in little things, you won't be honest with greater responsibilities," he spoke to me. It's as if I forget that nothing is hidden from God. If I cannot make and keep small promises to myself, then how can I be faithful with the things of God?

It's easy to rationalize my behavior by saying the little things don't matter, but small steps off the path can lead to my becoming completely lost. What I need to remember is that nothing is a small thing to God.

This false teaching is like a little yeast that spreads through the whole batch of dough! (Galatians 5:9)

How can you be more faithful in the small things?

Heavenly Father, make me mindful that how I handle little things is an illustration of my faithfulness to you. Obeying you helps me to know your will even more. Give me the strength of will to be faithful even in the smallest things. Amen.

October 28 ✠ Luke 17–18

Jesus reminds us that we are to serve him in Luke 17:7-10. It is our duty. In fact, his description of the servant's work is that we serve him before tending to ourselves.

Sometimes we don't want to spend time thinking of ourselves as servants. But when I call Jesus "Lord" and "Master," I use language that puts me in the role of a servant. Humility is not a trait that comes easily to me. Pride, yes, but not humility. These verses remind me that being obedient doesn't elevate me—it's simply what I'm supposed to do.

No, O people, the Lord has told you what is good,
and this is what he requires of you:
to do what is right, to love mercy,
and to walk humbly with your God. (Micah 6:8)

What roadblocks do you face in living a humble life?

Dear Master, I am your servant. May I always do what I am supposed to do in my service to you. Amen.

October 29 ✠ Luke 19–20

Tax collectors were described many ways, but never as generous. Yet Zacchaeus showed generosity that could only be the result of his love for Jesus.

He was generous in his hospitality. I admire that Zacchaeus didn't flinch when Jesus announced that he was coming to be a guest in his home. Instead, Luke says Zacchaeus "took Jesus to his house in great excitement and joy."

Zacchaeus was generous in his repentance. Instead of merely turning away from his past behavior, he sought to make restitution to any he had cheated, and not just by returning to them what he had taken, but four times as much.

Zacchaeus was generous in his gifts to God. He proclaimed to Jesus that he would give half his wealth to the Lord, when Jewish law only required 10 percent.

Zacchaeus realized what he had received from Jesus—grace and forgiveness—and his priorities changed completely from that day forward.

Don't forget to show hospitality to strangers, for some who have done this have entertained angels without realizing it! (Hebrews 13:2)

In what ways do you serve Christ by serving others?

Lord, grant me a generous spirit—a spirit like that of Zacchaeus—whose joy at knowing you prompted an outpouring of generosity. Thank you for your unending generosity to me. Amen.

October 30 ✠ Luke 21–22

I am familiar with Peter's denial of Jesus and the cock crowing. The story makes me think of the ways I can deny knowing Jesus and the times when I may feel uncomfortable being associated with him.

Am I uncomfortable asking a blessing before a meal in a restaurant, especially with people whose faith is unknown to me?

When I seek God's guidance and receive it, do I share the great news with others?

Am I willing to voice my opinion based on my beliefs when it is contrary to the general "wisdom" of the world?

Do I fear being labeled as fanatical or weird and how it will affect my career if I am vocal about my faith?

Am I quick to compromise my beliefs to ensure harmony at work, with friends, or with family members?

Have there been times in my life when I hid my faith and later felt as Peter did when he heard the rooster crow?

If anyone is ashamed of me and my message in these adulterous and sinful days, the Son of Man will be ashamed of that person when he returns in the glory of his Father with the holy angels. (Mark 8:38)

When have you been ashamed of your relationship with Jesus?

Lord, I don't want to deny you. Please help me to be bold in my faith, looking only to you for guidance, not falling away under peer pressure. Amen.

October 31 ✠ Luke 23–24

Herod was excited to see Jesus not because he wanted to hear him teach, but because he hoped Jesus would perform a miracle. Instead, Jesus did nothing and said nothing.

I cannot imagine what Jesus was thinking when this happened, but I wonder if he was tempted to do something, then and there, to prove who he was. Instead, he did not defend himself. He remained silent.

Sometimes I act like Herod acted. I want to see a miracle. I want Jesus to prove to me that he is who he says he is. I want a sign that he's really there. I want to know for certain that Jesus is real. Sometimes I get what Herod got—silence.

Silence may be what Jesus experienced from God in this time. But even if God was silent, Jesus still knew who God was and that God loved him. I should never take silence to mean that God is absent or not listening. When I experience silence, I should lean even harder on my faith.

If I had not confessed the sin in my heart,
  the Lord would not have listened.
But God did listen!
  He paid attention to my prayer.
Praise God, who did not ignore my prayer
  or withdraw his unfailing love from me. (Psalm 66:18-20)

When doubt overcomes you, how do you find your way back to the truth?

Lord, may I never be discouraged if I hear nothing but silence. You love me and always listen to me. Amen.

November 1 ✠ John 1–3

Sandwiched between the account of Jesus clearing the vendors out of the temple and his conversation with Nicodemus are three verses at the end of chapter 2: "Because of the miraculous signs Jesus did in Jerusalem at the Passover celebration, many began to trust in him. But Jesus didn't trust them, because he knew human nature. No one needed to tell him what mankind is really like" (John 2:23-25).

Faith based on miracles is not much faith. It's like seeing a tree and believing that we see the whole tree. If we judge the strength of a tree by what we see, we may be surprised when a storm comes along and the tree doesn't stand up to the wind. Roots make a difference, even though we cannot see roots.

In the same way, while miracles attracted a crowd to Jesus, he understood that miracles could not hold them there. We just read Luke's crucifixion account, which shows that while many may have believed, when Pilate called for Jesus' release, the crowds did not remain faithful.

What does Jesus think of me? He knows what I am really like.

To the faithful you show yourself faithful; to those with integrity you show integrity. (Psalm 18:25)

What does it mean to you that Jesus knows "what mankind is really like"?

Unchanging God, may I be faithful to you in all things. Amen.

November 2 ✠ John 4–5

"Then Jesus explained: 'My nourishment comes from doing the will of God, who sent me, and from finishing his work'" (John 4:34). What if I were nourished only by doing the will of God? I would like to say that I am completely satisfied by doing what God wants me to do. If I could say that, it would mean that all the things I fret over and worry about would no longer occupy my thoughts and my time. In truth, I will only be satisfied when I do God's will.

Unfortunately, I often go in many directions, do many things, and meet many obligations that satisfy others without considering if I am doing what God wants me to do.

And we can be sure that we know him if we obey his commandments. If someone claims, "I know God," but doesn't obey God's commandments, that person is a liar and is not living in the truth. But those who obey God's word truly show how completely they love him. That is how we know we are living in him. Those who say they live in God should live their lives as Jesus did. (1 John 2:3-6)

How hungry do you let your spirit grow before you choose the nourishment of doing God's will?

Lord, I want to do your will, which is the only way I can be truly satisfied. Amen.

November 3 ✠ John 6–8

"Jesus answered, 'If I want glory for myself, it doesn't count'" (John 8:54a).

The Covenant Prayer in the Wesleyan Tradition is a powerful prayer. One line of it says, "Let me be employed by thee or laid aside by thee, exalted for thee or brought low for thee."[13]

These are not easy words to pray. I want to be used for God's glory, but I secretly hope that I'll be glorified along the way. I like being recognized for my service to God. I know of a pastor who, a few years ago, wanted to recognize the congregation's "best Christian." Fortunately, members intervened and the plan quickly died.

Jesus, our example, says in John 8:50 that he has no wish to glorify himself. If the desire for glory is in my heart and in any way influences my actions, I have strayed from the example Jesus gave us. I think about what Jesus taught about prayer and fasting in the Sermon on the Mount. He said to do these without drawing attention to ourselves. If you receive the attention of others, that is your only reward.

All that I do should be for the glory of God, not to bring glory to myself. My eyes should never turn away from God to see if anyone else is watching.

Now all glory to God, who is able, through his mighty power at work within us, to accomplish infinitely more than we might ask or think. (Ephesians 3:20)

How does your concern for what others think hinder your work for God?

Lord, let me seek only to gain your approval, not that of the world. May I never take my gaze from you. Amen.

November 4 John 9–10

The Pharisees were so proud of their education and knowledge that they could not hear the wisdom of the man born blind. Their arrogance shows in John 9:34: "You were born a total sinner! Are you trying to teach us?"

Their pride in their education became a stumbling block to any further education. They felt they could learn nothing from this man whom Jesus had healed.

How many opportunities for learning do I miss because I allow pride or social standing to close my ears and my mind to God's word delivered through others?

Just as our bodies have many parts and each part has a special function, so it is with Christ's body. We are many parts of one body, and we all belong to each other. (Romans 12:4-5)

When have you noticed all the parts of the body of Christ working together in harmony?

Lord, open my ears and my mind to hear and embrace the words from others that allow me to learn more about you. Save me from spiritual arrogance that closes me off from what you want to teach me. Amen.

November 5 ✠ John 11-12

"Many people did believe in him, however, including some of the Jewish leaders. But they wouldn't admit it for fear that the Pharisees would expel them from the synagogue. For they loved human praise more than the praise of God" (John 12:42-43).

I see myself in the description of the Jewish leaders who believed in Jesus. I don't want to lose the human praise I receive. I don't want to give up some of the things that are of the world in order to become wholly God's.

But when I surrender to God, even if only temporarily, I get a taste of what my life could be like if I surrendered totally and completely. Do I trust that new life in Christ can be better than my life as it is now?

This means that anyone who belongs to Christ has become a new person. The old life is gone; a new life has begun! (2 Corinthians 5:17)

What would it take for you to let God create you as a new person?

O Lord, forgive me. I ask you to strengthen me to serve you—completely and wholeheartedly. I say with my mouth that I want to be wholly yours, but my actions show otherwise. Help me, Lord! Amen.

November 6 ✠ John 13-16

"So now I am giving you a new commandment: Love each other. Just as I have loved you, you should love each other. Your love for one another will prove to the world that you are my disciples" (John 13:34-35). It sounds so simple—love each other. But when I consider my judgmental thoughts about people, I know I fall short. When I get aggravated with other drivers and call them names because they cut me off, I do not love as Jesus commanded.

Jesus says our love for one another will prove to the world that we are his disciples. I wonder if people see anything in me that causes them to think I am a disciple of Jesus. How does my behavior describe me?

For God called you to do good, even if it means suffering, just as Christ suffered for you. He is your example, and you must follow in his steps. (1 Peter 2:21)

Who do people see when they look at you?

Lord, I want others to know I am your disciple. Let my words and actions and thoughts toward others always be loving. Amen.

November 7 ✠ John 17-18

Sometimes when I read the New Testament, I feel like an observer—on the outside looking in. The Gospels tell the story of Jesus, but Jesus spoke to his disciples or to those who gathered to hear him teach. I try to apply them to myself, but sometimes they seem not to speak to me directly.

But in John's Gospel, Jesus prays about *me*! In John 17:20, Jesus says he prays not only for his disciples, but also for all who will ever believe in him through their message. Reading those words gives me great joy! Jesus actually prayed for me!

> I will answer them before they even call to me.
>   While they are still talking about their needs,
>   I will go ahead and answer their prayers! (Isaiah 65:24)

How does it feel to know that Jesus prayed for you so long ago? Can you imagine him interceding to God on your behalf even now?

Gracious Lord, thank you for thinking of me when you walked on the earth. I am so blessed to have you as my savior and my best friend! Amen.

November 8 ✠ John 19–21

I write this at the end of an incredibly busy week. I've just returned from an out-of-town trip, and I leave again in three days for two more trips. Even as I recover and catch up from one trip, I prepare for two more. In the busyness of the week, it's sometimes hard to remember that God is in control.

I am reminded of that fact when I read Jesus' response to Pilate: "You would have no power over me at all unless it were given to you from above." I may be busy, but I shouldn't worry, because God is in control. If Jesus could know that and face Pilate calmly, then I should be able to remember that and face the relatively minor challenges of today.

> "Am I a God who is only close at hand?" says the Lord.
>   "No, I am far away at the same time.
> Can anyone hide from me in a secret place?
>   Am I not everywhere in all the heavens and earth?" says the Lord.
> (Jeremiah 23:23-24)

How difficult is it for you to accept that God is in control?

Lord, when I look at my calendar, I am often overwhelmed. Help me remember that my hours and minutes are in your hand and in your control. Amen.

November 9 ✦ Acts 1–3

I've read Acts 2:42-47 as a model for how our church should behave or how small groups should work within the church, but this morning as I read these verses, I realized that I have a responsibility to act as those early believers did. It's easy to avoid behavior when you look at group action because it seems impersonal. But I am called as a believer to devote myself to teaching, to fellowship, to sharing meals, and to prayer.

I have a responsibility to be hospitable as well. One of the activities of the early church was meeting and eating in homes. This is something I don't do but should. I think I often try to complicate hospitality. It should be less about the food or the setting and more about building relationships with others.

When God's people are in need, be ready to help them. Always be eager to practice hospitality. (Romans 12:13)

How can you practice hospitality today?

Lord, I want to follow the example of those early believers by showing hospitality to others, both in my home and in other places. Make me intentional about sharing your love with others. Amen.

November 10 ✦ Acts 4–6

"The apostles left the high council rejoicing that God had counted them worthy to suffer disgrace for the name of Jesus" (Acts 5:41). The apostles boldly proclaimed Jesus. They persisted even when threatened with prison. Why do I not have that same boldness in my life? I do not share Jesus with others as I should. I am timid and afraid of disgrace. I never rejoice at the thought of rejection.

What do I really fear? Am I more concerned with pleasing people than with pleasing God? If I love others as Jesus loved them, I should want them to know Christ for themselves.

Jesus said, "If anyone is ashamed of me and my message in these adulterous and sinful days, the Son of Man will be ashamed of that person when he returns in the glory of his Father with the holy angels" (Mark 8:38).

When I fail to share Jesus with others, I deprive them of a blessing and show contempt for what Jesus did for me. It sounds harsh, but Jesus' words in Mark are blunt.

Give thanks to the Lord and proclaim his greatness. Let the whole world know what he has done. (Psalm 105:1)

When have you boldly proclaimed your love for Jesus and shared him with others?

Lord, I want to be bold and loving in proclaiming you when I have the opportunity. Show me what you want me to do and give me the courage to do it. Amen.

November 11 ✠ Acts 7–8

As I read the text of Stephen's sermon in Acts 7, I began to think about the Old Testament accounts he mentioned. His sermon showed his knowledge of the Scriptures and his understanding of how the pieces fit together.

We sometimes dismiss the Old Testament because as Christians, we look to Jesus as our savior. But when we decline to study the Old Testament, we miss the buildup it provides to the good news of Jesus. Stephen used the Bible available to him, the Old Testament, to understand Jesus.

To me, the whole Bible, both Old and New Testaments, speaks to me about my faith. Truly it is the living Word of God, for each time I read it, I learn new truths and gain new insights, even in familiar passages.

Your word is a lamp to guide my feet and a light for my path. (Psalm 119:105)

How has your experience of reading the Bible changed over time?

Lord, you gave us your word, and you created our minds to understand it as you reveal it to us. Thank you for the Bible, both Old and New Testaments, that open my eyes to know you better. Amen.

November 12 ✠ Acts 9–10

I wish I knew more about Barnabas. He is one of my favorite people in the Bible. Maybe it's because I can relate to him. I love to encourage others, and I am a trusting person. I tend to expect the best from people.

Barnabas took Saul's conversion at face value, believing what others had told him about Saul. Before Barnabas intervened, the believers would not accept Saul or see him. They were afraid of him and could not accept his conversion as genuine. Enter Barnabas. He vouched for Saul and encouraged the believers to see him for what he was—a changed man.

What if there had been no Barnabas? Who would have stepped up to connect Saul with the believers? Without encouragers, many people would never succeed due to the roadblocks in their paths.

And let us not neglect our meeting together, as some people do, but encourage one another, especially now that the day of his return is drawing near. (Hebrews 10:25)

Who could you encourage today? Who regularly encourages you?

Lord, thank you for Barnabas. May I be a Barnabas for others. Amen.

November 13 ✠ Acts 11–13

Because of the prophecy of Agabus that a famine was coming, the believers in Antioch decided to send relief to the believers in Judea. The famine had not yet come, but they believed the prophecy, and acting in faith they sent relief even before the famine occurred.

I suspect that many observers thought the believers acted irrationally. Even today, we may scoff at those who warn us of environmental issues such as global warming, water shortages, and endangered species. Where I live, scientists have warned us for years about water shortage, yet until the drought arrived, many people ignored the warnings and continued to follow their normal patterns of water usage.

Just as in biblical times, prophets come in many forms and for many reasons. I pray for discernment to distinguish the false prophets from God's prophets. I also pray for the conviction to heed God's prophets, even when doing so may cause others to laugh at me.

The earth is the Lord's, and everything in it. The world and all its people belong to him. (Psalm 24:1)

What warnings should you heed regarding God's world? What can you do about them?

Creator God, may I be a good steward of all you have given me. Give me a heart to care for your creation and wisdom to know what to do. Amen.

November 14 ✠ Acts 14–16

When Paul and Barnabas preached, they reminded the believers that they must suffer many hardships before entering the kingdom of God. Just this morning I read about Joseph revealing his identity to his brothers when they came to purchase grain in Egypt. Joseph was not bitter or vengeful toward his brothers, even though they treated him terribly.

Instead, Joseph acknowledged that God placed him in Egypt. He did not allow his suffering to hamper his faith in God. He remained faithful in his suffering, even though he suffered much before Pharaoh gave him power.

Paul and Barnabas remind me that suffering is not separate from God. Suffering will draw us closer to God when we have faith that God is in control.

Dear friends, don't be surprised at the fiery trials you are going through, as if something strange were happening to you. Instead, be very glad— for these trials make you partners with Christ in his suffering, so that you will have the wonderful joy of seeing his glory when it is revealed to all the world. (1 Peter 4:12-13)

When has your suffering brought you closer to Christ?

Lord, may I never lose the joy of your presence in my life, even in the face of suffering. Amen.

November 15 ✣ Acts 17–19

In Acts 19, the Ephesians are concerned that Artemis will "be robbed of her great prestige." They feel they have to take action to preserve her status.

When Christ died for our sins, he freely gave up his status as God so that we might receive status as God's children. The difference between how Christ is elevated and the way the Ephesians tried to elevate Artemis is that we are to follow Christ's example of humility and serve others rather than elevating ourselves. Our Lord washed the feet of his disciples, the act of a servant, and he calls us to do the same. This is hardly an act of prestige!

But he was pierced for our rebellion,
  crushed for our sins.

He was beaten so we could be whole.
   He was whipped so we could be healed. (Isaiah 53:5)

How difficult is it for you to serve others with no expectation of anything in return?

Lord, you call me to serve others as you did, as a way to elevate your name in this world. I want to be faithful to your example so that your name is spread as others observe my behavior. Make me different from the world so that I honor your name. Amen.

November 16 ✠ Acts 20–22

Ananias had great faith. When he went to Saul, he knew Saul's history, yet he called him brother. Can I exhibit enough faith to minister to someone I fear?

In contrast, the Jews who heard Paul's preaching were unable to acknowledge his change. They could only accept what they already knew. Looking at the difference between the behavior of Ananias and of the Jews in Jerusalem reminds me that I need to be aware that God works in ways that may challenge my traditional beliefs. If I am unwilling to see beyond what I know, I can miss new lessons from God. Worse yet, I may stagnate and become useless as a disciple.

Then they scoffed, "He's just a carpenter, the son of Mary and the brother of James, Joseph, Judas, and Simon. And his sisters live right here among us." They were deeply offended and refused to believe in him. (Mark 6:3)

What sometimes keeps you from fully believing in Jesus?

Open my eyes, Lord, that I may see your work in unlikely places. Open my heart to accept the changes you make in others. Open my arms to embrace the evidence of your grace I see in those around me. Amen.

November 17 ✠ Acts 23–25

From reading Acts 24, it sounds as though Felix got close to becoming a follower of Christ. But Acts 24:25 says Felix became frightened. He told Paul that he would call him back when it was more convenient.

There are times in my life when I do the same thing. I want Christ to come back at a more convenient time. Whether out of fear of ridicule, a desire to do something that I know is incompatible with my faith, or just because I already have my day mapped out, there are times I find it inconvenient to obey Christ.

Felix did not move up to governor by embracing unconventional beliefs. His fear may have been due to the possible reaction if he became a follower of Christ. It could mean loss of position and persecution.

Can I follow Christ even when doing so is inconvenient?

But Jesus told him, "Anyone who puts a hand to the plow and then looks back is not fit for the Kingdom of God." (Luke 9:62)

What does it take for you to move ahead with Christ and not look back?

O Lord, it hurts me to think of how I act sometimes. I know I grieve your spirit when I don't do what you want me to do. Help me to be stronger and bolder in living my faith. Amen.

November 18 ✠ Acts 26–28

Paul's great desire, as expressed in Acts, was to get to Rome to preach the gospel. And he did, though as a prisoner instead of a free man. While the path to accomplishing his goal was not what he might have imagined, he had faith in God and remained steadfast in his faith throughout his adversity. He not only knew who he was, but he knew *whose* he was.

Reading Acts, it's easy to see God's hand in Paul's circumstances. Can I as easily see God's hand in the circumstances of my own life? Can I trust God and therefore remain calm when storms rage around me? I need to remember Paul when I have difficulty seeing God in what happens in my life. I need to remember that God is in control, even over the tiniest detail.

O God, your ways are holy.
Is there any god as mighty as you?
You are the God of great wonders!
You demonstrate your awesome power among the nations.
(Psalm 77:13-14)

How can you remember whose you are, even in the most difficult times?

Lord, let me always lean on you and trust you, even when I cannot see where your path leads. You are the everlasting God! Amen.

November 19 Romans 1–3

"For everyone has sinned; we all fall short of God's glorious standard" (Romans 3:23). I am familiar with this verse, but familiarity can cause me to take it lightly. I am often too quick to dismiss my sins or to view them as less sinful than they truly are. I usually fall into this trap when I compare myself to others. Making fun of someone to my husband or children doesn't seem nearly as bad as committing murder or adultery. But I am not to use other people as my gauge. I am to use God as my standard, exemplified in the behavior of Jesus. When I hold up my actions to the standard he has set, I am less likely to rate my sins as trivial. If I am truly to appreciate the sacrifice Jesus made for me, I need to remember that I fall short of God's standard.

Our society places so much emphasis on self-esteem that I believe it is especially difficult to see myself as a sinner, not worthy even to be in the presence of God. I have to remind myself frequently of how little I deserve his grace so that I can be grateful for it.

God saved you by his grace when you believed. And you can't take credit for this; it is a gift from God. Salvation is not a reward for the good things we have done, so none of us can boast about it. (Ephesians 2:8-9)

When are you tempted to rank sins from small to great? When are you tempted to deny God's grace to others?

Lord, I never want to take my salvation for granted. Make me mindful of your grace. Do not allow me to compare myself with anyone but Jesus. Amen.

November 20 ✚ Romans 4–7

I can relate to Paul's struggle with sin as described in Romans 7:14-25. He attributes his propensity to do wrong not to himself, but to the sin living in him. At first blush, this sounds like a copout. When our oldest son was little, he would say that the reason he could not pick up his toys was because "the ant took my hands." Paul's musings sound a lot like our son's.

As I ponder the notion Paul presents, I wonder if the real message is not one of excusing sin but instead the idea that we should not beat ourselves up over our sin. I am going to sin because I am human. Satan delights whenever we think we are too bad for Christ to redeem because not only do we turn away from Christ, but we end up wallowing in a sea of self-pity and anger at our own unworthiness.

But Paul tells us that Jesus saved us from the *destructiveness* caused by sin. We will still sin because we are incapable of doing otherwise. But when we accept what Jesus did for us, we are freed from beating ourselves up when we sin.

You gave me life and showed me your unfailing love. My life was preserved by your care. (Job 10:12)

How does accepting that you are a sinner free you?

Lord, I am going to sin. I know it. But you sent Jesus so that his death atones for all of my sin. I want to bury my sin with him and be raised with him to a new life that is free of guilt, self-pity, and destructiveness. Thank you for your great mercy. Amen.

November 21 ✠ Romans 8–10

I absolutely love Romans 8. I am reading it from the New Living Translation for the first time, so the words sound new and fresh to me today. Verses 35-37 are particularly inspiring because of the perspective they give to suffering.

We will have trouble and calamity, and we may be persecuted, hungry or destitute, but that doesn't mean Christ does not love us. No matter how bad things get, Christ still loves me. And because of that, I can rejoice! So even when it seems that I have lost, I have still won! Praise God!

Rejoice, you people of Jerusalem!
Rejoice in the Lord your God!
For the rain he sends demonstrates his faithfulness.
Once more the autumn rains will come,
as well as the rains of spring. (Joel 2:23)

In what ways do you rejoice in the Lord?

Almighty and Glorious God, I praise you for who you are. I am always a winner because you love me. Amen.

November 22 ✦ Romans 11–13

I believe Romans 12 summarizes everything I need to do to be a faithful follower of God. It's uncanny how everything ties together. I recently felt that God was showing me three sins in particular that I needed to address in my life. I felt he was showing me that I needed to be more compassionate, hospitable, and intentional. When I read Romans 12, I found that Paul addressed each of these three areas.

Romans 12:11 focuses on *intentionality*: Never be lazy, but work hard and serve the Lord enthusiastically. Verse 13 talks about *compassion* and *hospitality*: When God's people are in need, be ready to help them. Always be eager to practice hospitality. Enthusiasm and eagerness—perhaps those are the keys to what we should be for Christ!

For I know how eager you are to help, and I have been boasting to the churches in Macedonia that you in Greece were ready to send an offering a year ago. In fact, it was your enthusiasm that stirred up many of the Macedonian believers to begin giving. (2 Corinthians 9:2)

How has Scripture spoken specifically to you?

Lord, may I enthusiastically and eagerly serve you. Amen.

November 23 ✦ Romans 14–16

I find it easy to get caught up in rules—what is right and wrong—in my Christian walk. There are so many things for which the Bible either offers no clear-cut direction or seems to give contradictory direction. Paul cuts to the chase in the final sentence of Romans 14: If you do anything you believe is not right, you are sinning.

My gauge is not what is right for others but what is right for me. Remembering this, I don't have to get bogged down in rules. If it doesn't feel right to me, it doesn't matter if it is permitted. God is showing me that I am not to do it, so if I ignore my conscience and do it anyway, I sin.

Dear friends, if we don't feel guilty, we can come to God with bold confidence. (1 John 3:21)

In what ways does God speak directly to you, regardless of standard "rules"?

Omniscient God, you know all about me. I cannot hide behind rules. May I always listen to you and obey what you call me to do and be. Amen.

November 24 ✠ 1 Corinthians 1–4

From what I've read of Corinth, I know it was a hub of activity in Paul's day. As an important crossroads of Greece, Corinth was a mix of people and ideas. When Paul spoke of worldly wisdom, he considered the readers of his letter.

I've been reading *Fresh Wind, Fresh Fire*, by Jim Cymbala, pastor of the Brooklyn Tabernacle. He says churches today have taken their focus off the central truth of Christ and instead focus on blending into the world.[14] In light of this, Paul's message to the Corinthians seems especially timely. In 1 Corinthians 1:21-23, Paul offers no apologies for his message, even though neither the Jews nor the Greeks can accept it.

I should live according to the gospel, not according to some watered-down version that is sanitized to make it palatable to the world. I don't want to follow a lukewarm messenger or live according to a lukewarm message. I want to be enthusiastic about Christ and his message. I want to be like Peter, asking God to wash all of me, not just my feet!

Come, let us sing to the Lord!
Let us shout joyfully to the Rock of our salvation.
Let us come to him with thanksgiving.
Let us sing psalms of praise to him. (Psalm 95:1-2)

How difficult is it for you to follow the true gospel instead of the world's watered-down version?

Lord, show me how you want me to live and give me the courage to do it. Let me boldly live and proclaim you to others. I don't want to be pressured to conform to the world. I want to be transformed by you. Amen.

November 25 ✠ 1 Corinthians 5-9

Paul's opinion about Christians and lawsuits is radical in today's society. He asks, "Why not just accept the injustice and leave it at that? Why not let yourselves be cheated?"

Which is the greater prize—to win a lawsuit or to turn the other cheek and inherit the kingdom of God? It's not difficult to find stories of people who won a lawsuit but still feel as if they lost.

Whenever I focus on how another person wronged me, I take my mind off God and am not able to find the peace he desires for me. No amount of money or legal victories can compare to the peace Christ can give me if I seek him in all things. Accepting, even rejoicing in suffering, draws me closer to God, a blessing much greater than any court can give me!

Sensible people control their temper; they earn respect by overlooking wrongs. (Proverbs 19:11)

How can you discern when to strive for mercy over justice?

Lord, your sayings are often difficult and hard to accept in our world. Help me to be different by loving others and by not seeking my own justice. Instead, let me seek you. Amen.

November 26 ✠ 1 Cor 10-13

So much of Paul's message in 1 Corinthians leads to chapter 13. When he tells the people to consider the conscience of those who believe it is wrong to eat or drink certain things, his message is to let love govern their behavior. When he talks about spiritual gifts in chapter 12, he says love is even more important than any spiritual gift.

Love should govern all I do, all I say, and all my relationships. Lord, let it be so!

In view of all this, make every effort to respond to God's promises. Supplement your faith with a generous provision of moral excellence, and moral excellence with knowledge, and knowledge with self-control, and self-control with patient endurance, and patient endurance with godliness, and godliness with brotherly affection, and brotherly affection with love for everyone. (2 Peter 1:5-7)

Why is love the greatest of all gifts?

Lord, help me to love everyone, even those I find particularly unlovable. May I look for you in each person I meet. Amen.

November 27 ✥ 1 Cor 14–16

"For to your shame I say that some of you don't know God at all" (1 Corinthians 15:34b).

After Paul discusses how the Corinthian church should live as the body of Christ, he says some of them, even though a part of the church, don't know God at all. Ouch!

Being part of the church, a name on the church roll, does not gain me spiritual status. I can attend regularly, serve diligently, and give faithfully and still not know God. If I don't seek him and seek to know him, I am no different from the Jews Jesus criticized for assuming that their status as children of Abraham gave them a free pass.

Spiritual laziness can occur even when I work diligently in the church. It is not my action that draws me close to God; it's my stillness—time spent in study, prayer, and quiet. I cannot hear God speak to me if I am consumed with activity, even when my motivation is to serve him.

My people will live in safety, quietly at home. They will be at rest. (Isaiah 32:18)

What will you do today to seek God?

Lord, I don't ever want to be far from you. I long to know you more and better. Help me to be quiet and rest in your presence. Amen.

November 28 ✚ 2 Corinthians 1–4

"We now have this light shining in our hearts, but we ourselves are like fragile clay jars containing this great treasure. This makes it clear that our great power is from God, not from ourselves" (2 Corinthians 4:7). This is such a beautiful way to describe a Christian. We have such a special treasure inside because the glory of Christ resides within us. Yet, because it lives in a clay jar, it is not always visible to others. What others see is nothing special, an ordinary person. But just as you can view a clay jar's contents when you look inside, God can see what is inside me, and as others get closer to me, they can see what is inside me as well.

I often long to do something profound for Christ. This passage reminds me that an ordinary clay jar is something special as long as it is filled with treasure from God. Instead of concerning myself with doing something great and profound, I should focus on becoming more like Christ, filling my clay jar fuller than it is now. The fuller the jar, the easier others can see its contents.

In the same way, let your good deeds shine out for all to see, so that everyone will praise your heavenly Father. (Matthew 5:16)

How can you make your treasure—Christ's glory—more visible to others?

Lord, let me not forget that the treasure inside is important rather than the jar that holds it. Keep me focused on becoming more like you so others can easily see the treasure I have. Amen.

November 29 ✠ 2 Corinthians 5–8

I love my family. I am happy in my church community. I enjoy where I live and find great beauty in my neighborhood and city. I feel blessed with my life.

When I read 2 Corinthians 5:1-10, I have to stop and think if I am able to agree with Paul about being ready to be at home with the Lord. When things are going well in this life, I am not as eager to go home to be with the Lord. And yet, when I am suffering, heaven is a much more appealing place.

I do get excited about heaven when I stop and think of what will and won't be there. The thought of spending all my time praising God and leaving behind hurt and tears and need gives me incredible hope. It is a great encouragement to me when I am worried or hurt or suffering to know that this life is just a small part of my *whole* life.

Even the sparrow finds a home,
and the swallow builds her nest and raises her young
at a place near your altar,
O Lord of Heaven's Armies, my King and my God!
What joy for those who can live in your house,
always singing your praises. (Psalm 84:3-4)

How can you live an abundant life here on earth and also keep your sights set on heaven?

Gracious Father, as much as you have given me, you have promised me even more. I thank you for the hope that fills my heart and the place you have made for me in heaven. Amen.

November 30 ✢ 2 Cor 9–13

"You must each decide in your heart how much to give. And don't give reluctantly or in response to pressure. For God loves a person who gives cheerfully" (2 Corinthians 9:7). Sometimes I feel pressure to give either my time or money to a cause. The cause may be worthy, but it may not be right for my gifts. In this verse, I believe Paul gives me permission not to feel guilty about withholding as long as I am generous to *someone.*

Giving should bless the recipient, the giver, and God. If I am unhappy about giving either my time or money to a cause, the cause may benefit, but I may be resentful. My resentment can impair my relationship with God.

This is why I need to seek God's guidance in all things, especially where I give my time and money. I can miss what God plans for me when I do things I should not do.

There is a path before each person that seems right, but it ends in death. (Proverbs 14:12)

How do you decide where to use your time, gifts, and money?

Lord, give me a discerning mind and heart to know where you want me to serve you. There is so much need in the world. May I do what you desire. Amen.

December 1 ✢ Galatians 1–3

Take a moment to reflect on Paul's words in the first chapter of Galatians: "But even before I was born, God chose me and called me by his marvelous grace. Then it pleased him to reveal his Son to me so that I would proclaim the Good News about Jesus to the Gentiles" (Galatians 1:15-16).

When I consider the life Paul led before his Damascus Road experience, I'm surprised he says God chose him before he was born.

These words are overwhelming to me. Before birth, I was chosen by God and called by him. That means I am never too small or insignificant to escape God's notice. If I was chosen before birth, then I have never been out of God's grip.

This means no one is ever out of the reach of God. We may turn away when we see God, but he chose us. The question is not whether God chose me but how I choose to respond to him.

You didn't choose me. I chose you. I appointed you to go and produce lasting fruit, so that the Father will give you whatever you ask for, using my name. (John 15:16)

How does it encourage you to know that God chose you as his own before you were even born?

Lord, it's incredible that when I was unknown and too tiny to see, you saw me and chose me. I can never go anywhere or do anything away from your presence. Thank you for loving me so deeply and fully. Amen.

December 2 ✤ Galatians 4–6

Salvation only comes through the cross of Christ. Nothing I can do will save me. When I accept and believe that, I am *free* from rules. Galatians 5:13 says, "For you have been called to live in freedom, my brothers and sisters. But don't use your freedom to satisfy your sinful nature. Instead, use your freedom to serve one another in love."

I am free, but I must guard against following the desires of the world. I cannot allow the things of this world to enslave me, for then my freedom is for nothing. While I am free, I am to follow the guidance of the Holy Spirit, because even though I am free, someone—either the Holy Spirit or the sinful nature—will still lead me.

The sinful nature rules when gluttony, hostility, selfishness, and impurity influence my behavior. I must always be on guard to fight these characteristics. When I am joyful, at peace, and practicing self-control, I am allowing the Holy Spirit to rule in my life.

And you will know the truth, and the truth will set you free. (John 8:32)

How do you show that you are grateful for the freedom God gives you?

Lord, I want to use my freedom for good. I want the Holy Spirit to guide my behavior. Make me strong to stand against my sinful nature. Amen.

December 3 ✠ Ephesians 1–3

Before reading the chapters from Ephesians today, I struggled with an issue that many of us face: more month than money. It affected my ability to quiet my mind and read God's word. As is usually the case, when I put off getting into God's message, I realize that, when I finally read it, the words speak to me where I am.

"I pray that from his glorious, unlimited resources he will empower you with inner strength through his Spirit" (Ephesians 3:16).

Today, I need God's glorious, unlimited resources. I need them every day, but today I feel especially needy as I consider holiday expenses and current bills. I long for increased trust in God to supply my needs. I am comforted in knowing that life is more than the cares of this world, but I also know that I can call on God for help with these cares.

Your word is a lamp to guide my feet and a light for my path. (Psalm 119:105)

When have you claimed the strength of the Spirit to help you through a difficult situation?

Lord, I struggle with the small details of life that don't seem small in my limited ability. I know you are greater than anything I face, and I want the peace that comes from knowing and believing that. Help me through this day, O Lord. Amen.

December 4 ✠ Ephesians 4–6

In the book, *A Long Obedience in the Same Direction*, author Eugene Peterson talks about the "everyday religion" we get from friends, talk show hosts, politicians, those in the media, and counselors.[15] As I read Ephesians, I thought about how Paul's advice contradicts what we hear touted as common sense or everyday religion.

Paul says, "Let everything you say be good and helpful, so that your words will be an encouragement to others." Yet we are encouraged to "tell it like it is," without regard for how our words affect the recipient. An entire media industry grew around trashing celebrities. We cannot stand in a grocery store checkout line without reading negative headlines. Strangely absent is an equal amount of coverage for those who use their fame to raise awareness about the plight of the hungry, homeless, children, and victims of war and natural disasters.

Paul says to be "tenderhearted, forgiving one another just as God through Christ forgave you." What we often hear is, "Don't let others take advantage of you. Stand up for your rights. You must be tough to be successful. It's a dog-eat-dog world." We are told it's fine to give, but make sure you get the tax deduction. Paul tells us to "give generously to others in need."

You have heard that our ancestors were told, "You must not murder. If you commit murder, you are subject to judgment." But I say, if you are even angry with someone, you are subject to judgment! If you call someone an idiot, you are in danger of being brought before the court. And if you curse someone, you are in danger of the fires of hell. (Matthew 5:21-22)

How seriously do you take the Bible's teachings, which are so contradictory to those in our world?

Lord, keep me strong against the darkness of the world. Let me remain in the light. Amen.

December 5 ✠ Philippians 1–4

Paul, in Philippians 3, talks about his "pedigree." He shares things we consider important in this world and in our society: family connection, education, social status, career success. Yet he calls all these things worthless garbage. He gave up his religious pedigree to serve Christ.

What is of more value in my eyes—social standing, respect, education, material wealth, even my position in my church—or knowing Jesus Christ and living for him?

Store your treasures in heaven, where moths and rust cannot destroy, and thieves do not break in and steal. Wherever your treasure is, there the desires of your heart will also be. (Matthew 6:20-21)

How can you make a conscious, daily effort to store your treasures in heaven?

Lord, I don't want anything to get between you and me. I don't want to hold on to what this world values. Instead I want to cling to you always. Let my every thought and action be something that pleases you. Amen.

December 6 ✠ Colossians 1–4

"And whatever you do or say, do it as a representative of the Lord Jesus, giving thanks through him to God the Father" (Colossians 3:17). Reading this verse gives me a sense of great responsibility.

Being a representative of the Lord sounds more powerful than living to please God. A representative's job is to stand in for someone else. Our representative form of government makes those we elect responsible for accurately conveying our wishes in the policies and laws they make. It's not about what they personally want; instead, it is about what the people they represent want.

In the same way, if we live as representatives of the Lord, our own wishes and desires are subordinate to what God wants.

A good representative does not lose focus or get distracted by political pressure that opposes the will of his or her constituents. In the same way, representing Christ may put us in opposition to what others think we should do. We must stay focused and faithful as Christ's representatives.

For I have come down from heaven to do the will of God who sent me, not to do my own will. (John 6:38)

What does it mean to you that you represent Jesus Christ in the world?

Lord, I want to be your representative in the world. Help me to listen to you so I know what you desire me to do. Keep me focused and faithful. Amen.

December 7 ✠ 1 Thessalonians 1–5

"So you received the message with joy from the Holy Spirit in spite of the severe suffering it brought you. In this way, you imitated both us and the Lord" (1 Thessalonians 1:6). To accept Christ when it results in peace and joy is one thing, but to receive him with joy when suffering results is something completely different. I tend to think of enduring suffering as requiring a certain maturity of faith that happens over a period of time. But the Thessalonians apparently knew, even as they received the message, that they faced severe suffering as a result. Yet they received it with joy!

I want to be strong in my faith so that I can endure suffering and remain faithful to Jesus. But I have trouble being faithful even in small things.

The master said, "Well done, my good and faithful servant. You have been faithful in handling this small amount, so now I will give you many more responsibilities. Let's celebrate together!" (Matthew 25:23)

How can you dedicate yourself today to being faithful even in the small things?

Lord, give me the strength to be faithful to you in all ways, big and small. May I look to the example of the Thessalonians, Paul, and especially Jesus. Amen.

December 8 ✠ 2 Thessalonians 1–3

Second Thessalonians 2 warns of the evil that goes on in the world. Paul says the evil one will deceive people.

I am often too quick to dismiss such passages of Scripture. Because we have an image of Satan in a red suit with a pitchfork, it's hard to take him too seriously. And yet, that may be part of his plan to get us to minimize him.

As I read this passage, I thought of all the ways we so-called Christians twist words to meet our own agendas. We can turn others off to our faith because we are more judgmental than loving, but also because we don't stand firm in matters of faith.

I want to spend my time and energy seeking to know God better, not debating the unclear issues that separate denominations. I don't want to believe that just being a good person is enough. I want to grow always in the image of Christ and not be distracted by people or beliefs that take my focus off God.

"My thoughts are nothing like your thoughts," says the Lord.
    "And my ways are far beyond anything you could imagine.

For just as the heavens are higher than the earth,
  so my ways are higher than your ways
and my thoughts higher than your thoughts." (Isaiah 55:8-9)

How can you find the balance between questioning and accepting what you know of God?

Lord, I rejoice that you will destroy the evil one with the breath of your mouth. Make me serious and strong to withstand his attack. Don't let me become distracted, but keep me focused on you. Amen.

December 9 ✣ 1 Timothy 1–6

First Timothy 6 contains valuable instruction about money. Verses 8 and 9 focus on a desire for wealth. Paul says that when we long for wealth, we take our eyes off God and fall away from the faith.

In verses 17-19, Paul says those who are rich should not trust in their money but trust in God. Their wealth gives them the responsibility to share with others.

Perhaps the verses that best capture God's goal for our attitude about money are 6-8. Paul says we should be content with what we have if we have enough food and clothing. Can I say that I am content? As catalogs fill my mailbox and advertisers urge me to purchase their products, can I say with confidence that I am content?

Better to have little, with godliness, than to be rich and dishonest. (Proverbs 16:8)

How can you temper your desire to acquire more with the realization that you already have the greatest treasure of all?

Lord, thank you for these words written to Timothy and also to me. I need to remember to focus on what I have, which is more than sufficient, instead of what I don't have, which is superfluous. Amen.

December 10 ✠ 2 Timothy 1–4

I am rarely consumed with thoughts about the "last days." God has told us that we don't know when it is, and anyway, I should obey him all the time, not only when I think he will show up.

But the 2 Timothy 3:1-5 struck a nerve with me. The examples Paul gives of wrong living are ones I see all around me, and I hope others don't see them in me:

• Love of only self and money
• Boastful and proud, scoffing at God, ungrateful
• Considering nothing sacred
• Slandering others and having no self-control
• Acting religious but rejecting the power that makes one godly

The last one worries me. I can do all the things that make me look outwardly religious, but if I do not give total control to God, then I gain nothing but pride (which Paul actually mentions twice in this passage). Surrendering my whole self to God is accepting the power that makes me godly.

My old self has been crucified with Christ. It is no longer I who live, but Christ lives in me. So I live in this earthly body by trusting in the Son of God, who loved me and gave himself for me. (Galatians 2:20)

In what ways can you claim the true power of God today?

Lord, keep me from pride. May I totally surrender to you. Amen.

December 11 ✠ Titus 1–Philemon 1

I cannot be a lone Christian. Paul's letter to Titus reminds me that I am to support and encourage others. In Titus 2, Paul instructs men and women on how to live, and he gives specific instructions to both older and younger people.

At a conference I attended during the summer, the pastor said there is no such thing as a retired Christian. It's not a career with a finite lifespan. Paul understood this, and he frequently singled out older and younger people for different instructions.

We are often saddened by news that someone has died shortly after retirement. We say it is unfair that they did not get to enjoy their retirement. That should not be said of us regarding our faith. We should rejoice that a person served God up to the end of his or her life.

Even in old age they will still produce fruit; they will remain vital and green. (Psalm 92:14)

How can you recognize that God uses you at every stage of life?

Lord, I am inspired by those who joyfully serve you even though they are advanced in years. May I learn from their example to never tire of being faithful to you. Amen.

December 12 ✠ Hebrews 1–4

Hebrews 2:1 warns us against drifting away from the truth of Jesus. We are to "listen very carefully" because the noise that is not Truth is louder than God. God's Truth is unchanging, but we tend to be attracted by the latest new thing. It seems especially that way during the Christmas season. "Must-have" gifts fill the sale papers and TV ads. We rush from store to store to get the things we think will bring joy to someone's life.

But joy cannot be found in things. We seek joy in the wrong places. Joy happens when we know that no matter what comes, whether blessings or sorrow, God is there. He is steadfast in his love for us and eternally faithful.

Even as the bustle and rush of this season threatens to pull me away from the Truth, I need to listen very carefully to the angel's message: "I bring you good news" (Luke 2:10).

I have the only gift I need: a Savior! Praise God!

"I, the Lord, have called you to demonstrate my righteousness.
I will take you by the hand and guard you,
and I will give you to my people, Israel,
as a symbol of my covenant with them.
And you will be a light to guide the nations.
You will open the eyes of the blind.
You will free the captives from prison,
releasing those who sit in dark dungeons." (Isaiah 42:6-7)

In what ways can you listen carefully to the good news from God today?

Gracious God, thank you for the greatest gift of all—your Son. May I remember that because I have him, I have everything I need. Amen.

December 13 ✠ Hebrews 5–7

The author of Hebrews points out that a stagnant faith in God will not satisfy me. In 5:11–6:3, the author says we should not remain babies in our faith, but should grow and strengthen our devotion to Christ. We are to learn more so we can understand more and become mature in our relationship with God.

A good analogy of our faith is a tree—it's either growing or dying. If I merely attend a service on Sunday, pray in a crisis, and donate an amount that is insignificant to me, then I am not growing. I may do this year after year, so it may seem as if I am stagnant. However, every day moves me closer to death, where I will see God face to face. Do I want to face him as a stranger or as my dearest friend?

When the master of the house has locked the door, it will be too late. You will stand outside knocking and pleading, "Lord, open the door for us!" But he will reply, "I don't know you or where you come from." Then you will say, "But we ate and drank with you, and you taught in our streets." And he will reply, "I tell you, I don't know you or where you come from. Get away from me, all you who do evil." (Luke 13:25-27)

Would God recognize you right now? Would you recognize God?

Lord, I love to know you better. You are my God and my closest companion. Keep me always in your care. Amen.

December 14 ✠ Hebrews 8–10

I am having lunch today with a friend who has endured a rough time this year. The last time we had lunch together, a couple of months ago, she felt bitter about losing her job and had stopped going to church. I hope that she is feeling better, and I've prayed about our time together.

I thought of my friend as I read Hebrews 10:32-36. The author not only recalls the suffering the readers endured, but also how they helped others who suffered. In all cases they remained faithful to God.

I can lose nothing on this earth that has eternal consequences. As long as I remain faithful, I have all I need. What an incredible blessing!

Don't be afraid, for I am with you.
Don't be discouraged, for I am your God.
I will strengthen you and help you.
I will hold you up with my victorious right hand. (Isaiah 41:10)

When have you lost everything? Were you able to cling to God, or did you turn away?

Lord, thank you for your faithfulness to me. May I have the attitude of those to whom Hebrews was addressed, so that no matter what happens, I remain joyful because I know you. Amen.

December 15 ✠ Hebrews 11–13

"Think of all the hostility he endured from sinful people, then you won't become weary and give up. After all, you have not yet given your lives in your struggle against sin" (Hebrews 12:3-4). This is a blunt statement. I often mentally place myself on a pedestal because I am a good person and do things for others. I like to rest on my good deeds, and when I compare my behavior with lots of other people, I look good. So I climb up on my pedestal, content with myself and hoping that others notice just how good I am. I enjoy basking in the praise I receive.

These verses knock me off my pedestal in an almost mocking way. They confront me as I sit back and rest from my good deeds.

Jesus pressed on. He did not reach a quota of good deeds and then call it quits. He did not stop to admire his miracles and give others time to form a receiving line to express their gratitude to him. When he withdrew, it wasn't to bask in admiration. It was to pray, to stay in close touch with his Father. It was to keep his focus on God, not on his good deeds.

When I hold my life and deeds up to those of Jesus, I realize there is no place in my life for sitting on a pedestal.

And they sang in a mighty chorus:
"Worthy is the Lamb that was slaughtered—
to receive power and riches
and wisdom and strength
and honor and glory and blessing." (Revelation 5:12)

In what ways are you tempted to bask in the praise of others rather than moving forward in your service to God?

Holy God, I am nothing without you. May I never think I accomplish anything on my own, but always acknowledge your power in my life. Amen.

December 16 ✠ James 1–5

"And even when you ask, you don't get it because your motives are all wrong—you want only what will give you pleasure" (James 4:3).

Like many, I pray for material goods, promotions, a winning team, etc. However, as I read this verse, I thought of a different prayer request. I need to consider my motives when I pray for others. If I pray for my sons to do well on exams, is my prayer for them, or is it connected to the pride I feel in their accomplishments?

Later in chapter 4, James warns about making plans without considering if they are what God wants us to do. How often I make decisions without consulting God! Then, when things don't go well, I pray to God for help!

Pray like this:
Our Father in heaven,
    may your name be kept holy.
May your kingdom come soon.
May your will be done on earth,
    as it is in heaven.
Give us today the food we need,
    and forgive us our sins,
    as we have forgiven those who sin against us.
And don't let us yield to temptation,
    but rescue us from the evil one. (Matthew 6:9-13)

What motivates you to pray?

Father in heaven, teach me to pray so that my prayers are focused on others, not on what gives me pleasure. Amen.

December 17 ✠ 1 Peter 1–2

In John Maxwell's book *Today Matters*, he emphasizes that values must prevail over feelings.[16] In 1 Peter 1:14, that point is made in a different, but similar way: "Don't slip back into your old ways of living to satisfy your own desires."

No matter how tempting the old ways are, no matter how comfortable and familiar they feel, I must behave according to what I value, regardless of the comfort level I experience when doing so. I don't always feel like being different, but Peter says that if I *value* my faith, I should *crave* spiritual milk (1 Peter 2:2). If I want to grow in my faith, I have to get past the baby stage. I must subordinate feelings to values.

And so, dear brothers and sisters, I plead with you to give your bodies to God because of all he has done for you. Let them be a living and holy sacrifice—the kind he will find acceptable. This is truly the way to worship him. Don't copy the behavior and customs of this world, but let God transform you into a new person by changing the way you think. Then you will learn to know God's will for you, which is good and pleasing and perfect. (Romans 12:1-2)

When are you tempted to "slip back into your old ways of living"? What reminds you of your status as a new person in Christ?

Lord, I long to know you better. Even when the world tempts me otherwise, keep my mind and my will strong for you. Make my behavior consistent with what I value, which is knowing you and serving you. Amen.

December 18 ✦ 1 Peter 3–5

"Be tenderhearted, and keep a humble attitude. Don't repay evil for evil. Don't retaliate with insults when people insult you. Instead, pay them back with a blessing. That is what God has called you to do, and he will bless you for it" (1 Peter 3:8b-9). *Tenderhearted.* This word says so much to me. I picture someone whose heart is so fragile that every injustice causes the person to ache deeply for the one wronged. But more than that, the ache extends to the one inflicting the pain or injustice. I think of someone who is as gentle with a boor as with a baby, who suffers along with the suffering, who sees only the pain in others and never in herself.

At first glance, a tenderhearted person may seem weak and weepy, given to being pushed around by others, and incredibly insignificant. But on deeper inspection, I see it takes tremendous strength and courage to be tenderhearted. Who would willingly choose to suffer with others, to return insult with blessing, to embrace the pain of others as his or her own? This is not a decision lightly made. To bear the burdens of others, the tenderhearted person must have strength beyond that of an athlete. Only inner strength, given by God, will prevent tenderhearted people from collapsing under the weight of the suffering they take upon themselves.

Get rid of all bitterness, rage, anger, harsh words, and slander, as well as all types of evil behavior. Instead, be kind to each other, tenderhearted, forgiving one another, just as God through Christ has forgiven you. (Ephesians 4:31-32)

Are you strong enough to be tenderhearted?

Lord, give me the strength I need to be tenderhearted. Please address my fears by showing me the blessing that comes from serving you as a tenderhearted disciple. Amen.

December 19 ✠ 2 Peter 1–3

"For you are a slave to whatever controls you" (2 Peter 2:19b). The opening sentence of 2 Peter says, "This letter is from Simon Peter, a slave and apostle of Jesus Christ."

Peter describes himself as a slave, and then, tucked away in the letter, he says we are slaves to whatever controls us. Because he claims to be a slave of Jesus Christ, he implies that Christ controls him. I'm not sure I can make the same claim Peter made—that I am a slave and apostle of Jesus. Many things compete for control of my life—food, relaxation, service, money, pride. I can name these so easily that it frightens me.

While some of these things are not bad in and of themselves, they are dangerous when I choose them over Christ. I can say that Christ controls me, but do my actions bear it out?

Seek the kingdom of God above all else, and live righteously, and he will give you everything you need. (Matthew 6:33)

What enslaves you?

Jesus, I want to be a slave and apostle to you. May I let nothing control me other than the desire to do your will. Amen.

December 20 ✠ 1 John 1–3

"If someone has enough money to live well and sees a brother or sister in need but shows no compassion—how can God's love be in that person?" (1 John 3:17)

I struggle with this verse because the words "enough" and "well" are not clearly defined. I would like to ask John what he meant by these words, just as Jesus was asked what he meant by the word "neighbor." I want a formula to use so that I can know whether or not I am living well, especially when I find myself in what feels like a financial bind.

Maybe I should focus on the word "compassion." When I take my attention off my own situation and instead focus on the needs of others, compassion takes the lead over the focus on my own needs.

Give to those who ask, and don't turn away from those who want to borrow. (Matthew 5:42)

In what ways do you struggle with financial burdens? In what ways do you hold back from those who are in need?

Lord, please show me how to live to please you. Loosen my grip on the things of this world. Give me a generous heart and reveal to me how to use it to bless others. Amen.

December 21 ✣ 1 John 4–5

First John 4:7-21 instructs us that we are to love others and also love God. It's not something that's either/or; it's both/and. When we truly love God, we love others because they are made in the image of God and are also the children of God, just as we are. We are all part of the family.

Eugene Peterson, in *A Long Obedience in the Same Direction*, says no Christian is an only child. We are part of the family whether we participate or not.[17] As part of a Christian community, we flourish when we love each other and expect the best from each other. Do I see each person in my church as beloved of God?

And a voice from heaven said, "You are my dearly loved Son, and you bring me great joy." (Mark 1:11)

In what ways do you struggle to live out the words of 1 John 4:7-8?

Heavenly Father, I am your child, and you have blessed me by surrounding me with brothers and sisters. Help me to love both you and them with an unshakable love. Amen.

December 22 ✣ 2 John 1–Jude 1

The church to whom Jude wrote dealt with an issue that remains common today—the reconciliation of behavior with God's grace. An expression I often hear is "once saved, always saved." Whether this is true or not is not the issue. Obedience is the issue.

If I give myself to God, part of my gift is my obedience. If I give myself to God out of love and gratitude for what he has done for me, then my desire is to obey. It's not a grudging act; instead, it is a joyful lifestyle.

If that is the grounds for my obedience, then I don't have the issues Jude describes. If I choose to obey God, acting immorally will not interest me. When people use God's grace to justify their immoral behavior, I know they do not serve God joyfully and gratefully. Otherwise, why would they want to act immorally?

Because I love God, I want to please him, not myself. His approval means more to me than any immoral act.

If you love me, obey my commandments. (John 14:15)

How do you discern what acts are in obedience to God and what acts are immoral in God's sight?

Lord, I love you, and my desire is to obey to you. I don't want to grieve you by my behavior. Continue to teach me your ways. Amen.

December 23 ✠ Revelation 1–2

In Revelation 2:1-7, God gives a message to the church at Ephesus. Their enthusiasm for God had waned from when they first believed. They got comfortable in their faith, and in their comfort they allowed their love for God to cool.

In *The Seven Habits of Highly Effective People*, Stephen Covey reminds us that love is a verb. He says that when you feel you don't love someone anymore, it's because you rely on a feeling, not an action. To make love a verb, Covey says to act loving, to be intentional about loving another.[18]

The same is true with God. To keep my love strong for him, I must actively love him—offering praise, serving him, seeing the ways in which he reveals himself to me. I must keep my faith fresh, or it will gradually die.

Others were given in exchange for you.
I traded their lives for yours
because you are precious to me.
You are honored, and I love you. (Isaiah 43:4)

When have you felt that your faith was dying? How did God help you revitalize it?

Loving Father, I want your comfort, but I don't want to become so comfortable that I take you and your blessings for granted. May I demonstrate your love for me in the way I respond to others. Amen.

December 24 ✠ Revelation 3–5

"For you were slaughtered, and your blood has ransomed people for God from every tribe and language and people and nation" (Revelation 5:9b). It is an interesting contrast to read Revelation on Christmas Eve, especially to read the praise of the Lamb in Revelation 5 and know that this is the same Jesus who was born as a baby.

The wonder of it all—that God would not only come to earth in human form, but would come as a baby and be the same Lamb who is praised in Revelation. It is almost too marvelous to comprehend!

Look at my servant, whom I strengthen.
He is my chosen one, who pleases me.
I have put my Spirit upon him.
He will bring justice to the nations.
He will not shout
or raise his voice in public.
He will not crush the weakest reed
or put out a flickering candle.
He will bring justice to all who have been wronged. (Isaiah 42:1-3)

Take a few moments to marvel at the wonder of God's love for you. How can you fully claim it this Christmas?

Wonderful God, your love for me is too amazing to comprehend. You gave your Son for me, for all of us, for now and to eternity. Glory in the highest! Amen.

December 25 ✠ Revelation 6–8

Revelation 7 describes those who died in the great tribulation and who now stand in front of the throne and praise the Lamb. They are "from every nation and tribe and people and language." Because they suffered on earth, they are honored in heaven.

It is encouraging to read those words, but not because I can count myself as one who has suffered. Indeed, I truly haven't. But when I think of the plight of so many of God's children in the world, and how overwhelming the need is, it gives me comfort to know how God tenderly loves those who suffer and that they will have special treatment in heaven. This doesn't lessen the need to act on earth, but it would be easy to become discouraged if our vision ended with death.

Reading Revelation 7 helps us maintain hope and a view of life that extends beyond the grave.

He will feed his flock like a shepherd.
He will carry the lambs in his arms,
holding them close to his heart.
He will gently lead the mother sheep with their young.
(Isaiah 40:11)

How does it comfort you to know that God will one day right all injustices?

Lord, thank you for sending your Son to live among us. Thank you that we have the hope of eternal life because he died for us. Help me to have vision that extends beyond the grave, so that I remain confident in you. Amen.

December 26 ✠ Revelation 9–11

While Revelation includes lots of imagery, some parts contain observations about people that don't seem to change. Revelation 9:20-21 tells of people who were not affected by the plagues mentioned earlier in chapter 9. Because they were not directly affected, they refuse to change their behavior.

We hear that it is better to learn from the mistakes of others than to make the same mistakes ourselves, but we are often too quick to rationalize that a choice will turn out differently for us. We believe we are more competent, better prepared, more aware of the pitfalls than someone else. As a consequence, we continue in ignorance until we suffer directly for our mistakes.

God places us within a community so we can share and learn from each other. To discount the experiences of those around us is to be arrogant and prideful.

Let us think of ways to motivate one another to acts of love and good works. And let us not neglect our meeting together, as some people do, but encourage one another, especially now that the day of his return is drawing near. (Hebrews 10:24-25)

How are you encouraged, uplifted, and held accountable by your spiritual community?

Lord, open my eyes to the lessons you teach me, from whatever source. May I remember that you are all-powerful and are able to use others to teach me. Amen.

December 27 ✤ Revelation 12-13

Could I remain faithful to God if I were conquered by one whose rule completely opposed God? What if my faithfulness excluded me from the ability to buy and sell anything?

I hope I would be faithful, but I can't answer those questions with certainty because I have not experienced either circumstance. I hope I never will!

Enduring is part of my Christian journey, but "enduring" is not a term used often in the world today. The media does not glorify endurance so much as it glorifies a quick rise to the top. The temptation is strong in our society to discount patience and endurance.

But even if you suffer for doing what is right, God will reward you for it. So don't worry or be afraid of their threats. Instead, you must worship Christ as Lord of your life. And if someone asks about your Christian hope, always be ready to explain it. (1 Peter 3:14-15)

How have you been able to endure in the past? What will help you endure today?

Lord, I pray that I will never be shaken from my firm foundation in you. May I always abide in your presence and be faithful even in difficult circumstances. Amen.

December 28 ✦ Revelation 14–16

Again, in Revelation 14:12, John reminds us that we are to endure persecution patiently. We are to remain obedient and faithful to Jesus.

Sometimes persecution comes in the form of criticism. Recently I read a newspaper column written by an atheist high school student. It appeared on Christmas Day. This morning I read a letter to the editor in response and was relieved by how sweetly it was written. Often, the response is to attack, which does nothing positive for either party.

John reminds us to be patient, to endure persecution. He does not say to lash out at those who persecute us. Violence begets violence. Anger begets anger. By enduring patiently, we can break the cycle.

What blessings await you when people hate you and exclude you and mock you and curse you as evil because you follow the Son of Man. When that happens, be happy! Yes, leap for joy! For a great reward awaits you in heaven. And remember, their ancestors treated the ancient prophets that same way. (Luke 6:22-23)

How difficult is it for you to react in compassion when others criticize your faith?

Faithful God, I pray for strength to not retaliate when I am criticized. Instead, I want to respond in love. Amen.

December 29 ✠ Revelation 17–18

The account of the destruction of Babylon in Revelation 18 should make me pause and think about how quickly things can change. We tend to become complacent because so much change happens gradually. Yet natural disasters and military events can happen suddenly and unexpectedly. The results often have a huge impact, affecting thousands of people.

Just as the merchants and shipbuilders were affected by the fall of Babylon, many are affected even if they do not live in a devastated community. As much as we like to think of ourselves as independent, we are actually all interdependent. What affects one affects many, and we are often affected by actions that occur in faraway places.

Revelation 18 reminds us how quickly our circumstances can change. Because there is so much we cannot predict or know, it is important to cling to God. No matter what happens in the world, he is there and is the same always. His love for us is constant and unchanging, and he will not leave us alone—ever.

The Lord directs the steps of the godly.
   He delights in every detail of their lives.
Though they stumble, they will never fall,
   for the Lord holds them by the hand. (Psalm 37:23-24)

How have you held to the unchanging God in times of great upheaval?

Lord, help me to put my faith only in you—not in governments or countries or structures or people—but you and you alone. May I cling to you and not to possessions. Amen.

December 30 ✠ Revelation 19-20

I am not sure I appreciated the continual praise in Revelation until a couple of years ago when I acknowledged the magnitude of my sins. When I took the time to contemplate over my lifetime the many ways I had defied God, I truly came to appreciate what he has done for me. There is truth to the words Jesus speaks in Luke 7:47: "But a person who is forgiven little shows only little love."

I feel I have been forgiven much, and when I stop and think of my sins and what God did for me through Jesus' death, I am overwhelmed! I can lift my voice in the praise given to the Lord in Revelation 19 because I have experienced that "salvation and glory and power belong to our God."

If we claim we have no sin, we are only fooling ourselves and not living in the truth. But if we confess our sins to him, he is faithful and just to forgive us our sins and to cleanse us from all wickedness. (1 John 1:8-9)

How often do you confess your sins to God?

Lord, much in the book of Revelation is hard for me to understand, but I do understand the desire to praise you constantly. Thank you for rescuing me from my sins. I could not do it myself. Amen.

December 31 ✠ Revelation 21-22

"And the one sitting on the throne said, 'Look, I am making everything new!'" (Revelation 21:5a)

As I walked this morning, I reflected on the year and thanked God for the hope of a new year. Reading the above verse gives me great encouragement for the future that begins *today*.

This time of year, it's easy to think about all things being new because a new year is beginning. Yet, with every new day, there is the opportunity to make all things new. Each day can be different from the past, and for the Christian, each day should be different because it offers a new opportunity to draw ever closer to God.

John Wesley spoke of moving toward perfection, and every day is an opportunity for that. While it is good to reflect at the end of the year, I should reflect at the end of each day. Have I grown in my faith or stayed the same? Have I learned more of God, or have I been too busy to listen and allow God to teach me? These are some of the questions I should ask myself each day.

With every sunrise, the Lord tells me, "Look, I am making everything new!" May I listen to him and view each day as a fresh opportunity to learn and grow.

Great is his faithfulness, his mercies begin afresh each morning. (Lamentations 3:23)

How did God make everything new for you today?

Creator of everything, make me new! I want to be washed in the blood of Jesus, die to myself, and live eternally in Christ. Amen.

Notes

1. James Rowe, "Love Lifted Me," *The Broadman Hymnal* (Nashville: Broadman Press, 1940) 352.

2. Oswald Chambers, *My Utmost for His Highest: An Updated Edition*, ed. James Reimann (Grand Rapids MI: Discovery House Publishers, 1992) February 27.

3. Henri J. M. Nouwen, *Life of the Beloved* (New York: The Crossroad Publishing Company, 1992) 57.

4. Chambers, *My Utmost for His Highest*, March 12.

5. Rick Warren, *Rick Warren's Bible Study Methods* (Grand Rapids MI: Zondervan, 2006) 247.

6. Chambers, *My Utmost for His Highest*, July 4.

7. Edward Mote, "My Hope Is Built," *The United Methodist Hymnal* (Nashville: The United Methodist Publishing House, 1989) 368.

8. Joanna Weaver, *Having a Mary Heart in a Martha World* (Colorado Springs: Waterbrook Press, 2000) 48.

9. Chambers, *My Utmost for His Highest*, August 20.

10. James Weldon Johnson (1871–1938), song, "Dem Bones."

11. Weaver, *Having a Mary Heart in a Martha World*, 70.

12. Found in *The United Methodist Hymnal*, 607.

13. Found in *The United Methodist Hymnal*, 607.

14. Jim Cymbala and Dean Merrill, *Fresh Wind, Fresh Fire* (Grand Rapids MI: Zondervan, 1997) 97.

15. Eugene H. Peterson, *A Long Obedience in the Same Direction* (Downers Grove IL: IVP Books, 2000) 44.

16. John C. Maxwell, *Today Matters* (New York: Center Street, 2004) 269.

17. Peterson, *A Long Obedience in the Same Direction*, 175.

18. Stephen R. Covey, *The Seven Habits of Highly Effective People* (New York: Fireside Books, 1989) 80.